African Adventurer's Guide To

BOTSWANA

African Adventurer's Guide To
BOTSWANA

Mike Main

Struik Publishers
(a division of New Holland Publishing (South Africa) (Pty) Ltd)
80 McKenzie Street, Cape Town, South Africa
London • Cape Town • Sydney • Auckland
New Holland Publishing is a member of Johnnic Communications Ltd

First edition published by Southern Book Publishers in 1999
Second edition published by Struik Publishers in 2001

ISBN 1 86872 576 6

10 9 8 7 6 5 4 3

Edited by Peter Joyce
Cover design by Illana Fridkin
Designed and typeset by Illana Fridkin
Maps by Mike Main: some originals by Cartcom
Index by Helen Keevy
Proofread by Inge du Plessis

Reproduction by Creda Communications (Pty) Ltd, Cape Town.
Printed and bound by Creda Communications (Pty) Ltd, Cape Town.

Mike Main's book *Kalahari: Life's Variety in Dune and Delta*, originally published
by Southern Book Publishers, is still available but only through the author. If you
would like to purchase copies of this title, you are welcome to contact the
author at: PO Box 2265, Gaborone, Botswana, or email mmain@info.bw.

PREFACE

This book was originally published as *Visitors' Guide to Botswana*, co-authored by John and Sandra Fowkes. I took over the project in the mid-1990s, and in the preface to the third edition I wrote:

'In the decade and a half of my time here I have seen significant changes, many of them a source of concern. Fuelled by diamond wealth, the country is rapidly hauling itself out of the 18th century and into the 21st with all the social, economic and political difficulties associated with such a traumatic shift. For a people who traditionally saw wild animals only as a food resource their aesthetic value is presently of marginal concern. Due to a combination of factors such as veterinary fences, devastating drought, poorly controlled hunting and, above all, man's steady encroachment into the Kalahari, wildlife numbers have dramatically collapsed and animals are now largely confined to reserved areas. It is unlikely that populations will ever recover to former levels.'

Well, things are looking up. The Department of Wildlife and National Parks are improving their service. Recent game censuses indicate that numbers are increasing.

But these very successes contain within them a new and unforeseen threat. To many, the unique attraction of Botswana is the freedom of its uninhabited (or sparsely inhabited) wilderness: here it is possible to experience, in unfettered isolation, the vastness of Africa. Like everything else, though, this is changing. 'Use it or lose it' we all used to cry, decades ago. 'Make it pay or it will be lost' we said. So, recently, in pursuit of just this kind of thinking, large chunks of Botswana have been identified (and old areas rationalised), turned into concession areas and rented out, at very high rates, to the highest approved bidders.

These concession holders must therefore invest and develop their concessions in order to create the large revenues needed to sustain the whole operation. As a result, public right of access to these areas is controversial to say the least. Almost all of the Okavango and much of Chobe District is covered by concessions or national parks, and the right of the independent traveller to go where they will, without payment, is now less sure, more open to question. To protect its wilderness, Botswana has engulfed and, inevitably, changed it. Soon, to enjoy the freedom of the past will become a very expensive experience indeed. This must be progress!

Despite this, there are still huge areas of true wilderness; any place along the way where one chooses to stop is a campsite (provided it is not in a concession area!). Bureaucracy and regulations, like elsewhere, understandably blanket the national parks and game reserves, but there is as much to enjoy outside these places as there is within. While the Okavango is now largely available only if you are prepared to pay for it,

Makgadikgadi, the vastness of the Kalahari, Tsodilo Hills, Gcwihabe Caves, fossil rivers, ancient dune-fields, remote and beautiful woodlands – all still await you. But be quick. Kubu Island is now under the management of the local community, Tsodilo looks set to follow quickly. I suspect Gcwihabe will not be far behind. In a way, this is right and necessary. A year or so ago there were rumours of a commercially organised millennium party at Kubu and talk of tens of thousands of guests! I can understand why – it is the most perfect setting for such an occasion – but can you imagine the environmental impact of so many people?

Botswana remains special because its wilderness is still seductive; it still whispers the call to excitement, adventure, challenge and self-discovery. But it is not going to stay that way for long.

Lastly, remember too, as Sandra Fowkes once wrote: 'Of those who consult this book, those who seek the soul solace of earth untrammelled by city man, I ask only this: Be thoughtful of your actions that you might not so selfishly enjoy and use the wild areas that you destroy or change them for those who will follow you.'

Mike Main

ACKNOWLEDGEMENTS

It is difficult to look back through 13 years and four editions to select particular individuals from the many who, in countless ways, have made this work possible. One, however, continues to stand out above all others. To Alec Campbell, friend, mentor and guide, I again offer a humble and sincere 'thank you' for still more years of patience, thoughtfulness and an endless outpouring of fascinating knowledge.

It would be wrong, too, to fail to acknowledge the continued support and assistance of Philip Welch, who still works magic with the mysterious innards of the internal combustion engine and its four driving wheels.

I would also like to acknowledge the contribution of Michelle Cooke, who efficiently undertook much of the data collection, especially for the Okavango and Tuli areas. My new-found wife, Kerstin, did much important groundwork for which I am especially grateful. Phil Marshall of the Department of Wildlife and National Parks was extraordinarily helpful not only in providing important data but also in reading and correcting much of the text. Friends of long standing, Patrick and Veronica Jonsson, provided vital information for many of the maps and I thank them for their interest and input. In response to my request in the last edition for ideas, suggestions and general feedback I have received many comments and for these I thank you all.

As I emphasise elsewhere, I really do encourage comments, criticisms, updates and suggestions. You can contact me – email, post, fax or phone – at the addresses and numbers given below. (One small point: I much prefer talking to writing – call me direct for a chat rather than leave messages or enter into correspondence. I hope you'll understand).

Mike Main
PO Box 2265
Gaborone
Botswana

Tel & fax (267) 397-5433
Email: mmain@info.bw

INTRODUCTION

Botswana is a very special place, rightly renowned for its wildlife. It is the big animals that immediately come to mind, and on a visit to the national parks of Moremi and Chobe, for example, you are likely to see many different kinds of antelope, elephant and hippo, giraffe, lion, jackal and hyena, monkeys and baboons. With luck you could see leopard and cheetah. If you delight in birds you won't be disappointed, and you'll keep your companions entertained as they witness your dilemma when you try to choose between binoculars to get a better look at a new bird, a camera to photograph another and a bird book to try to find out what they both are!

If your wildlife interests are even more specialised, Botswana offers a great diversity of plants, insects and reptiles. Some are as yet unnamed – and could even bear your name if you introduce them to science.

Add to this array of plants and animals a unique geographical feature, the Okavango Delta, where a river runs into a semi-desert, spills its contents over of 13 000 km^2 of waterways and then quietly disappears under the thirsty sands, and you have another excellent reason to explore Botswana. Throw in the Kalahari Desert and the Makgadikgadi Pans and the reasons multiply.

Although the Okavango Delta is perhaps the best known and most visited area, Botswana has a great deal more to offer. The desert that finally swallows the waters of the Okavango River, for instance, exerts a strong pull, as do the culturally diverse people of the country as a whole.

Striking contrasts and new wilderness experiences are Botswana's two main attractions. You will not find many countries on the African continent that are so different from the urban environment familiar to the average American or European traveller.

MM

CONTENTS

HOW TO USE THIS GUIDE

This book grew out of the author's experience in answering people's questions about how to get to Botswana and what to do when they were there. It is written primarily for the person who is travelling in a private party rather than with a tour operator, although there is a section in Chapter 5 devoted to the latter. Chapter 1 provides an overview of the country, its people, its past and present. Chapter 2 gives some good reasons why you should visit the country; Chapter 3 discusses aspects of planning your visit; Chapters 4 and 5 summarise the nuts-and-bolts of travel to and around the country, accommodation, visitor facilities and services, and so forth; Chapters 6 and 7 profile the main tourist destinations; Chapter 8 recommends routes to follow; Chapter 9 covers accommodation. You'll find, in these pages, plenty of useful tips on what to carry with you, what you can expect at the border posts and ways of communicating with the Batswana people.

Before planning your trip, turn to Chapter 3, then work out the time you have available, decide on the way you want to travel (that is, either in your own two-wheel-drive vehicle, or a four-wheel-drive, or with an operator) and the venues and activities that interest you most. This information will give your trip a shape. Now you can decide where on your route to stay.

Maps of routes and towns

This edition of *African Adventurer's Guide to Botswana* is innovative in several ways. Among new features is the inclusion of GPS (Global Positioning System) reference points and route maps. It is important to be quite clear about the role of the maps. I am assuming those who use this book will either be well acquainted with Botswana's main road network or will have with them a standard national road map of some sort.

For this reason, few of the main roads are included on the maps. Most of the maps are of remote, off-road parts of the country that do not normally appear in ordinary maps, or at least not in sufficient detail.

Our maps are mostly schematic, and they are not to scale. North is always shown, but it does not always point to the top of the page, as convention demands, because the route needs to fit neatly into the page shape and size (though you can always, of course, rotate the book).

The maps have been tested by a number of travellers, who have found them quite satisfactory, and I believe and trust that you will have no difficulty using them either.

Distances and times

Times and distances given in the text are only approximate – and cannot be otherwise. I have driven one route in two hours and a year later taken 4.5 hours over the same journey. Many variables affect one's time over a given distance of sand or dirt road. Is it wet or dry? What season is it? Is it morning or night when the sand is cool and firm, or 3 pm when it's hot and loose? What was the wheel-track width of the last vehicle before you to travel along a sandy road? Are you heavily laden or carrying a light load? Did the vehicle stop for a break? Everything makes a difference. Once, driving to Xade in the Central Kalahari Game Reserve, I followed some wide-track four-wheel-drive water tankers. They had so churned up the road that what should have taken five or six hours took nearly two days!

Time estimates given in the text are what I think the ordinary driver will take if they are not in a frantic hurry and conditions are pretty much like they were when I last went that way.

Distances are also something of a problem. Variations occur in the maps appearing in different publications, official and otherwise, and the numbers don't always match the distance on your odometer.

I've come to learn that a bit of wheel-spin here and there does not seem to make a great deal of difference over long journeys. A much more significant contributory factor is the variation in odometers themselves. A one or one-and-a-half per cent error does not sound much but wait until you are lost and that 'vital' turn-off does not appear after two, three, five ... kilometres! Thanks to modern GPS technology I have also discovered that my speedometer consistently reads about 9 or 10 per cent over, and that others seem to have the same built-in error.

I believe that tyre pressure, air temperature, road conditions and equipment error all contribute to differences in distance covered. I have checked all the data included here as carefully as I can. There are, so far as I know, no major errors (but bear in mind that bush tracks are constantly changing).

Feedback

Occasionally, readers work their way through the publisher's post to me and I am always happy to supply extra information wherever possible. I can be contacted at the following address:

PO Box 2265, Gaborone, Botswana; tel and fax (267) 397-5433 (office), email: mmain@info.bw.

Botswana is a large country and I cannot keep up to date with every route and change of track so, if you have any new information, any new routes or corrections or alterations to existing information, I shall be very happy to have it. It will be incorporated in future revisions, with an acknowledgement. If you supply a GPS position, please remember to let me have the datum on which your machine is set .

I look forward to hearing from you.

MM

INTRODUCTION TO BOTSWANA

Geography

Botswana is a landlocked country, in the centre of southern Africa, bordered by Zimbabwe, South Africa, Namibia and Zambia. It is relatively flat, with an average elevation of about 1 000 m (just over 3 000 feet) above sea level. The tropic of Capricorn crosses the lower third of the country.

Basically, the country is formed of two main drainage systems, one towards the north, the other to the south, separated by a slightly elevated ridge that runs from Lobatse northwest towards Ghanzi and Namibia. Another ridge of somewhat hilly country in the east separates these great basins from the watershed of the Limpopo River.

The Okavango River flows from the highlands of Angola into the northern basin. Much of this huge quantity of water evaporates, but a trickle sometimes escapes to make its way via the Boteti River to the great, ancient lake-bed of the Makgadikgadi Pans, which dominates the northern part of Botswana.

The southern region is largely waterless, but such drainage lines as there are all lead southwards towards the ephemeral Molopo River, which flows south into the Gariep (until recently known as the Orange) River and thence into the cold Atlantic in the far west.

Despite its considerable size (it is only slightly smaller than the Northern, Western and Eastern Cape provinces of South Africa combined, and a little larger than France). Botswana has no standing water except in the Okavango Delta in the northwest, along the Chobe/Zambezi in the north and the Limpopo River in the east. In addition, the evaporation rate is extremely high, averaging just a little under 2 m from an open water surface during the course of a year. As a matter of interest, nowhere in the country does the amount of rainfall exceed the amount lost by evaporation! These factors make Botswana an extremely dry country, and this is reflected not only in the fascinating adaptations of the flora and fauna but also in the way its inhabitants have modified their life styles to a difficult climate.

Climate

The wet season runs from November through to April, the rain brought by with impressive thunderstorms, sometimes accompanied by hail (which is quite common, especially in the earlier part of the season). Average rainfall diminishes as you travel across Botswana from the northeast to the southwest. Some 650 mm can be expected around Chobe in the north each year but the average for the Kgalagadi Transfrontier Park (the amalgamation of the former Gemsbok National and Kalahari Gemsbok national parks) in the south is only 150 mm. The Okavango region averages about 550–600 mm per year.

More important than averages, perhaps, is variability, and this too changes as one moves across the country. Towards the north, variability is about 25 per cent – i.e. one can expect as much as 25 per cent more or less rain about the average. In the south, this figure is 80 per cent! In other words, rainfall in the south is extremely variable, and unpredictable.

The dry period extends from May through to the end of October, but droughts are common and that period may well be much longer. While summer temperatures can reach 45 °C, July – the coldest month – can be bitter. Frost occurs at this time, especially in the southern part of Botswana, and there have been occasional reports of isolated snowfalls. These, though, are very much the exception.

Temperatures can be quite extreme in Botswana, with the greatest range occurring in the south. The following table shows the mean maximum and minimum temperatures, in degrees Celsius, in four months of the year at five locations in Botswana.

	April	July	Nov	Jan
Kasane	30/15	25/8	33/19	30/19
Maun	30/15	26/6	34/20	30/19
Francistown	28/14	24/5	32/18	31/18
Gaborone	28/12	22/2	32/16	32/18
Tshabong	28/12	22/1	33/16	35/19

It is important to realise that these figures are only averages, and that actual maximums and minimums can be very different. For example, there have been several reports of snow in the Kalahari and it is not uncommon for small quantities of water to freeze solid overnight in winter. On the other hand, maximum temperatures, especially in the hot months of October and November, can sometimes reach 40 °C and more.

For reasons related to the climate, May through to July/August is the period when the bulk of overseas visitors come to Botswana.

History

The pre-colonial era

The original inhabitants of Botswana, the 'First People' as their descendants now like to describe them, were the Khoesan-speakers, or Basarwa, known more widely as Bushmen or San. So far as we know, and certainly within the last 40 000 years (that is, in Late Stone Age times) they were the only inhabitants of southern and parts of eastern Africa. Their life style was that of the nomadic hunter-gatherer, though there is growing evidence that at least some of the groups (those who would be called Khoe as opposed to San) – especially those who lived along the Ghanzi Ridge, in the Okavango, beside the Boteti River and Sowa Pan – possessed livestock. Interestingly, their languages include words, for instance, those for 'cow', 'milk', 'pot' and 'sheep', that are not borrowed from other languages. It is the Khoesan who are responsible for the rock art for which Botswana is so famous.

Bantu-speaking people from central-west Africa began filtering east, west and south through the continent about 7 000 years ago, eventually crossing the Zambezi at about the start of the Christian era, some 2 000 years ago. They brought with them stock, the practice of building houses, the widespread use of pottery, skills in growing crops and, perhaps most important of all, knowledge of how to find, smelt and forge iron into useful implements. The earliest of these Iron Age people so far recorded in Botswana arrived around AD 450. Since that date, successive groups of Bantu-speakers have settled in what is now Botswana, which, today, is home to more than 20 language groups.

Modern history

Bechuanaland, as most of the country was called in colonial times, came into formal existence in several stages. The first occurred early in 1884, when missionary John Mackenzie declared a protectorate over an area south of the Molopo River (Botswana's present southern border). This was not recognised initially, but in January of the following year the region so proclaimed by Mackenzie did come under formal British protection and, at the same time, administrative jurisdiction was extended, for whites only, to latitude 22 South (which included approximately the lower third of modern Botswana).

In September 1885 the Protectorate status of the area south of the Molopo changed again: it was declared a British Territory (and thus a colony) and named British Bechuanaland. The area north of the river, formerly classed only as 'within the British sphere', became a Protectorate.

These measures had serious consequences for the Ngwato people: their lands were cut in half. For six years, no further changes took place but then, in May 1891, two more steps were taken on the route to the establishment of modern Botswana. British Bechuanaland, the colony to the south of the Molopo, ceased to exist when it was incorporated as part of the Colony of the Cape of Good Hope.

The Protectorate – that is, the portion north of the Molopo to latitude 22 – was extended northwards to the Chobe River but excluded the Tati Concession. This was the area, around modern Francistown, where gold had been found and for which an exclusive mining concession had been granted, by Lobengula, the Matabele king, to the Northern Light Company.

The boundaries of the newly expanded Protectorate were also deliberately vague about the area known as the 'Disputed Territory', the land between the Shashe and Motloutse rivers, which was claimed both by Lobengula and by Khama, ruler of the Ngwato. However, in September 1892, both these areas were included in the Protectorate and, in 1899, the final boundary between Bechuanaland and Rhodesia was settled.

During those early years, indeed right up to 1965, Bechuanaland was administered from outside its own borders (in fact it was one of the very few countries in the world, perhaps the only one, to have an external capital!).

Initially, the administrative capital was at Vryburg in the Cape colony but, on the incorporation of British Bechuanaland into that Colony, it moved to the town of Mafeking, 35 km beyond the Protectorate's borders but still part of the Cape (note that this town also changed its name, from Mafeking to Mafikeng). The capital city of Gaborone was practically built from scratch to house the new government that assumed office following independence on 30 September 1966.

At this time Botswana was counted among the ten poorest nations on earth, and no-one could have predicted the great treasure of diamonds which was to be discovered in the late 1960s and 1970s. This great bounty has turned Botswana into one of the wealthiest countries in Africa, the third-largest producer of diamonds in the world, generating a growth rate and economic progress seldom paralleled elsewhere. At the time of writing, this growth continues unabated. Today, Botswana is a unified, peaceful, prosperous and democratic nation with a successful modern economy supported by an efficient infrastructure of roads, railways, telecommunications, water and electricity (see Economy, page 22).

Population

Botswana is home to some 1.6 million inhabitants, a population that is growing at the rate of approximately 2.8 per cent per annum.

Considerable problems are associated with this rapid birth rate and, as is common elsewhere, the gap between rich and poor appears to be growing alarmingly while the need for rapid economic growth, to provide jobs for school leavers, remains as pressing as ever. The HIV/Aids pandemic is, however, having a dramatic effect. The death rate has risen sharply and life expectancy has fallen from over 60 years to a level now fast approaching 46.

Botswana is a country in transition. In 1966, when independence was obtained, it was exceedingly under-developed. With a population, only 30 years ago, of 543 000 people, it had no government secondary schools, no industry or economy to speak of, and only 8 km of tarmac road! Its achievements since then have been quite remarkable – but there has been a high price to pay. The cultural life of the people has been severely battered by the demands of a 20th-century existence and the fight for a place in the world economy. Traditions are disappearing overnight, family structures are under enormous pressure, urban drift has become an unstoppable flood, population growth exponential and the generation gap has become a gulf separating father and son, mother and daughter. Botswana has accepted this, perhaps the greatest challenge it has yet to face, and is bent on stepping forward with determination into the 21st century. Given the successes of the recent past and the willingness of its people, there is every hope it will succeed, despite the pain and frustrations that can be expected on the journey.

Language

While the country is known as Botswana, residents are properly referred to as Batswana (singular, Motswana) and the language is Setswana. Although Setswana is the national and English the official language, the former is not the home tongue of all the people. Indeed, the population is made up of a surprisingly wide number of tribal groupings; Setswana speakers include the Bangwato, Ngwaketse, Bakwena, Bakgatla, Barolong, Bahurutse, Batawana, Batlokwa and Balete to mention a few. Setswana has become the effective lingua franca but there are equally as many groups whose home language is not Setswana. These include Hambukushu, Bayei, Basubiya, Ovaherero, Bakalanga, Bakgalagadi and Basarwa (the Bushmen).

Every language and culture has its own norms and customs of behaviour. Politeness in one society may be the height of rudeness in another. A good place to start is with simple courtesy and respect for the person with whom you are dealing. Using a few phrases of the local language can also help to smooth the flow of communication.

Greetings

Despite the many different languages spoken in Botswana, greetings in Setswana, the official language, will be understood throughout the country. Some basic definitions will help you unravel the difference between Botswana, Batswana, Motswana and Setswana. The root 'tswana' takes on various meanings when different prefixes are added to it. Thus, Botswana is the country; Motswana means one of the people of the country; Batswana is the plural, meaning more than one person of the country; Setswana is the language of the country.

Batswana set great store by courteous greetings, and you don't have to be a great linguist to take your first step – it must be one of the easiest of all languages in which to be polite. Go back to one of the first words that you ever uttered – 'Ma'. Lengthen the 'm' sound as though you were about to start humming. Say 'Mma' and you have learnt the correct form of addressing women. Adding 'Mma' onto a communication in English immediately makes it sound more polite – 'How much is this basket, Mma?' The courteous form of addressing men is 'Rra' (lengthen the 'r' sound to produce 'Rra').

The equivalent of 'Hello' in Setswana is 'Dumela', the stress placed on the middle syllable. Marry your new word with the appropriate form of address and you have made a useful investment in communication. If you have no further linguistic ambitions, the only other phrase you should learn is `Go siame', an all-purpose end to a conversation meaning 'It's all right'.

Economy

At the time of independence (September 1966), Botswana ranked among the ten poorest nations in the world. It possessed just 8 km of tarmac road (one in Francistown and seven in Lobatse), no government secondary schools, and a tiny population of about 500 000. The country was, apparently, without significant mineral deposits and woefully short of skilled labour and appropriate human resources. To survive alone looked like a major challenge.

The development of the copper and nickel matt mines at Selebi-Phikwe, and a generous beef deal with the European Union, began the long upward journey to wealth, but it was the discovery of diamonds that really moved Botswana out from among the beggars into Africa's Super League. Botswana is now a top producer of diamonds, possessing one of the wealthiest gem-quality mines in the world.

To its credit, the government has tended to spend the windfall wisely. It is generally agreed that Botswana has a world-class road network, an excellent telephone system and a reliable electricity grid.

But success has brought its own problems. The single most important message to emerge from a recent International Monetary Fund survey was the need to reduce dependence on diamonds. Only 70 per cent of world diamond sales are controlled by De Beers' Central Selling Organisation, and that figure may decline. With less and less centralised control of the market, there is increased variation in price and this – when diamonds account for nearly a third of Botswana gross domestic product and some 70 per cent of export earnings – has a direct effect on the country's economy. In short, Botswana is vulnerable to the movement of diamond prices.

After diamonds, the next major contributor to Botswana's prosperity, surprisingly enough, is interest earned on foreign holdings. I am told it is conventional for countries to hold two to three months' 'cover' of foreign purchases. As a measure of its present wealth, Botswana has between two and three years' cover! Tourism, the cattle industry and mining (apart from diamonds) account for most of the other earnings, with tourism making an ever more significant contribution.

Industrialisation is a major challenge, especially with South Africa as a giant neighbour. Yet the imperative is relentless. Despite the ravages of AIDs, population pressures are intense; more than 25 000 students arrive on the labour market each year, jobs must be found for them, and this means diversifying the economy. The diversification programme is still in its infancy but it appears to be holding its own, though a country-wide shortage of skilled labour poses yet more challenges.

Government

Botswana is a practising democracy, its constitution based on the Westminster model. All adults over the age of 18 have the vote, and elections are held every five years. The executive president is appointed by the ruling party. There are 40 elected seats in the National Assembly; an additional four members are specially appointed. In the 1999 national elections the Botswana Democratic Party, which has been in power since independence, won 33 seats, the opposition National Front gained six and the Botswana Congress Party one. The cabinet, over which the President presides, comprises 13 ministers, with four assistant ministers. A 15-member House of Chiefs acts in a purely advisory capacity to the government.

Until fairly recently there was no limit to the number of terms a president could serve, but changes to the constitution now restrict an incumbent to two five-year periods. The first to hold the office was Sir Seretse Khama, who died in 1980 after 14 years in the saddle. Sir Seretse's place was taken by Sir Ketumile Masire, who voluntarily relinquished the presidency after 18 years. He was succeeded by Mr Festus Mogae.

2

WHY VISIT BOTSWANA?

People come to Botswana principally to visit the Okavango, to see game, and to explore and enjoy the wilderness.

The country is unique within southern Africa in a number of ways. In the Okavango it boasts what is arguably the world's largest and certainly most beautiful inland delta. The Tsodilo Hills and their heritage are without parallel in the realm of rock art. The great paleo-lake of Makgadikgadi must be one of the least known and most unsung of the subcontinent's exotic venues. And then there's the Kalahari, a vast expanse of wilderness wreathed in legend, home to San and other once-nomadic peoples and a mecca for explorers and travellers for the past two centuries.

Indeed, one thing that makes Botswana so different is its huge abundance of wilderness. Intrinsically there is nothing special about the great spaces: they are, after all, just 'empty land'. The point is that in most of the rest of southern Africa, by comparison, there is so little empty land. Driving outside Botswana, you'll notice how all the roads are fenced and the gates locked. We in Botswana, for safety reasons, now have in place a programme to fence our main roads, but this is more to keep cattle off the roads than restrict human movement (though the animals still manage to wander onto them, so drive with extra care). There are plenty of gates and few, if any, are locked – mainly because there is very little privately owned land in the country.

Over 17 per cent of the country has been set aside as game reserves and national parks. Only 4 per cent comprises freehold farms. The state owns sizeable areas, but by far the greatest part of Botswana is tribal land administered by tribal land boards and remains, mostly, unfenced and undeveloped. Access to tribal areas is not controlled, and it is these large tracts of unoccupied land that help make the country so special.

Essentially, there are two ways to see Botswana. Either you self-drive in a 4x4 or you pay a safari company (or the lodge the company owns) to transport you. Hitch-hiking between anything other than the main centres is not really an option: few people will take a stranger 'on safari' with them.

Large and exclusive concessions are being granted to commercial operators in accordance with the policy aimed at making the wilderness pay for itself. Each concession diminishes the amount of uncontrolled land accessible to the public at large – understandably, managers of these tracts, which are set aside specifically for hunting or photographic safaris (or both; see further on), do not want to encourage casual visitors.

In Botswana, conservation is succeeding, but perhaps for reasons which we did not anticipate: the high cost of conserving and protecting the environment means large entry fees for non-citizens, which limits access to areas we want to preserve, and thus safeguards them, to a relatively small number of wealthy people (citizens are charged a lot less, but must have a particular purpose in mind;i.e gathering honey, cutting grass, collecting firewood are among a number of unrestricted activities.)

Visitors have access, of course, to the proclaimed game reserves and national parks, but it is now difficult to get into the Okavango, and into the Linyanti and Chobe areas, except in the company of a licensed operator. However, much of the rest of the country is still there for the adventurous: a lot of the Ngamiland and most of Ghanzi, Kgalagadi and Central districts are open to would-be explorers – which I think is more than enough to satisfy those in quest of unspoilt Africa.

Parks and wildlife

Botswana's sanctuaries need little introduction. They are areas to which, on payment (see Fee Structure, page 209), the public have access. Privately owned safari lodges and hotels have been established in or near most of them but, apart from these, accommodation at the time of writing is for campers only. Despite relatively high fees, the demand for entry permits continues to rise and, some years ago, a booking system was introduced. This has not been successful, and has led to a great many complaints. I have been informed that the system is being overhauled and that we may now expect much improved service.

For the independent traveller, a four-wheel-drive vehicle (4x4) is I believe at least desirable, if not essential, for travel within almost all the parks. It certainly is so for Chobe and Savute, Khutse, the Central Kalahari and Nxai Pan (unless the entrance road receives an unexpected upgrade) sanctuaries. On the other hand, in good conditions one might manage with a saloon car in Moremi and certainly the main 'river roads' in the Kgalagadi Transfrontier Park would present no difficulty. To travel away from them would, however, be impossible without a 4x4.

Perhaps the best known of the sanctuaries is the Chobe National Park, in the north of Botswana. Gems within this are the Chobe river-front where, as the dry season deepens, game numbers steadily increase as the animals concentrate near the only water left in the region. They are not, however, confined to the riverine area: even though the famed but ephemeral Savute Channel to the south has long since ceased to flow, artificial waterholes have kept game in the region, which is famous for its elephant, lion, hyaena and for its magnificent, sweeping views.

Thrusting deep into the Okavango Delta area is Moremi Game Reserve. This has recently been enlarged to include all of Chief's Island. Public vehicular access is from the eastern side (the western approaches are blocked by rivers and lagoons). Chief's Island itself is reached by courtesy of the various safari camps in the concession areas. Moremi, being so abundantly provided with water, has a splendid complement of game animals.

The two great sanctuaries that lay on either side of the Maun–Nata road have now been combined to form the Nxai Pan and Makgadikgadi National Park. There is no open, standing water in this region, and the two areas (one a grassed-over lake-bed set about with glorious acacia trees, the other a treeless grassland), though visually spectacular, are very seasonal in their offerings. There is always wildlife of one sort or another to be seen at Nxai Pan, but the last two-thirds of wet season is definitely the best time to visit.

The old game reserve of Mabuasehube, in the south, is no more: some years ago it was incorporated into the much larger Gemsbok National Park, on whose boundary it lay. Recently, the Gemsbok National Park itself ended its days as a separate entity: in a new and exciting initiative the park and South Africa's Kalahari Gemsbok National Park were combined in what is now called the Kgalagadi Transfrontier Park (KTP).

The idea of a transfrontier park had been discussed for many years and great credit is due to both countries for putting into practice so challenging a concept. It is important for conservation that the scheme succeeds, for it can blaze the trail for dozens of other similar projects, not only in Africa but around the world. The challenges are considerable, and, inevitably, there are unexpected difficulties. New Customs posts, roads, offices and staff quarters have to be built, prices standardised and geared to relative currency values. Policies and methods may have to be changed, sometimes from extreme positions, to reach a commonly acceptable management system.

Bird life

There is an abundance of birds to be seen in Botswana at all times of the year, although fewer of them are around in the colder months: between April and September you'll see mostly resident birds and a small number of winter visitors, but no European migrants. The warmer months, there-fore, are best for bird-watching. The presence or absence of water also strongly influences the number and species of birds in a given area. The drier the region, and the poorer the rainy season, the fewer the birds.

There are seasonal concentrations of birds, but they're difficult to pre-dict. At Lake Ngami, for example, you'll see very little if the 'lake' is dry, which it usually is these days. Conversely, a water-filled Ngami is one of the most prolific bird localities in Africa. The same holds true for Botswana's salt pans. In short, bird life is very rich if there is water, virtually non-existent if there is none and, at these times, your visit can be disappointing. This variability is particularly striking around the Makgadikgadi Pans, especially Sowa Pan in the northeast. Here, if there have been adequate rains, millions of birds congregate towards the end of the season, notably flamingos, pelicans and wild ducks. If there's no flooding, though, you won't see much.

Good birding areas include the Chobe and Okavango regions in the north and the Limpopo valley in the southeast. An experienced bird-watcher in the former two may expect to see up to 200 species in a week, among them slatey egrets, shoebills and wattled cranes. Specials include half-collared kingfishers, the Pels fishing owl and the African finfoot. In the Limpopo valley, it would not be surprising to see 150 species in the same period of time. By contrast, in a dry part of the Kalahari – Mabuasehube, for example – you might spot just 30 to 50 species.

Botswana does boast one or two birds of particular interest to the spe-cialist. The southeast is one of only two localities in southern Africa where the short-clawed lark occurs, and the black-faced babbler has been sight-ed in Ngamiland. Namibia is the only other place where the latter is found.

The bird club in Gaborone organises regular walks from the National Museum on the first Sunday of every month, starting at 6.30 am in the summer and 7.15 am in the winter. The secretary and committee wel-come visiting bird enthusiasts and will assist them in any way they can. Contact details: Private Bag 00300, Gaborone; tel and fax 397-1584.

Fishing

Three primary fishing areas occur in Botswana – along the Chobe River, in the Okavango Delta and in the Limpopo valley to the southeast. Much of the better fishing in the Limpopo is on private land and thus not easily accessible to visitors. Tiger-fishing is rewarding in the Okavango and Chobe throughout the year but is at its best from August to February when the water is low (although the annual flood can sometimes produce excel-lent sport). Other good catches include bream, tilapia and barbel.

It is difficult to be more precise about the best months for fishing, especially in the Okavango region. Much depends upon what part of the Delta one is visiting. The size and time of the flood has a major impact upon the quality of fishing. The flood can take five or six months to work its way through the entire system and varies greatly in volume from year to year, and in its time of arrival. Having decided on a fishing holiday, the best course of action is to contact some of the fishing camps mentioned in this guide (see Chapter 9, page 206) and ask their advice.

The Chobe/Zambezi area hosts more than 91 species of fish of which 24 are sought after, but most visiting fishermen are mainly interested in just two species: tigerfish and bream. Chobe's present tiger record is 9.8 kg; 5–6-kg catches are common, and the Chobe tiger are lighter, leaner and said by many to be better fighters than, for example, those from Kariba. Other popular catches include pike, squeaker, western bottle-nose, many dwarf species and yellowfish. This last, found both in the rapids at Kasane and in the upper Zambezi, offers a very exciting challenge to the expert.

The fairly new sport of fly-fishing, still in its infancy but immensely popular in South Africa, is spreading quickly into the more secluded parts of the subcontinent. The Chobe is no exception.

No licences are required for fishing in waters outside a national park. Until recently one could apply for a licence to fish at designated places within their boundaries, but this facility has been suspended for the time being (the embargo doesn't apply to subsistence fishermen) and an investigation into control measures is underway. New regulations may be published this year (2001). This moratorium does not affect fishing elsewhere in Botswana. Arrangements can be made with local fishing companies to try your luck in Caprivi and Zambian waters. These enterprises will also take care of licensing, rod levy, immigration and other formal matters.

Trees and other snags on the bottom of the rivers and channels will lay heavy claims on your line, spoons and hooks so it's advisable to have a large supply on hand. Steel trace and swivels are essential if tigerfish are your quarry. Do remember that crocodile and hippo still abound in large numbers, particularly in the Okavango and in the Chobe. It would be foolish to take unnecessary risks.

Due to the aquatic weed control measures in force in Botswana, you may bring your boat in only through certain designated points, where the craft will be sprayed and a permit issued. In fact, such a permit is required for all boats – regardless of whether they come from inside or outside the country – when they are moved between zones within Botswana. Applications for import permits can be lodged with The Water Registrar, Department of Water Affairs, P/Bag 0029, Gaborone; tel 360-7340/1, fax 390-3508. Boats can be hired at Kasane.

Elephant safaris

Riding through the Botswana bush on the back of an elephant is a top-of-the-range experience, and quite an extraordinary one. I was privileged to be a guest at the camp – Abu Camp (see page 234) – for several days and can speak for the quality of the facilities there: they were outstanding. The high point, though, is being with the elephants themselves. Personally I found riding the animals less thrilling than running with and among them. I was researching material for a publication, and taking photographs, so perhaps this was the reason I was given such freedom of movement. I will not forget standing between Abu's tusks and looking up into his cavernous mouth, nor the lessons I learned trying to photograph young elephants enjoying a mud bath. It appears that taking photographs and standing among mud-bathing juveniles are not compatible activities!

Hunting safaris

Hunting safaris are the real roots of tourism in Botswana. In the 1950s and 1960s many of the great hunting names (of both companies and individuals) from Kenya came to Botswana, established themselves and, some of them, remained. A list can be found on page 63. 'Photographic tourism' has now far overtaken hunting in terms of numbers and revenues but the latter is still an important element of the tourism industry.

I recently spoke to Chris Collins, one of the 'old time' hunters who lives in Maun and is still in business. I wanted to know what makes Botswana special from a hunting point of view. His answer can be summed up in one word: quality. Although the quotas are presently somewhat limited, lion and leopard are considered to be unusually good, and elephant ivory recently caused something of a sensation. One tusk came in at 45 kg (100 lbs), an exceptional weight and, apparently, every hunter's dream.

While trophy quality is one drawcard, elephant hunting is another. Botswana banned the hunting of these animals nearly 20 years ago and, since then, herd numbers have risen dramatically to the point, arguably, where the country has too many elephant. Two or three years ago the ban was lifted and these animals are now on licence once more.

Many hunters consider Botswana a good destination not only for the quality of its game and the availability of elephant but also for other reasons. The infrastructure is generally excellent and complements good game-management systems (all hunting takes place on very large private concessions), and movement to find the different species is much less demanding than in other countries.

Elephant population control

This will be a sensitive issue to many readers, and I don't want to get too involved in controversy in these pages, but the bare facts present a difficult problem which will have to be faced square-on sooner or later. Hunting is a small but important part of the equation.

Botswana's game herds were extensive in the early years of the 19th century. Foreigners began hunting around 1830; one report suggests that in 1850 alone exports of wildlife products included 10 000 elephant tusks and 3 000 leopard skins. By the end of the century certain, much sought-after species were facing regional extinction; elephant had disappeared from southern Botswana and were very scarce in the north. Numbers slowly increased over the decades that followed but it was not until a ban on elephant hunting came into effect in the 1980s that the situation underwent fundamental change.

In 1981 the national elephant herd was estimated at about 40 000 animals. Ten years later it was thought to be in the 65 000 –70 000 range; by the end of the millennium it was acknowledged that the number had risen to nearly 105 000. An annual rate of increase of about 5 per cent is not unreasonable, so we can easily calculate what the future might look like.

Every report confirms my own experience that elephant are spreading ever more widely, back into areas they last occupied decades ago. At first glance this might be seen as a good thing but unfortunately there are problems: areas long ago cleared of elephant are now occupied by humankind and its cattle. The return of the former occupants, impelled by population pressures and scarcity of food, provokes conflict – a conflict that humans always win.

In simple terms, we cannot allow our elephant herds to go on increasing annually by some 5 000 head. So what to do? Nobody knows. You can't simply 'truck-out' 5 000 animals a year. You can't herd them for hundreds of kilometres to new homes. Birth-control measures have not proved effective.

It's hard to avoid the unpleasant alternative, but it certainly looks as if culling will have to be considered. And if the elephants are going to die anyway, the country might at least make some much needed money by allowing the hunters in.

All that said, though, hunting does not of course make much of an impact on herd sizes. We banned it for so long that the market collapsed. In the first year after the ban was lifted, I believe, Botswana struggled to sell 50 licences; in 2000, about 180 licences were issued. Presumably the number will steadily increase, but it will never approach the 5 000 needed just to keep the elephant population where it is.

Photography

Bright sunlight throughout the year makes it possible to use low ASA films. I use 100 ASA almost exclusively and seldom experience light problems. Such film avoids the 'graininess' one sometimes experiences with the higher ratings. Again, because of the brightness of the light, an 81A is a useful (but not essential) addition. A standard skylight/UV filter is also handy and protects the lens.

Dust is a serious problem in Botswana: it gets in everywhere and special precautions need to be taken. I keep my equipment in a plastic bag in a camera case. However you approach the problem, though, it does need to be addressed. Makgadikgadi is an especially difficult area in this regard: the lake deposits are aeolian, finer than talc and able to infiltrate the most unlikely places!

Clouds are important in some types of photography, and for this reason the winter months are often not the best. They are the coolest, of course – and hence the most popular from a visitor's point of view – but they're generally cloud-free. October, November and December (depending on when the rains start, if at all) are wonderfully dramatic, as indeed is the entire rainy season. The first three months bring thunderstorms, and when those blue-black rain clouds come over the horizon towards evening they create the most spectacular photographic backdrop imaginable. The towering masses of cumulus that preside over these sudden storms create stunning sunsets. It will be especially hot at that time of year, so cameras need to be kept out of the sun and film kept as cool as possible.

Photographing the local people can be tricky, and the polite thing to do is to ask first. In some cases a small gratuity will be expected.

Other activities

Tourism is relatively undeveloped in Botswana. The country offers game and wilderness but there are no organised trails (open to the public at large: no 'managed' 4x4 routes, rock climbing, caving, water sports or the like. Ballooning has been dreamt of by many but the Civil Aviation and National Parks authorities have not encouraged it in the past and, indeed, the vegetation, and vast tracts of land devoid of roads, militate against the sport. Certainly one can enjoy a mokoro trip or a game walk but, in 99 per cent of the cases, you have to be a guest with a safari organisation.

Many of these 'add-on' activities will come in time. Indeed some are available in embryonic form. At the time of writing (late 2000) two horseback safari companies were operating in the Okavango, and I understand that this is a wonderful and extraordinary experience (see page 63).

Culture

Botswana is a country of surprisingly diverse cultures. At first glance, it seems to be a unilingual nation of Bantu-speakers, but in fact more than 20 major languages are spoken here (see page 21). English and Setswana are the two official means of communication, of which Setswana is the more widespread – some 80 per cent of the population use it as their first language and almost everybody understands it. Most people outside the remotest rural areas also speak and understand English.

Cultural groups are as varied as language, the diversity reflecting the fascinating turns of history over the past 2 000-odd years.

The original inhabitants were the Khoesan (sometimes spelt Khoisan, and popularly referred to as San or Bushmen). It is estimated that 40 000 members of this group still live in Botswana, but many regard this number with some suspicion, largely because of the difficulties of definition. So-called Bushman genes have spread widely through the population at large and it is hard to say with precision who is and who is not a Bushman. The main criterion is how the individual concerned describes her- or himself.

San culture is still, for the most part, alive and well. That it stands apart as that of the pristine hunter-gather, remaining untainted over the centuries by outside influences, is rubbish. The San have always been part of the mainstream of life in this country. In the past 100 to 150 years, however, the role they have played on that stage has tended to be that of the underdog, the marginalised and the exploited. In a way this has served to protect many aspects of their culture. Even today, San tend to live within their own communities and, for this reason, have kept alive their cultural traditions, beliefs and, to some extent, their knowledge. However, visitors will find it difficult to get to and observe the traditional Bushman communities (but not impossible: see below, and page 96).

In the past this country has been extremely sensitive about what is increasingly becoming known as 'cultural tourism'. Terms such as this are awkward because of their imprecision, and because what they represent is so quickly prostituted. I notice that the word 'eco-tourism' seems to mean many different things to many different people and perhaps, for that reason, one does not hear it as much as one used to. Personally, I think cultural tourism means meeting the indigenous people of a country and seeing how they live – how they eat, drink, cook, sleep, plant, reap and sow. Throughout my long association with the periphery of tourism I have many times been confronted with visitors' demands to 'meet the people'. On those rare occasions when the requests have been fulfilled, I have seen bridges built between cultures; I have seen an expansion of understanding and mutual acceptance.

The occasions have been infrequent because of the Botswana government's suspicion about this kind of tourism. And those suspicions have often, understandably, been fuelled by reports of abuse of one kind of another, especially with regard to the Bushmen. So cultural tourism has hardly developed in Botswana. But attitudes are slowly changing. A small but growing number of operators are, with government blessing, providing opportunities for guests to meet the 'locals', and where meet-and-mix happens it is very successful. You'll find the names of those who provide such introductions on page 96.

This relaxation affects more than the Bushman community, for there are many other groups with fascinating cultures. Among them are the Kwena, Ngawaketse and Ngwato (all three are of Tswana stock), the Herero, Kalanga, Pedi, Lete, Hambukushu, Subiya, Kgalagadi – to name but a few. Each group has its own heritage and language, and each offers much of interest to the visitor.

PLANNING YOUR TRIP

Basically, there are only two ways in which to see Botswana. You either drive yourself around, plan your own route and, subject to what is said elsewhere (about concession areas, the hazards of going it alone and so forth), wander where you will. Most of this country is classed as Tribal Land and, generally speaking, you may camp anywhere. Alternatively, you may use your car or an airline to get to your starting point, from where you travel onwards with a safari operator.

Almost all the Okavango and Chobe camps are fly-in. This means that you head for Maun or Kasane and, from there, travel to your camp by vehicle or light aircraft. You cannot just 'drive through the Okavango and admire the views and the animals'. More and more wilderness camps are opening up around the country and they are, almost by definition in remote places and therefore, invariably, hard to get to. I suspect that they too will become 'fly-ins'. I know there is talk of establishing safari lodges near or in the Kgalagadi Transfrontier Park and the Central Kalahari Game Reserve but, at best, these will be served by 4x4-type roads. Many lodge owners deliberately maintain their remoteness in order to discourage casual callers.

Outside the safari lodges and national parks there is much of what I believe makes Botswana special, namely the wilderness and what it holds. I am talking here of such places as the Kalahari Desert itself, the Okwa River, Hunter's Road, Makgadikgadi, the Western Woodlands, Drotsky's Cave, the Tsodilo Hills and a thousand other destinations, some of which I myself have yet to explore.

The important point about all these places is that they are not items on the commercial tourist menu. This means you have to do it all yourself. You decide what you want to see, you decide which routes to take, you decide how much time to invest, you take responsibility for yourself. You need a reliable 4x4 vehicle, experience, common sense, self-reliance and a sense of adventure. You have to be prepared to look after yourself because nobody else is going to.

If it is to be a safari lodge, camp or hotel, the preparation is as straightforward and minimal as making a booking through a travel agent. If, however, you are organising your own trip, then much greater effort is required. A journey to and through the routine venues – national parks, game reserves, a trip from Maun into the Delta and back – is not particularly complicated. But a foray to one of the more unexplored parts of the country is not to be taken lightly. It needs careful planning and preparation and some sensible back-up precautions. I cannot stress this too much. We see plenty of evidence of near-disaster, of people who don't listen to advice and totally underestimate the potential hostility of the Kalahari. In a recent incident some bright sparks drove off into the sands in an ordinary saloon car. They were found and rescued after a massive ten-day search – but only through good luck and the efforts of a large number of people and institutions who gave of their valuable time and expertise.

Although there is no real substitute for experience, it should not be necessary for those embarking on their first safari into the wilds, especially the wilds of Botswana to, as it were, reinvent the wheel. The aim here is to provide some useful basic information so that you will be suitably prepared and equipped for a safari. There is nothing more frustrating, when you have arrived at a point 200 km from nowhere, than to find that, say, the salt, toilet paper, tin opener, or films for the camera have been forgotten!

Ultimately, what you carry on safari is your personal choice and what is suggested below should be regarded simply as a guideline. There may be little of use here to the experienced traveller, but those who have not safaried extensively may well find this section helpful. These are the three golden rules worth keeping in mind:
• Keep everything simple. You've come to see and enjoy; to take a break from home, not to take home with you. Many an abandoned vehicle on the sides of Botswana's roads have collapsed and died from overweight!
• Never leave a water point without filling all your containers. You should allow roughly 5 litres of water per person per day. This includes a small allowance for washing.
• Never leave a filling station (fuel outlet) without replenishing your petrol or diesel – you may meet somebody who needs an emergency supply.

Major parks and reserves: timing your visit

Botswana's national parks and game reserves have their own particular attractions at any time of year. However, if your specific objective is to see game and to witness the great migratory herds, the following is a guide to the best visiting times.

Chobe National Park

The river front at Kasane and Linyanti are good all year round but best from May to October. Away from the river, and the Savute area, are best from November through to May, although, if the Savute Channel is flooded or the Mababe Depression contains long-standing water, May to October also offers excellent viewing. See page 110.

Moremi Game Reserve

Viewing here can be good all year round but the dry season, from May to November, is usually the best. See page 125.

Okavango Delta

The Okavango is a vast wetland, the size of which varies through the year because it is shaped and controlled, largely, by the rains which fall in Angola to the northwest and which are brought down along the Okavango River. The floods arrive at Mohembo, at the northwestern end of the Delta, as early as December, building up to a peak between January and March, but occasionally as late as May. These same floods slowly work their way through the vastness of the Delta in the succeeding months so that the highest levels in Maun, at the opposite end of the wetlands, are not recorded until July or August, sometimes even in September. The Delta is at its largest during the months of June and July and at its minimum extent in December and January. Although fishing can be good throughout the year, the best months seem to be from August to February, while the best game-viewing months are from July to October. See page 128.

Nxai Pan National Park

Successful game-viewing in this national park depends very much upon whether or not rain has fallen. If the rains have been good, December to early April are excellent months, especially for zebra and gemsbok . If the rains have failed, a visit to the park can be very disappointing from the point of view of seeing game. However, a good time to visit this park is June and July (which are usually dry months), during the springbok mating season. Khori bustard are plentiful all year round. Incidentally, the water at Nxai Pan is not only potable but also tastes good. Still, it's a good idea to travel with extra water. You'll also need a 4x4 to get to Nxai Pan, and to get around the park in the wet season. See page 123.

Makgadikgadi Pans Game Reserve

This reserve is set in beautiful countryside and should be enjoyed for that. From the first rain (which usually falls in November) onwards until April,

May and sometimes early June, the grasslands are occupied by herds of migrating antelope and their attendant predators. But the animals are very skittish and hard to find as there has been a lot of poaching on the outskirts of the park – which is difficult to control as the reserve is surrounded by cattle posts.

Also, lions are perceived as a threat as they sometimes take livestock. And it is difficult, with the limited number of game guards stationed here, to keep out the donkeys and goats that wander into the park. In the wet season large herds of zebra can be found in the eastern part of the reserve. It is also a good place to see raptors. It is advisable to bring your own drinking water: that within the reserve is very salty and quite sulphurous. See page 123.

Central Kalahari Game Reserve (CKGR)

Drought has severely reduced many of Botswana's game species and too much must not be expected of this reserve. As with Khutse (see below and page 120) several good rain years need to have elapsed before we can hope for the return of game in substantial numbers. However, six watering points have been established in the northern half of the CKGR, from Deception Valley to Pipers Pan, and game of some kind will always be encountered. In the wet season animals are more dispersed. See page 106.

Khutse Game Reserve

It is unusual to see significant quantities of game in this reserve, particularly of late (November 2000) owing to the prolonged drought. There need to have been several good years of rain before the game is likely to return in large numbers. Khutse is renowned for its excellent bird life. Game will most likely be found in the vicinity of pans at any time of year, but October to April is usually best. See page 120.

Mannyelanong Game Reserve

Here there's a nesting colony of Cape vultures; the birds are best seen in the winter months, from May to August or September. See page 217.

Mabuasehube area

This is now part of the Kgalagadi Transfrontier Park (see below). The largest concentrations of game will be seen in the vicinity of its pans during the rainy season, from October through to April. See page 122.

Kgalagadi Transfrontier Park

The park is divided by two major rivers, the Auob and the Nossob. Game-viewing is always good. However, it is particularly good along the Auob from June to October. The same is also true for the Nossob, but from January until April. It is well worth paying a visit to the great dune-fields that stretch between the two rivers during the rainy months. Covered with lush vegetation, they make a most striking sight. See page 118.

Suggested touring itineraries

What Botswana has to offer does not readily lend itself to easily presented travel packages. The following are, however, some suggestions which may help you with your planning.

Obviously, for fly-in travellers, the itinerary is going to be dictated by the time available and the size of their pockets. While the same may be true for the self-drive and self-sufficient visitor, money can be stretched a lot further and time becomes the principal limiting factor.

As a general rule, plan to spend a minimum of two nights in the Okavango, whichever of the two types of traveller you are. This means you'll probably be in camp by lunchtime, certainly by 4 pm, on the first day, which will give you a late afternoon and/or evening opportunity to explore, plus the whole of the following day. If your plane leaves the next morning you won't be able to squeeze much else in.

This comment holds true for many of the more isolated destinations. It is certainly true for places such as Drotsky's Cave and Tsodilo Hills. It usually takes the best part of a day to get to these places from almost anywhere, and to leave again the following morning is a sheer waste of time. Like the Okavango, Tsodilo, in my opinion, is worth three nights or even more; two is the absolute minimum.

Most of the places described in the chapters that follow give some indication, where appropriate, of how much time you should set aside.

Suggestions: two-wheel-drive

It is now possible for ordinary saloon cars to penetrate, and for their drivers and passengers to explore, large parts of Botswana. At the last count the Department of Roads were responsible for maintaining nearly 5 000 km of tar, 2 000 of gravel and 2 700 of earth and sand surfaces. In addition to this there are 10 000 km of tracks of various kinds, within the nine district councils, that are not maintained at all (many different up-to-date road maps are available, which should be used in planning your routes).

Of course, in spite of the ever-growing number of tarred kilometres, there are limitations. Although combis (mini-buses) have been known to negotiate the heart of the rough country, don't take chances. For example, the route between Maun and Kasane, through the Moremi Game Reserve via Savute, is a no-go area for anything other than a 4x4, certainly for the less intrepid traveller.

It is possible to travel on tarmac from Maun all the way up the western side of the Okavango Delta to the border gate at Mohembo, beyond Shakawe, and along the southeastern side to Shorobe. Maun itself is connected by tarred road to Nata; the Nata–Kasane section has been tarred for some years. The main road from Gaborone to Ghanzi is now complete, and so is the connection to Maun. The tarred short-cut from Gaborone through Thamaga to Kanye considerably reduces the time and distance to Jwaneng on the Ghanzi route. From the village of Sekoma a narrow but excellent tarred road runs through Werda to Tsabong, helping make the Kgalagadi Transfrontier Park more easily (and quickly) accessible, just as the tarmac road to Letlhakeng did for Khutse Game Reserve and the Central Kalahari.

These changes enable one to see much of what Botswana has to offer, notably the attractions of the arid southern and central Kalahari as well as the game-rich northern regions. The water-world of the Okavango and the northern parts of Chobe National Park are even more accessible.

For example, drive the Francistown–Nata–Maun route; leave your vehicle in Maun and fly into the Delta. Once there you have a number of options; camps range from the ultra-luxurious to the basic (and much cheaper) venue, and a traditional canoe, or mokoro, will get you around. Information on the various choices is available from travel agents in Maun and on page 258 of this guide.

From Maun, drive back to Nata and then head north on the tarmac road to Kasane. This is the gateway to the big-game world (although you cannot enter Chobe National Park in a saloon car and must arrange a game drive with one of the local safari companies). Either camp in the Chobe National Park or stay outside its boundary, at Chobe Safari Lodge or Kubu Lodge.

From Chobe, plan an overnight excursion into Zimbabwe, taking the excellent tarred road to Victoria Falls. Continue through Hwange National Park to Bulawayo, then turn south and make your way to South Africa via Beit Bridge. The alternative is to return to Botswana and head southwards to Francistown.

For the independent traveller there are one or two 'standard' routes through Botswana, popular itineraries that travel agents will know about, and which are covered elsewhere in this book.

Four-wheel-drive: the shorter trip

A great many options are open to you if you're an independent traveller with a 4x4 vehicle and limited time at your disposal. Possible routes are covered in detail in Chapter 8, and specific venues in Chapter 7. These are a couple of suggestions linking more than one destination:

Maun to Kasane via Victoria Falls. This is one of a great many options, an approximate 450-km journey which should take you six days to complete. You'll be camping, so self-sufficiency is the keyword. Start from Maun, spend one night at least at a Moremi Game Reserve campsite, two nights at Savute and three nights in one of the campsites around Kasane. In Kasane, enjoy a morning game drive and, in the afternoon, take a commercial boat-trip into the park. On your second day, either repeat the Chobe National Park experience (see page 39) or cross into Zimbabwe and spend the day at Victoria Falls, which is only 70 km away.

Maun to Tsodilo Hills and Shakawe. Four days, 900 km; camping. Spend the first night at Tsodilo Hills (400 km). Again, you will need to be self-sufficient. The first 350 km is tarred, the last 50 km unadulterated hell – two hours and more of low range first or at best second gear and 10–20 km/h all the way! But it will be worth it. Spend at least two nights at Tsodilo, then make your way back along Hell Run and up to Shakawe. There are several lodges and campsites here, and depending on your preference and pocket you can either slum it or live it up for a night (a shower, after what you've been through, will I'm told be a bit like heaven on earth!). From here it is an easy day's drive back to Maun.

Four-wheel-drive: the longer trip

For those with more time to spare, there's a splendid choice of lengthier expeditions. The following, again, is simply a representative sample of the options available to you.

Extension of the Maun–Kasane route. Two weeks; camping. Overnight in Maun, refuel, stock up and head northwards to Moremi South Gate. Spend four nights in the Moremi Game Reserve, dividing your time between the Third Bridge and Xakanaxa campsites (remember, you now have to book in advance). Then drive north to Savute and spend a couple of nights there. Head north again to Ihaha campsite in Chobe National Park. The final two nights before the journey home can be spent at Victoria Falls in Zimbabwe.

At the start of the trip, when you get to Maun, you will probably be eager to be up and at the big-game country, and reluctant to waste an afternoon. However, if the Thamalakane River is flowing, use the time to wander among the water lilies and take in the phenomenal bird life of the area's waterways. Or hire a mokoro (traditional canoe) and let your poler guide you through the quietness and peace. You'll find it well worthwhile.

Options from Maun. With more time to spend, all kinds of possibilities are open to the visitor with a four-wheel-drive vehicle, including visits to the Nxai Pan and Makgadikgadi National Park – especially rewarding if your visit coincides with the game migration. Or you can leave your vehicle in Maun and fly into the Delta for two or three days' camping and canoeing.

Remember that Maun is the last place where you can hire a mokoro if you follow the Moremi–Savute–Chobe itinerary (see pages 196 and 198). Take the standard route through Moremi to Savute, but then head north to the campsite on the Linyanti River. Alternatively, stop at Tjinga or Nogatsha, both pleasing but lesser-known campsites, in the Chobe National Park, on the way to Ihaha.

The Caprivi route. This takes you from Kasane over the Ngoma Bridge through Katima Mulilo, Popa Falls and Mohembo Gate to Shakawe. There is an excellent road that runs through the Caprivi enabling you to travel speedily and smoothly from one side of the Delta to the other. The route is varied and interesting, and I shall describe it in some detail. The assumption is that you will be travelling from east to west. As the trip takes you out of Botswana and into Namibia, you will have to clear Immigration at the Ngoma Bridge. It is also a good idea to check on the security situation, which has been somewhat volatile of late.

Unless you want to enjoy some last-minute game-viewing along the river bank, take the main tarmac road to Kachikau. This leads along the higher ground and then drops down to the river's floodplain, from where the Ngoma Bridge, which links Botswana and Namibia, is clearly visible. The distance from Kasane to the Ngoma Bridge is 64 km and will take you less than an hour.

Your next destination is Katima Mulilo, 67 km from the Ngoma Bridge border post. Here you'll find yourself, quite clearly, in a different country. Katima Mulilo is a bustling centre where you can pick up any spare parts needed, and stock up with excellent Windhoek beer! Note that Namibia has its own currency – the Namibian dollar – but that, at the time of writing (November 2000), the South African rand was still used and South African credit cards were valid. If it is likely to be important to you, it would be as well to check ahead of time.

From Katima Mulilo to the Kwando River is a run of about 120 km on a good-quality road that then continues for the remaining 212 km to the Popa Falls campsite. The latter, an appealing venue, is run by Namibia's Department of Nature Conservation. Petrol is available at Andara junction, not very far up the road from Popa Falls. In a real emergency, one might try one's luck at the safari camp south of Shakawe, but the camp is not in the petrol business so plan to refuel either at Andara or before leaving Botswana at Etsha-6 .

From the Popa Falls campsite you can walk and 'boulder-hop' your way to the main body of water. It's about half a kilometre wide, and its flow is eventually transformed into the whole of that magical, unique, 13 000-km^2 wetland paradise, the Okavango Delta – quite a thought.

Begin your return journey at the Andara junction. The road will take you through the Mhlango Game Reserve to the Mohembo Gate, which is the border between Botswana and Namibia. Here, you clear Customs and Immigration. The distance from the junction to the border is approximately 35 km.

What to take

Clothing

Whatever the time of the year, a shirt or blouse, shorts or a light skirt are all that are really necessary. Jeans or slacks, a long-sleeved cotton shirt and bathing costume are useful on safari; a jersey or jacket are handy for evenings and mornings; in winter, a warm hat or balaclava and a sleeveless waistcoat or tank-top would be a sensible combination (if your head and chest are warm, the rest of your body also feels warm).

Dun colours are generally the most suitable as they attract less attention and, it is said, do not draw tsetse fly to them as readily as do brighter colours. White is not really practical. Clothes should be of a durable material – opportunities for laundering may not be as frequent as one might wish, and thorns are a constant menace to delicate fabrics.

Day-wear is quite appropriate for summer evenings. In winter, however, and especially from May through to August, it can get very cold at night, so cold in fact that a small canister of water may freeze solid. So a change of warm clothing is highly recommended.

For the same reason, campers should pack warm sleeping bags. Tracksuits are useful since they help to build up layers of insulation as the temperature drops, and they are a comfortable alternative to pyjamas. Winter also demands warm socks, gloves and a hat, cap or, as mentioned, a balaclava, especially for those a little thin on top!

Shoes

There are as many opinions on correct footwear for the Kalahari as there are makes and types of shoe. The choice is yours, but a word or two might help you decide. It is not recommended that visitors go barefoot: the sand can get too hot to walk on and your feet can actually blister. Thorns, insects and scorpions are among other hazards. Heavy boots are a matter of preference but something lighter is really more practical. Choose a shoe that can be easily removed (so that the sand can be emptied out!) and which is made of a porous material, something that is easy to wash and which allows the foot to breathe. Open sandals and 'tackies' (running shoes) are suitable; a pair of 'flip-flops' handy, as it were, around camp.

Accessories

If animals, birds, the stars or endless vistas are what you are interested in, binoculars are an absolute must. So, too, is a camera. Recommended for larger game is a 200-mm lens; for birds, you'll need a lens of a minimum 400 mm. A wide-angle lens of 35 mm or less is helpful if you want to do justice to the magnificent views.

A word of warning, though, about optical equipment. Prodigious quantities of sand and dust are synonymous with Botswana in general and the Kalahari in particular. Take the greatest care, therefore, to protect delicate equipment. Here, you will need considerable ingenuity and effort to be successful – merely carrying your equipment in its container or a cloth bag is not enough. The dust will get in. Some people keep their cameras and binoculars inside sealed plastic bags, and bring along a spare supply of the bags. Professional photographers never wipe dust from a lens but, instead, blow the dust off with compressed air, small canisters of which can be obtained from photographic shops.

Hats, sunburn creams (especially of the barrier type) and sunglasses are essential, particularly if you are not used to the heat and the glare – both of which can be formidable. Insects can be a nuisance and repellents are recommended. Don't forget antimalarial tablets (Larium or Chloroquine), which are recommended for Botswana.

Some people regard a compass as a panacea to all problems of navigation: it is not. A compass (like the sun, if it's shining) will only tell you where north, south, east and west are. For good navigation in a country like Botswana – so lacking in landmarks – you need to (a) know where you are to start with; (b) have maps of the area you are in; (c) know how to use a map and compass; and (d) be able to work by dead-reckoning (because there are very few landmarks to help you).

YOUR VISIT: THE PRACTICALITIES

Entering Botswana

Many visitors arrive in Botswana by road. Unfortunately, direct flights from Europe are now no longer possible: you have to complete your journey through one of the neighbouring countries. Most traffic comes through Johannesburg, a route which Air Botswana, the national air carrier, shares with South African Airways. There are daily links and connections with Windhoek (Namibia), Victoria Falls (Zimbabwe) and Harare (Zimbabwe).

Entry documents

Passports All visitors require passports and, where applicable (see below) visas. They also need sufficient funds to support themselves for three months and, if arriving by air, a return ticket.

Visas are not required of passport holders from the following countries: all Commonwealth members, Austria, Belgium, Denmark, Germany, Finland, France, Greece, Italy, Liechtenstein, Luxembourg, Namibia, Netherlands, Norway, Pakistan, Republic of Ireland, Samoa (Western), San Marino, Sweden, Switzerland, United States of America, Uruguay and Yugoslavia.

Nationals of all other countries are required to obtain a visa. They should do so at least three months in advance of their intended visit, by writing to The Chief Immigration Officer, PO Box 942, Gaborone. Passport-size photographs are required for visa applications.

Length of visit The maximum time a non-resident may spend in Botswana is three months in any calendar year. However, it is usual practice, at the point of entry, to grant an initial period of one month. Once in the country, the period of stay can be extended by applying at any Immigration office.

Customs formalities

All goods acquired outside Botswana must be declared on entry into the country. Goods acquired from within the Southern African Common Customs Area (SACCA) – Botswana, South Africa, Swaziland, Namibia and Lesotho – are free from duty but may be liable to sales tax and additional levies. Visitors may bring into Botswana, duty free, the following:

Wine: 2 litres. *Spirits and alcoholic beverages:* 1 litre plus 6 x 340 ml cans of beer. *Cigarettes:* 400. Cigars: 50. Tobacco: 250 g. *Perfume:* 50 ml. *Toilet water:* 250 ml. Other new or used goods of a total value not exceeding 1 250 Units of Account (UA) per person. A Unit of Account is equal to R1.00. Minors – that is, children under the age of 18 – may claim these concessions except in respect of tobacco and alcohol.

Sales tax is payable on most consumable items and is usually 10 per cent of the item's value. It does vary, especially in respect of various alcoholic beverages. Note that sales tax is charged on spare fuel carried in containers.

Permits

Some imported items require special permits, which are obtainable from the ministries concerned (among them Wildlife, Mines and Agriculture). If you are not sure whether a permit is necessary for a particular item, contact the Customs authorities at the Department of Customs and Excise, P/Bag 0041, Gaborone; tel 391-2455.

If your vehicle is equipped with a two-way radio, a citizen band radio or a mobile telephone set you will need to obtain a permit from the Radio Licence Office, Botswana Telecommunications Corporation, PO Box 700, Gaborone; tel 395-8246/395-8000, fax 391-3355. Allow one month for the processing of the application.

Health certificates

Currently, yellow fever inoculation certificates are not required unless you come from an African country north of the Zambezi, or from Angola or northern Namibia, where the fever is endemic. You should be inoculated at least 10 days before entering Botswana and it is valid for 10 years.

It is advisable for all travellers going beyond Gaborone to be inoculated against the following diseases and to carry an International Certificate of Vaccination: hepatitis A (now available for children as well as adults); rabies; typhoid; tetanus; polio (adults require boosters); meningitis (children under 6 years of age). By all accounts the risk is extremely low, but it may be as well for foreigners to be on the safe side.

Border Posts
Botswana/Republic of South Africa

Border Post	Times of operation
Pont Drift	7.30 to 16.30 daily
Platjan	7.30 to 16.30 daily
Zanzibar	7.30 to 16.30 daily
Martins Drift	8.00 to 18.00 daily
Parrs Halt	8.00 to 18.00 daily
Sikwane	7.00 to 19.00 daily
Tlokweng Gate	7.00 to 22.00 daily
Ramotswa	7.00 to 19.00 daily
Pioneer Gate	7.00 to 19.00 daily
Ramatlabama	7.00 to 20.00 daily
Phitshane Molopo	7.30 to 16.30 daily
Bray	7.00 to 16.00 daily
Middlepits	8.00 to 18.00 daily
Bokspits	report to South African/Botswana Police
McCarthy's Rust	8.00 to 16.00 daily
Kgalagadi Transfrontier Park	*Note:* Customs facilities are now available

Botswana/Namibia

Mamuno	7.00 to 22.00 daily
Mohembo	6.00 to 18.00 daily
Ngoma	8.00 to 16.00 daily

Botswana/Zimbabwe

Mpandamatenga	8.00 to 16.00 daily (for non-commercial purposes only since there are no forwarding agents at this post)
Matsiloje	6.00 to 18.00
Ramokwebane	6.00 to 20.00 daily
Kazungula Road	6.00 to 18.00 daily

Botswana/Zambia

Kazungula Ferry	7.00 to 18.00 daily

Border Posts

There are a number of additional entry points, but with no border posts on the Botswana side. In these instances you are required to report to the nearest police station immediately. Such points of entry include Bokspits, Baines' Drift and Buffel's Drift. Visitors should also note that there are no bridges across the Molopo River in the south, and that there are no high-level bridges across the Limpopo. Both rivers are liable to flooding, and at those times access may not be possible.

It is important to remember that border posts will be especially crowded on the evening before, and on the first morning and last night of, a public holiday (see page 59). Even though the staff try to prevent long delays they are usually unavoidable. Don't plan to rush through as soon as the post opens – you probably won't get far, and certainly if you're on a main transport route because freight trucks queue during the night. Either alter your travel times or try one of the lesser used border posts. The longest delays can be expected at Ramokwebane, Ramatlabama and Tlokweng.

Airports in Botswana

Location	Times of operation
Sir Seretse Khama, Gaborone	6.00 to 22.00 daily
Maun	6.30 to 20.00 year round
Francistown	7.00 to 19.00 year round
Selebi-Phikwe	6.00 to 18.00 summer
	7.00 to 18.00 winter
Kasane	6.00 to 18.30 daily
Jwaneng	7.30 to 16.30 weekdays only
Orapa	7.30 to 16.30 weekdays only

Currency

Payment in only the following types of currency is accepted by the Customs authorities: cash or traveller's cheques in rand, sterling and United States dollars. In the case of Zimbabwe dollars, payment will only be accepted if tendered in traveller's cheques. When entering or leaving the country, visitors and residents are pemitted to carry with them, without prior authorisation, pula notes and coins and/or foreign currency notes and coins up to a total of P10 000 per person.

Vehicle licences and insurance

Motor vehicles, caravans and trailers that are legitimately licensed and registered in their country of origin can be brought into Botswana by visitors and used by them for a period of six months. As in many other countries, vehicle owners are required to hold a minimum third party insurance. Third party insurance valid within the Southern African Customs Union (SACCA) is also valid in Botswana. Only road tax (see below) is therefore payable in respect of vehicles from these countries.

Third party insurance can be obtained at the border post. Owners of vehicles from outside the SACCA also need to obtain a Temporary Import Permit, which is valid for six months and which can be renewed at the Customs offices.

Driver's licences Foreign driver's licences are valid in Botswana for a period of six months. Licences not printed in English should be accompanied by a written translation. Carry your driver's licence with you at all times when behind the wheel.

Road tax for all foreign vehicles entering the country is currently P5 (or R10, from which you receive P1.60 change). Visitors arriving by road from either Zambia and Zimbabwe are required to pay both the tax and a sum for insurance cover, a combined amount of P15. This must be paid either in rand or pula (Zimbabwean or Zambian currencies are not accepted).

Firearms

The control of firearms in Botswana is very strict. There is a total restriction on the importation of side-arms, automatic weapons and small-bore (.22 calibre, for example) rifles. An import permit is required for any weapon allowed in. The permit may be obtained by writing in advance to The Officer in Charge, Central Arms Registry, P/Bag 0012, Gaborone; tel 395-1161 ext. 2466.

Boats

In order to control the spread of aquatic weeds, the authorities require that a permit be obtained for each boat brought into the country. This must be applied for in advance from the Department of Water Affairs, P/Bag 0029, Gaborone; tel 360-7100.

Similarly, permits are required for boats that are being transported from one zone of the country to another. These too may be obtained from the Department of Water Affairs.

Food

Foodstuffs, including fresh meat, may be imported only if they are for immediate and personal consumption. You are limited to 25 kg of meat per vehicle. In certain cases importation of dairy and uncooked meat may be prohibited (for instance, in the event of outbreaks of foot and mouth disease) unless an import certificate is obtained from the Veterinary Department, P/Bag 0032, Gaborone; tel 395-0500.

Please note that it is *not* necessary to have a health permit from the Veterinary Department in order to transport meat for personal consumption within Botswana. There are certain rules, however, with which you should familiarise yourself if this is relevant to your trip (basically, meat can be taken north but not brought back to the south).

Pets

It is possible to bring domestic pets into Botswana with very little difficulty (my Jack Russell goes everywhere with me!). For both dogs and cats you will need a movement permit issued by a state veterinarian indicating that the animal has been inoculated against rabies. The rabies vaccine must have been administered not more than one year before the end of the intended journey and not less than one month before it commences. A certificate from a state veterinarian, certifying that the animal is in good health, is also required.

Pro forma movement permits have been drawn up by the authorities and are available in Botswana, Lesotho, Swaziland, South Africa, Namibia and Zimbabwe. With this form, which is valid for 60 days, dogs and cats can be carried freely between and among these countries. If you bring a dog or cat into Botswana and intend that it should travel around with you, it is essential that you carry a valid movement permit. You may have to produce it at the numerous veterinary cordon fences through which you will pass. If you do not have such a permit, you may not be allowed to proceed. Visitors from Zambia who produce equivalent documents will also be allowed to enter the country with their pets.

It should be noted, however, that dogs and cats are *not* allowed into national parks and game reserves. There are kennelling facilities for both these kinds of pet in Gaborone and Selebi-Phikwe.

To bring a horse into Botswana, you'll need to obtain temporary export and import permits, which must be arranged, well in advance of the intended visit, through the veterinary and animal health departments of both in the country of origin and of Botswana. This will require a dourine test on mares within 21 days of travelling.

Veterinary services Limited services are available in Botswana. State vets may be found in many of the main centres but there are private veterinary clinics only in Francistown and Gaborone. Gaborone's Veterinary and Agricultural Consultants offer a good, reliable 24-hour service, and may be contacted at: PO Box 41010, Gaborone; tel and fax 392-8689. They are situated in Tlokweng, on the outskirts of town on the main road to the South African border. A second veterinary practice operates close to Gaborone's main mall; phone Dr I. Ndzinge on 392-6817.

Plant material

Seeds, bulbs, plants and trees may be imported subject to restrictions. Contact the Chief Agricultural Research Officer, P/Bag 0033, Gaborone.

Health

Diseases

Malaria, a disease transmitted by infected mosquitoes, is encountered in all parts of Botswana and visitors are urged to take anti-malaria tablets. The type of malaria most commonly encountered is falciparum, one of the complications of which is cerebral malaria, a very serious condition indeed. Generally, the malarial threat is worst in the north of the country and here visitors are advised to take anti-malaria tablets throughout the year.

There are two major schools of thought concerning malaria. One option is to take nothing and treat it when you get it. Many locals adopt this approach, ignoring the prophylactics because they are not 100 per cent guaranteed and could mask the symptoms (a more dangerous situation because infection might not be correctly diagnosed in time). The alternative is to try and protect yourself against it – although some argue here that, if you contract the infection, it may not be recognized due to the symptoms being masked by the drugs you are taking to prevent getting it!

You must make your own choice – but always be aware that malaria is prevalent in Botswana, and that many unprotected residents die of it each year. Visitors who have come from a non-malarial region should not expose themselves to unnecessary risks and should take a prophylactic.

Botswana pharmacists recommend the following procedure:

• Seven days before arrival in the country, take one Larium tablet (active ingredient Mefloquine), followed by one a week during the visit and for four weeks after the visit. There have been reports of side-effects with this new drug but these can be reduced if the tablet is taken with a meal. Larium is not recommended for those with high blood pressure.

• If Larium is not the preferred choice, an alternative is two tablets of any Chloroquine-based prophylactic seven days before arrival, followed by two a week thereafter and for four weeks after the visit. This tablet regime should be accompanied by two Paludrine (active ingredient Proguanil) a day. Doses can be suitably reduced for children.

Malaria resistant to Chloroquine has been reported in Botswana. It is for this reason that Paludrine is taken as well, for stronger protection. It must be stressed that, in the opinion of Botswana medics, taking a Chloroquine-based tablet *without* the Paludrine back-up is extremely foolish.

Cerebral malaria is not a different variety of malaria. It is an infection so severe that the parasite has passed through the blood/brain barrier and is multiplying in the brain cells, which many drugs cannot reach. If it is caught early enough, it can be treated. Severe (if not fatal) difficulties will occur when there are long delays in diagnosis.

Some of the best advice I've heard for avoiding malaria sounded naïve to me at first, even though it came from one of Africa's leading authorities on the subject. 'Don't get bitten', he said! He went on to explain that sleeping under a net reduces the chances of being bitten by almost 80 per cent. Wearing long socks, long pants and long-sleeved shirts in the evening is another smart move. These steps, backed up by insect repellents, is probably the most effective thing you can do. Many regard Mylol as a better repellent than Tabard. Bayticol is also said to be excellent: it's expensive but (depending on how often you wash yourself) will last for days.

Regrettably, the country is now the **AIDS** capital of Africa. Routine precautions against contracting the HI virus are vitally important here. In Botswana, which is home to about 1.6 million people, it is now (November 2000) estimated that about 17 per cent of the total population are HIV-positive. Among adults – that is, residents between 15 and 49 years of age – the incidence is higher, probably nearer 30 per cent. In pregnant women, the group most commonly measured, rates vary from town to town but in some cases the figures are as high as 40–50 per cent. There is no need to go so far as to bring your own needles for use in the event of accident or emergency, although some people do. Doctors, hospitals and clinics are well versed on the now standard and effective, anti-AIDS procedures: I myself have witnessed the use of new needles and watched the destruction of used equipment at a hospital.

AIDS is an avoidable disease and there are no grounds for fear of catching it accidentally. Unprotected sex, of course, is simply asking for trouble: using condoms dramatically reduces the risk, as does abstaining from sex with strangers. It is not possible to catch AIDS from mosquitoes. Tests have shown that, although the insect does swallow human blood, the enzymes in its stomach destroy the virus so that it cannot be passed on to the person next bitten. There is no observable correlation between regions of malaria and the distribution of HIV/AIDS. There is therefore no need to tailor travel plans to HIV risk: just be careful.

Everything said about mosquitoes is applicable to **tsetse fly**.

Bilharzia is an ever-present threat in Africa, and Botswana, despite its reputation as desert country, is no exception. As a general rule, it is probably safe to assume that all rivers, streams and dams are infected, although not heavily. This is also true of the Okavango, especially around populated areas. The only way to avoid contracting the disease is not bathe or wade in water. Curiously, bilharzia cannot be caught by drinking untreated, infected water. Saliva is sufficient to prevent contamination. The disease is easily cured today. Symptoms take at least six weeks to develop.

Trypanosomiasis, or sleeping sickness, a disease transmitted by the bite of an infected tsetse fly, is a much reduced threat in modern Botswana. At its widest extent it occurs only in Ngamiland, in the Ngami, Okavango, Mababe and Chobe areas. The fly can inflict a painful bite and, if you should contract the disease, its symptoms, including headaches and a fever, develop only after about two weeks. A blood test can confirm if a patient is suffering from sleeping sickness. The condition is easily cured.

Rabies is endemic in many animal populations in Botswana, but remains rare. Its presence is often marked by unusual behaviour – an unprovoked attack on a human, for example, or unusual friendliness.

When a suspected rabid creature bites, it is important to get the patient to a hospital as soon as possible. A treatment is available which involves only five injections and which is extremely effective, if administered quickly enough after the bite – that is, within 24 hours. If it isn't, death will result. Strange as it may seem, the most effective immediate first-aid is to wash the wound with soap and water: soap kills the virus. Any soap will do, including dishwashing liquid. There is now a protective vaccination, but a rabid bite must still be treated.

Tick-bite fever affects many people, especially newcomers to the country and, therefore, visitors. It is prevalent in the wet season, particularly in March and April, and is passed on to humans from the bite of a tiny, pinhead sized tick. The disease incubates for seven days and then manifests itself. The symptoms include a severe aching of the bones, headaches, backaches and fever. Although it can be serious and exceedingly unpleasant, it is a self-limiting disease and will run its course in three to four days. Typically, other symptoms include swollen and painful glands. It's nearly always possible to locate an infected bite – the site will be marked by a raised yellow head with a small black central spot. There is much controversy about immunity, and whether this can be acquired by stoically enduring the pain until the body's system defeats the infection. Medical experts in Botswana suggest that there is no merit in following this questionable course and that the sufferer should report to a hospital, where the disease is easily controlled through a course of tetracycline.

Finding ticks on your body is an experience you might have to get used to. They are easily dislodged, though care should be taken that the embedded head as well as the body is removed in order to avoid infection. Removing very small ticks can be a problem. A useful way is to smear them with Vaseline, grease or a commercial sealant. A drop on the tick prompts it to release its hold and it can be pulled away when the sealant is removed.

Tampan ticks are one of the Kalahari's little unpleasant menaces. They are typically found living in the sand, under trees, usually but not always isolated trees, where game or cattle congregate. They are attracted by the carbon dioxide given off by our bodies, quickly emerge from their shelter and swarm up legs or over bodies. Rather than bite, they abraid the surface of the skin and engorge themselves on blood. They tend to release their hold and drop to the ground at the slightest movement.

They are much more unpleasant than they are harmful but you will most certainly want to avoid them. You can do this by not using trees where game and cattle obviously stand. If the ground is sandy and bare and big animals are about, the chances are that there will be tampan ticks.

Venoms

Scorpions are numerous in the sandveld of the Kalahari, and basic precautions include shaking out clothes and emptying out shoes before putting them on. The unwary are often bitten while picking up firewood, so it is wise to kick or knock the wood first. Many scorpions live in trees, especially under loose bark. A sting can be extremely painful but it is not generally dangerous, and within an hour or so the effects will have worn off. The best treatment is to cool the site of the sting and to administer a mild painkiller. Again and again, my Bushman friends insist that there is a more effective approach, namely to catch and kill the creature, squeeze its innards onto the palm of your hand, mix it up and rub it into the excoriated wound site. Experts scoff, Bushman smile forgivingly, and I'm still waiting for a friend to get stung so he or she can try it out.

Snakes Snakebite is a difficult issue to discuss in concise terms. Broad-spectrum anti-snakebite serums are available and, if you are travelling independently, you should consider taking one with you. They generally have a short shelf-life and need to be kept constantly cool, if not refrigerated. This is not always easy. And sometimes, an anti-venom injection has caused more problems than it has cured. If you're going to arm yourself with a kit, you'll need to know your snakes and how to use the serum.

An alternative to a snakebite kit is a new method of treating snakebite which, to me, seems a far more attractive choice. It is known as the Sutherland Method (after its Australian originator) or the Pressure Immobilisation System, and it involves only a few crepe bandages. It is not my intention here to explain the system in full but, essentially, it requires that the victim be rested, soothed and relaxed. The injured limb is completely bound – from one end to the other – with the bandages to exert firm but gentle pressure. The object is to restrict the movement of the lymph system in which the poison is transported. *No tourniquet is applied.*

One advantage of this procedure is that, in contrast to the tourniquet method (which can inhibit blood flow, with dangerous consequences), the affected limb is not at risk from blood depletion. Wolf Haacke, snake expert at the Transvaal Museum in Johannesburg, who is an exponent of the method, tells me that one can learn the details from Johan Marais' book *Snake versus Man,* and from snake parks. My advice is to study the method; it seems a valid compromise between risking the dangers of incorrectly administered serum and doing nothing at all.

Other risks and discomforts

Water in the towns and villages, reassuringly, is perfectly safe to drink. It is recommended to visitors, though – those who want to take sensible precautions – that they are vaccinated against **hepatitis A and B**, which are common diseases, before entering the country. An alternative is an injection of immune globulin that will provide protection for about three months. It is also advisable to have a **tetanus** and a **typhoid** booster. **Venereal infections** are quite common, especially gonorrhoea. The **sun** in the Kalahari is fierce, and those whose skins are not used to it should wear hats and apply sunburn creams, especially the kind with ultra-violet screening properties. The **dust** in the dry season will irritate unaccustomed eyes, so take eye-wash solution with you. Mild attacks of **diarrhoea** are not uncommon; Lomotil, a non-prescription medicine, is an effective cure.

Medical facilities

Botswana is well served by hospitals and health centres. General hospitals are located in or near Maun, Ghanzi, Gaborone, Francistown, Lobatse, Mahalapye, Serowe, Selebi-Phikwe, Molepolole, Kanye, Mmadinare, Mochudi, Ramotswa, Jwaneng and Orapa. Many of the villages throughout the country have medical clinics staffed by trained personnel. These clinics should be regarded as a resource not to be overlooked, especially for less serious complaints. Many are in radio contact with hospitals.

The state hospital in Gaborone is the Princess Marina (tel 395-3221); in Francistown the Jubilee (tel 241-2333). The Gaborone Private Hospital (P/Bag BR130, Gaborone; tel 391-0999, fax 390-1998) offers an excellent medical and emergency service.

Medical Rescue International (operating in Botswana since 1991) offers immediate, professional help in emergencies. The organisation operates a network of qualified medical staff, ambulances and Rapid Response services. Vehicles are equipped to Advanced Life Support Level and are able to provide medical air evacuations manned by trained flight personnel with appropriate equipment. Contact them at MRI Botswana, P/Bag BR256, Gaborone; tel 390-3066 (Admin) and 391-0601 (Emergency), or dial 911 (and, for Botswana mobile or cellphones, 112). The fax number is 390-2117.

First aid

If you intend to travel independently, and to the remoter areas, carry a first-aid handbook with you. Many lives have been lost unnecessarily through failure to take the simple precautions clearly outlined in such a book. You should also include a first-aid kit in your inventory. The Automobile Association, the Red Cross or any chemist will help you select suitable items for it. Heatstroke may prove to be a problem, and your first-aid equipment should include salt tablets. Some people may find that the intensely dry air of the Kalahari causes congestion in the sinuses; take along some kind of decongestant, too.

Infection can spread very rapidly, so keeping clean on safari is important. It is possible, with practice, to complete a respectable bath with only three mugs of water! Sweat-rashes often result from a combination of dirt and heat. Talcum powder will control the condition but cleanliness will help avoid it altogether. Another aid to controlling infection is a styptic pencil. Rubbed on bites, it reduces the irritation – and hence the scratching – and lessens the chance of infection from dirty fingernails.

Money

Currency and banks

Botswana's unit of currency is the pula, whose value is linked to a basket of four international currencies and the South African rand, and which has generally performed better than neighbouring currencies. In recent years its value has varied from 25 to 35 per cent above the rand, meaning that P1.00 will buy about R1.35 and, conversely, R1.35 is needed to buy P1.00. Visitors from the subregion will thus find Botswana expensive.

Bureaux de change are found in the larger centres and at some of the bigger border posts, while traveller's cheques and foreign currency can be changed at all banks, throughout the week and on Saturday mornings. Be warned that banking can be a time-consuming business in Botswana, especially at month's end. Foreign currencies are unlikely to be accepted over the counter. Generally speaking, hotels and tourist shops will accept US dollars, but will also take care not to lose over the exchange rate!

International credit cards

Botswana is not yet entirely credit-card conscious, although this is changing. Most of the travel agents, hotels and safari operators can and do accept credit cards. However, don't be surprised if you run into difficulties in chemists, supermarkets and the like. Petrol stations require cash. Using an international credit card, it is possible to draw up to P1 000.00 per day from automated teller machines (ATMs). Not every ATM is linked to all the banks; you need to check the machine itself for instructions.

Banks in Botswana

The country's four commercial banks are Barclays Bank of Botswana Ltd, Standard Chartered Bank of Botswana Ltd, First National Bank of Botswana Ltd and Stanbic Bank of Botswana Ltd. They provide high branch coverage backed up by agencies and ATMs in the major centres. Banks are not open on public holidays. Normal opening times are:*Barclays* main branches: Monday to Friday 8.30 am to 3.30 pm; Saturdays 8.15 am to 10.45 am. *First National Bank* main branches: Monday to Friday 9 am to 3.30 pm; Saturdays 9 am to 11 am. *Standard Chartered main branches:* Monday to Friday 8 am to 2.30 pm; Saturdays 9 am to 11am. *Stanbic* main branches: Monday to Friday 9 am to 3.30 pm; Saturday 8.30 am to 11 am.

Bank agencies around the country do not always observe standard hours of business, opening for shorter periods and are often closed on Saturdays. Agencies maintain current and savings accounts and will cash traveller's cheques. They do not, however, deal in foreign currencies, apart from the South African rand, except by special arrangement. They issue foreign exchange and traveller's cheques only by special arrangement.

Shopping

Eighty per cent of what we consume in Botswana is imported, and you'll find pretty well everything you need or want at prices slightly lower than elsewhere in southern Africa. Most day-to-day consumer items are readily available in the larger centres. Gaborone's retail sector is expanding, its modern shopping areas stocking the luxuries as well as the basics.

Good supermarkets can be found in Lobatse, Gaborone, Mahalapye, Palapye, Selebi-Phikwe, Francistown and Maun. Kasane, too, has a small supermarket. These towns also boast good clothing stores, liquor outlets, hardware shops, chemists, bookshops and gift (curio) shops. In the larger centres, imported fresh vegetables can usually be purchased without difficulty. Mondays and days following public holidays may sometimes present the shopper with temporary shortages, such as milk and vegetables.

Hours of trading are generally from 8 am until 5 pm, although bottle stores (liquor outlets) open at 10 am and close at 7 pm, Monday to Saturday. Some shops, especially those in the smaller centres, close for an hour at lunchtime. Some of the supermarkets in the larger centres open on Sundays. In most of the larger towns, too, at least one establishment, stocking the usual range of household requirements, remains open until as late as 8 or 9 pm, and it will invariably be open on public holidays as well.

All government offices, businesses, banks and most shops are closed during such holidays, although many of the supermarkets in the larger centres open for shortened periods.

Botswana does not have a sophisticated photographic market. If you are using specialist film, it is best to bring it with you. Colour-slide film is available only in the main centres and in some safari camps. There is a slight risk that this film might be over its sell-by date or has been ill-protected against the heat. Some centres can process colour prints on 'one hour' processing machines, but all colour slides and prints that do not fit these machines are sent outside the country for processing.

Shopping is a much more precarious business in small villages around the country. Almost every little centre has its store and a bottle store or 'Liquor Restaurant'. The range of goods in these outlets is sometimes amazing, at most times limited, but the basics will be available. Bottle (liquor) stores usually restrict themselves to soft drinks, beer and the cheaper spirits – but they are quite capable, occasionally, of unearthing an unexpected bottle of wine or a good whisky! Most of the stores on the main routes have refrigerators, but in the remoter areas you'll find nothing cold or fresh.

Business hours

There are two sets of business hours in Botswana: commercial enterprises generally open from 8 am to 5 pm although, in the smaller centres, some may close for lunch (1–2 pm). Government, post offices and all council and local government institutions, on the other hand, start work at 7.30 am and end at 4.30 pm, breaking for lunch from 12.30 pm to 1.45 pm.

Time

Botswana lies in the same time zone as South Africa. It does not have daylight saving, so there are no changes to the clocks during the course of a year. We are either one hour or two hours ahead of the United Kingdom (depending on their summer or winter time).

Electricity

Electricity is distributed through a standard 220 volt system but (annoyingly) there are two types of wall plug. Generally speaking, in the older houses you'll find 3-pin round-pin plugs; the more modern buildings will usually be fitted with 3-pin square-pin 13-amp plugs.

Post and telecommunications

Botswana has one of the most advanced telecommunications systems in Africa, with automatic telephone exchanges throughout the country, in both the larger towns and all those rural centres that have telephones. All are interconnected on an internal trunk-dialling system. International direct dialling facilities are available. In areas where there are no telephones, word of emergency can be communicated in two ways: the police will accept messages, including international telegrams, and most of the professional hunters and safari operators operate radio networks.

Telex and facsimile (fax) services Public services are on offer at post offices in Francistown, Gaborone, Lobatse, Palapye and Selebi-Phikwe. Facsimile terminals are available at the Botswana Telecommunication Corporation offices in Gaborone and Francistown. Many of the bigger hotels will also allow residents the use of their facsimile facilities.

Cellphones (mobile phones) The two operating companies are Orange and Mascom, whose coverage extends to most urban areas and along the main roads only. Roaming agreements are expanding the coverage.

Coin- and card-operated phones are distributed widely, and can be found even in some of the smaller villages. Cards can be purchased in many (but by no means all) shops.

Useful contacts

Lists of these appear in the Appendices (see page 254) and include details relating to government ministries and departments, to diplomatic and consular representation, to international organisations based in Botwana, and to the various service organisations.

Public holidays in Botswana

New Year's Day – 1 January
Public Holiday – 2 January or, if on a Sunday, 3 January
Good Friday (variable)
Public holiday on the Saturday following Good Friday
Easter Sunday
Easter Monday
Ascension Day (variable)
Sir Seretse Khama Day – 1 July
President's Day – 17 July
Public holiday on the working day following President's Day
Botswana Day – 30 September (if Botswana Day falls on a Saturday
or Sunday then it will be celebrated on the following Monday.)
Christmas Day – 25 December
Boxing Day – 26 December

Reading about Botswana

A great deal has been written about Botswana, and one researcher and writer merits special mention, namely Alec Campbell, formerly curator of the National Museum and Art Gallery and a resident of some 35 years' standing. His *Guide to Botswana*, and the booklet *Sites of Historic and National Interest in and around Gaborone*, are highly recommended.

Other recommended reading includes *Okavango* and *The Bushmen* (both by P. Johnson & A. Bannister); *Chobe Elephants* (Bruce Aiken); *Gaborone: the Complete City Guide* (by Patricia Farrow); *Guide to Gaborone* (Alec Campbell & Mike Main); *Exploring Tati: Places of Historic and Other Interest in and around Francistown* (C. van Waarden); *Birds of Southern Africa* (Kenneth Newman); *Roberts' Birds of Southern Africa* (Gordon Maclean); *Sasol Birds of Southern Africa* (Ian Sinclair); *Kalahari: Life's Variety in Dune and Delta* (Mike Main); *The Shell Field Guide to the Common Trees of Okavango Delta and Moremi Game Reserve, The Shell Field Guide to the Wild Flowers of Okavango Delta and Moremi Game Reserve, The Shell Map of Moremi Game Reserve; The Shell Map of Chobe National Park* (all by Veronica Roodt); *The Dangerous Snakes of Africa* (Stephen Spawls & Bill Branch); *Land Mammals of Southern Africa – a Field Guide* (Reay Smithers); *A Field Guide to the Mammals of Botswana* (Peter Comley & Salome Meyer); *A Field Guide to the Tracks & Signs of Southern & East African Wildlife* (Chris & Tilde Stuart), and *Wild Ways* (Peter Apps).

GETTING AROUND IN BOTSWANA

Mobile safari operators

If you are not able to provide your own transport for exploring Botswana, or if you prefer to make use of experts to take you off the beaten track, there are a number of operators who run mobile safaris in Botswana. A mobile safari is a commercial tour operation which moves from place to place by boat, vehicle or both, camping in the bush or using the facilities offered by some of the fixed camps or national park campsites.

Starting points

There are basically two categories of starting point: those outside Botswana, and those inside the country. The closer you can get to your main area of interest under your own steam, of course, the cheaper the safari costs will be. The main starting points in Botswana are Gaborone, Kasane and Maun.

A good-quality tarred road leads to Gaborone and Kasane and a reliable saloon car can get you there from South Africa, Zimbabwe or Zambia. Maun can be reached from Nata, or the track from Kasane via the Savute, and tar reaches both the Namibian border posts at Mohembo and Mamuno. The road from Nata to Maun is tarred; the road via Savute varies in condition depending upon the time of the year and how much traffic has been on it, but should not be undertaken in anything but a 4x4.

Trying to keep abreast of so mobile a population as these safari operators is a daunting task! On page 62 you'll find a list, with addresses and contact numbers, of all the well-known and reputable mobile safari operators known to me, including those based in Botswana as well as in neighbouring countries. It is now possible to go on a number of different, specialised and, in some cases, unusual types of safari (walking, elephant-back, horseback, birding, photographic safaris and so forth), and on the list I've also included brief information about these as well as the traditional safari operators. Certain variables affect cost, and you will need to consider these before making your final choice of safari operator.

Factors affecting price

Use the following list of variables to help you make your decision. Discuss them with a travel agent who is experienced in this field.

Do it yourself or full service: The degree to which you are prepared to participate physically in the day-to-day chores of safari life is a considerable factor influencing cost.

Level of service: Some companies ask you to 'help here and there', others want you to do nothing, while some go to the extremes in pampering you – as in the luxurious, legendary East African safaris of a now (almost) forgotten era.

Ready-made vs customised packages: Whether the safari is a standard package or one tailored to your precise requirements.

Number of days the safari lasts

Number of people in the group

Distance travelled on safari

Places visited: You pay extra for visiting expensive places like Chobe National Park and Moremi Game Reserve. You also pay for exclusivity, and for privacy.

Company's reputation: You can expect to pay a little more for the security of a good reputation, one based on many years of competent service.

Guide's reputation: Sometimes there's a premium on the group-leader or guide of your choice.

Inflation: High oil prices are working their way rapidly through the economy and are striking Maun as I write. Costs will definitely rise across the board, driven principally by increases in the price of Avgas and fuel for trucks and boats.

Add-on extras: There will be such additional costs as, for instance, a flight above the Victoria Falls, or an extra trip by mokoro – excursions which may not be part of the package. Try to pre-empt these.

Speciality tours: Price may be affected by the safari's specialised nature.

Gratuities: Although lodges state that their prices are 'all inclusive', this does not cover gratuities for general staff – nor tipping the guide!

I suggest that, after considering these factors, you contact your own travel agent, or one of those listed on page 258, and let their recommendations guide you to the final choice. After all, the agents are right on the spot (especially those in Maun), and most certainly know what is going on in the mobile safari business.

Mobile safari operators

(The figures in brackets indicate those companies that have been in operation for more than 10 years, and whose staff in Botswana are understood to hold Professional Guide licences; bear in mind that the list is not comprehensive.)

Afroventures (+20) PO Box 1200, Paulshof 2056, South Africa; tel (011) 807-3720, fax (011) 807-3480. PO Box 232, Kasane, Botswana; tel 625-0456, fax 625-0119.

Capricorn Safari (+10) Private Bag 21, Maun; tel 686-0351, fax 686-0571.

Crocodile Camp Safaris (+10) PO Box 46, Maun; tel 686-0265, fax 686-0493.

Drifters (+10) PO Box 48434, Roosevelt Park 2129, South Africa; tel (011) 486-1224, fax 486-1237.

Go Wild (+10) PO Box 56, Kasane; tel 625-0468, fax 625-1297.

Island Safaris PO Box 116, Maun; tel 686-0300, fax 686-0205.

Kitso Safaris (+10) PO Box 236, Maun; tel and fax 686-0493.

Nata Lodge (+10) Private Bag 10, Francistown; tel 621-1210, fax 621-1265.

Okavango Wilderness Safaris (+10) Private Bag 14, Maun, Botswana; tel 686-0086, fax 686-0632; Central Reservations PO Box 651171, Benmore 2010, South Africa; tel (011) 884-1458/9, fax (011) 883-6255.

Overland Safaris (+10) PO Box 82, Warden 9890, South Africa; tel (058) 643-0646, fax (058) 643-0670.

Penduka Safaris (+20) PO Box 55413, Northlands 2116, South Africa; tel and fax (011) 883-4303.

Wild Lifestyles (+15) PO Box 66, Maun; tel 686-3664, fax 686-1045, email: mikepenman@info.bw.

Ewan Masson Safaris (+15) Private Bag 257, Maun; tel and fax 686-2442, email: ensign@info.bw.

Specialised safaris

(Note that many of Botswana's lodges offer special excursions – for instance, mokoro trails, houseboat safaris and fishing safaris.)

Hunting
Blackbeard & Hepburn PO Box 104 Kasane; tel 625-0254, fax 625-0810, email: cbhsaf@botsnet.bw.
Safari South & Rann Safaris PO Box 40, Maun; tel 686-0211/ 686-0212/ 686-0213, fax 686-0379.

Horseback
Okavango Horse Safaris African Horse Safari Association, 36 12th Avenue, Parktown North 2193, South Africa; tel (011) 788-3923, fax (011) 880-8401.

Elephant-back
Elephant Back Safaris Private Bag 332, Maun; tel 686-1260, fax 686-1005.

Walking Trails
Linyanti Explorations PO Box 22, Kasane; tel 625-0505, fax 625-0352.

Canoeing Trails
Linyanti Explorations PO Box 22, Kasane; tel 625-0505, fax 625-0352.

Travel by air

Daily flights connect Gaborone, Francistown, Maun and Kasane. With the exception of Maun, all airports are a fair distance outside the town or city centre. In these cases there are no bus services and transport may be a bit of a problem if no prior arrangements have been made. However, most major hotels routinely collect in-coming and deliver out-going passengers, and they can be persuaded to help. If all else fails, phone for a taxi. Booking arrangements with safari lodges will automatically include charter flights from the local airport to the final destination. Among the air charter companies are those listed on page 259.

Aircraft maintenance

There are only two aircraft maintenance businesses in Botswana. In Gaborone, *Kalahari Air Service* and *Charter* offer full servicing for all types of aircraft, including jets. The servicing offered ranges from routine maintenance to 50-, 100- and 2 000-hour servicing and rebuilds. In Maun, *Northern Air* offers a general maintenance service which includes 50- and 100-hour servicing.

Travel by rail

There is a daily train – known as the 'night train' – connection from Mafikeng, in South Africa's Northern Cape province, through Gaborone in Botswana to Bulawayo in Zimbabwe and points further north. It is not expensive, nor is it luxurious and, beyond the fact that it does (usually) run once a day, it is no longer especially punctual. But people do use it, and it's an interesting way to travel for those for whom money is short, time abundant and punctuality unimportant.

The so-called night train, which offers economy and sleeper classes, departs from Mafikeng at 4.30 pm daily, stops at all the stations and arrives in Bulawayo around midday the next day. There is also a reverse service to Mafikeng, leaving Gaborone at about 9 pm to arrive in Francistown at 6–7 am the following morning. Daily trains also run between Gaborone and Francistown, departing at 10 am and arriving at about 4.30 pm, and offer first class and economy class facilities. Fares are very reasonable.

Travel by road

Access to Botswana by road is easy. The main entry points are (clockwise from the north) Kazungula, Ramokgwebana (Plumtree), Martin's Drift, Tlokweng, Lobatse, Ramatlabama and, in the west from Namibia, the Mamuno post. There are a number of smaller entry points and these should be considered for arrival or departure if this is planned for or very close to a public holiday. Those in the know find that it is often well worth travelling the extra 30 to 50 km in order to clear a quiet, uncrowded border point (using Ramotswa in preference to Tlokweng is a case in point). Passing through Ramokgwebana to Zimbabwe on the days around Christmas, for example, might take four to six hours and, believe me, it's an experience to be avoided! All these main access points are approached, and continue to Botswana's main centres, on tarred roads.

Bus and coach services

There are no reliable, scheduled and quality bus services into Botswana. At the time of writing (November 2000), Intercape Tours have just re-started their service between Johannesburg and Gaborone. It runs once a day in each direction, costs P120 per person one way and operates between Kudu Service Station in Gaborone's main Mall and Johannesburg's main railway station. Express Motorways have ceased their runs between Zimbabwe and Botswana but I understand a few local operators do provide a somewhat halting (in every sense of the word) service that connects Bulawayo with Francistown. A similar service links Mafikeng with Francistown via Gaborone.

In most cases the ubiquitous 'combis' (mini-buses) commute through the major border posts but these are informal services and schedule details are available only at the departure points. They are certainly fast and, apparently, quite safe.

Within the country, there are reliable long-distance bus services between the main towns and villages, and they give good value for money. Numerous buses work the routes in a somewhat unscheduled manner. To use them, one has to get oneself to a signposted stop on the route you wish to take – and simply wait. These facilities are far more common on the tarred roads and to villages close to the main towns. In the rural areas (along dirt roads), they exist hardly at all.

Most of the larger urban areas have a central bus terminus, the point from which almost all the buses start their journeys, and here it is much easier to find one going to your destination.

Taxi services

This kind of transport takes two forms. In the larger towns, 'combis' take the place of public buses that one might find elsewhere. They operate on fixed routes but not to fixed timetables. In theory they stop at designated stopping places but this is not true! There are no tickets, and one price fits all. At the moment, most journeys around Gaborone cost P1.50.

More conventional taxis do exist. It is not always easy to find them although, with the advent of cellular (mobile) phones it's a lot easier to make contact – provided you (or somebody else) knows the number to ring. Taxis in Botswana are not fitted with metres. Newcomers will be instantly recognised and seen as ripe targets for a rip-off. Here, there's not much advice I can give you; just be aware, try and negotiate a price beforehand, and perhaps ask local friends what kind of charge you might expect. This will at least provide a starting point!

Coach tours and safaris

As yet, there are no commercially organised coach tours of the country that I know of.

Vehicle hire

A list of vehice hire companies in Botswana appears below:

Gaborone
Avis Rent a Car Sir Seretse Khama Airport, PO Box 790, Gaborone; tel 391-3039, fax 391-2205, email avisgb@botsnet.bw.
Van & Truck Hire (vans, trucks, 4x4s) Plot 5649, Nakedi Road, Broadhurst, PO Box 916, Gaborone; tel and fax 395-6053.

Francistown
Avis Francistown Airport, PO Box 222, Francistown; tel 241-3901, fax 241-2867, email: avisfwn@botsnet.bw.

Maun
Avis Rent a Car opposite Maun Airport; PO Box 130, Maun; tel 686-0039, fax 686-1596.

Kasane
Avis Rent a Car Cresta Mowana Safari Lodge, PO Box 339, Kasane; tel 625-0144, fax 625-0145.

Hitch-hiking

Conditions for the hitch-hiker in Botswana are little different from those in Europe and elsewhere. No organisation exists for helping hitch-hikers, and there is an element of risk, which varies from time to time. It is more difficult to get a lift on the main routes than on the lesser ones, but this is compensated for by a higher volume of traffic. You will often be asked to contribute towards petrol costs. There is far less traffic in the rural areas but drivers seem more disposed towards giving lifts.

Driving in Botswana

Botswana has more than 5 000 km of first-class tarmac roads. It is now possible to drive from Johannesburg, Bulawayo or Windhoek, via Gaborone, Francistown or Ghanzi, to both Maun and Kasane and through Serowe to Orapa on a hard surface. In addition, the western Okavango highway is tarred from Maun to the border at Mohembo, as is that to Ghanzi and Mamuno on the Namibian border, from Ghanzi to Maun, and from Orapa to Motopi on the Nata–Maun road. Other, increasingly excellent roads are opening up the country to the motorist.

Not all roads, of course, are of such a high standard. There are many thousands of kilometres that range from rough or sandy tracks to gravelled surfaces and vary in quality from season to season, and from fair to execrable. If a good surface is critical to your journey, then you are advised to seek the most up-to-date information (see below).

Finding your way around

Never be without your driver's licence when driving. We here have an effective, if inconvenient, method of dealing with motorists who default in this respect. In addition to the imposition of a fine, your car (and everyone inside it) will be told to remain exactly where they stopped until a driver with a licence is produced, and there's no argument!

Having decided which areas in Botswana you wish to visit, the following notes will help you plan your journey. A number of routes are described in detail in Chapter 8 but, despite every effort, some of the information concerning the quality of road surfaces will not be accurate. Roads in Botswana change with the seasons and with the amount and type of traffic using them, and depending on how recently a grader has passed over them. The Roads Department does its best to maintain the surfaces but its task is monumental, and it simply cannot look after the thousands of kilometres of gravel and sand as well as it might wish to do.

A second factor that tends to make information on road surfaces less reliable than one desires is the problem of definition. What to one person is a fair surface may well be considered execrable by another. There is no standard by which a convenient measurement can be made. The specific comments on road conditions that appear in this book reflect, as far as possible, what general opinion was at the time when the road was last used.

The same subjectiveness also plagues the task of assessing travelling times. There are many factors which will influence speed, and no two people will complete the same journey in the same time. At best, then, you are asked to accept descriptions of road quality and time taken as simply an indication of what to expect.

Be warned: if you pride yourself on your ability to get from A to B in Botswana with the use of maps, by employing logical deduction and by following instructions to the letter, you are in for a new experience. Direction finding in the remoter areas requires boldness, common sense, perseverance and more than a modicum of faith. Even if there were accurate maps, there's absolutely no guarantee that the roads would be the same as they were when the maps were drawn. This is understandable, when you think about it: a herd of elephants passes by, demolishing trees as it does so. One of the trees falls over the road and the next vehicle to arrive finds its own random way around the obstacle, creating a new track that may only rejoin the previous one many kilometres further on.

Then there are the dreaded sand ridges. Your speed drops, the whine of the engine rises higher and higher as it strains with greater and greater effort. As a last resort, you swing off the track, hoping to get better purchase on the vegetation alongside. A new road is created.

All this poses problems for the writers of guidebooks who try to furnish helpful, clear and concise directions. My approach here is to give you a general description of the lie of the land and approximate direction and distance. It's suggested you use the 'decision-point' approach – that is, establish how fast you can or want to travel, calculate how long it should take to reach your destination, and keep the general direction in mind. Drive in that direction for that length of time, keeping a note of landmarks and durations. If you haven't arrived at your destination in the time estimated, then take a break for reassessment and a cup of tea or coffee!

Petrol and diesel

Fuel is widely available in Botswana; the oil companies are Caltex, Engen, Shell and Total. Prices frequently change and there is a price variation across the country. In general terms, the more remote the supply, the more expensive it will be. The greatest increase is about 15 per cent above the lowest price (Gaborone). Petrol and diesel are about the same price.

Fuel is available on all the main routes (and at an increasing number of outlets) and, in Gaborone, Francistown, Mahalapye and Serowe, on a 24-hour basis. Opening times at other centres are usually (and roughly) from 6 am to 6 pm. However, it is generally true that the more remote the area the more amenable the owner will be to negotiation on this point.

The following list details the remoter places at which fuel is available. Generally speaking, pumps operate from 7 am to 6 pm; some are closed for lunch, some on Saturday afternoons and Sundays. The places are Artesia, Bokspits, Bray, Charles Hill, Dukwi, Etsha, Kang, Kanye, Lerala, Masunga, Metlobo, Metsemotlhaba, Mmadinare, Mmathethe, Mochudi, Mosopa (Moshupa), Nata, Parr's Halt, Phepeng, Pitsane, Phitshane-Molopo, Ramokgwebane, Sefophe, Sekoma, Sherwood Ranch, Shoshong, Sikwane, Takatokwane, Tonotha, Tsabong, Tshesebe, Tutume and Werda.

Speed limits

All main roads carry an upper limit of 120 km/h. In towns and villages, the general limit is 60 km/h rising, in some of the throughroutes, to

80 km/h. All speed limits are signposted. National parks and game reserves impose their own restrictions, which are indicated en route. Botswana police regularly set speed traps and offenders are prosecuted. New radar equipment has been acquired and the police are prone to sudden bursts of activity. Sophisticated arguments will avail you nothing and, regretfully, the fact that you are in a foreign registered vehicle is likely to work to your detriment rather than in your favour. Traps are often set in unlikely places on main roads, mostly in 80-km/h or 60-km/h zones as one passes through small roadside villages.

Problems and hazards

Safety belts

It is compulsory to wear these (where the vehicle is appropriately fitted). A fine of between P10 and P30 is usually imposed; the maximum penalty is a fine of P200.

Riding on the roof

A vehicle's roof is an ideal position for game spotting and general viewing. The practice, though, is against the law in towns and villages. The police can be rather vigilant and will impose fines.

Children in the bush

Parents should think very carefully about taking younger children on holiday into the wildlife areas of Botswana. Apart from the long and often uncomfortable distances to be travelled, there is an element of danger.

Public campsites in the national parks are usually unfenced (although an electric fence has in the past been used at Savute and may reappear) and there are no areas in which small children can play unattended, so constant watchfulness on the part of adults is required.

Some private operators refuse children under 12 and only reluctantly accept children over 12, and there are no reduced rates for children. Botswana's national parks and game reserves, however, allow children of 8 years and below free entry, and offer a reduced rate for those between 8 and 16 (see page 209).

Cautionary tale: Savute campsite is situated next to the Savute channel, which for the past few years has been quite dry. Some 50 m across the channel from one of the camping places there used to be the skeleton of a crashed aircraft.

The wreck was an instant drawcard to the four children who had just arrived. With parents engrossed in setting up camp, the four bounded straight to the plane, explored and played around it.

But the underground water and the trees of Savute channel are a constant attraction for thirsty elephants that regularly visit the area, and the inevitable happened. The children and a young bull were in the same place at the same time, and by the time that parents and children emerged from their busy oblivion, the elephant's looming bulk separated the two groups. The romance of the wild was suddenly a very frightening and threatening reality for the inexperienced city dwellers. Fortunately, sheer fright froze all movement (though the emotions, and the rush of adrenaline, can be imagined). Perhaps that was what made the elephant quietly move on and away, averting a potentially very nasty situation.

Animals on the road

The motorist is warned to keep a very close watch for wildlife and stock on the road. This is a particular hazard in Botswana, and many lives have been lost to accidents caused by collisions. Whether a road is fenced or not, there is always the possibility of cattle, donkeys, goats and game straying onto it. Often they are deliberately herded there to take advantage of grazing that otherwise would go to waste. At night the hazard is even greater, particularly in the cooler months, when animals seek the warmth of the tarmac and when, even with spotlights, dark shapes on a dark road are extremely difficult for tired eyes to see. *The danger that animals represent cannot be stressed too strongly.*

I would like, especially, to emphasise the dangers of driving on high-speed roads at night. Many residents of Botswana consider a night drive on the Gaborone–Francistown highway to be suicidal. I am sure that the road to Maun is regarded in much the same way. Despite fencing, livestock will stray onto the road. Numerous people have died tragically in the past few years through collisions with animals. Please be careful. Try not to drive at night on the main roads or, if you do, make sure you have very good lights and exercise the greatest caution. Drop your speed by 20 km/h and arrive alive.

Accidents: what to do

The laws in Botswana relating to the reporting of accidents are similar to those elsewhere in southern Africa. If, as a result of a vehicle accident, there is any injury to persons or damage to property, it must be reported to the nearest police station or police officer 'as soon as is reasonably practical and in any event, within 48 hours'. Where there is minor damage only and no injury to persons, it is sufficient, with the agreement of all the parties involved, to exchange names and addresses. Where an accident has taken place it is the duty of the driver to stop. Parties involved have a legal right to demand from each other names and addresses, details of vehicle registration numbers and ownership, insurance particulars and the names and addresses of any passengers who may be potential witnesses.

A difficulty often arises in cases where livestock has been killed or injured. Basically, there are two situations in which this can happen, namely where the road is fenced, and where it is not. In the former case – that is, on most but not all of the tarred main roads and few (if any) of the gravel and sand roads – the owner of the livestock is theoretically responsible for any death, injury or damage caused by the presence of their animals. It is in fact an offence for a stock owner to allow their animals to stray onto the road. Thus it may seem, on the face of it, that there is a good chance of a successful claim against them. In practice, however, such claims are usually dismissed because of the many defences that are open to the stock owner and the counter-claim of some contributory negligence on the part of the driver.

On an unfenced road it becomes even more difficult to determine responsibility for damages. In both cases therefore, being aware of the dangers, the most practical solution is to try to avoid an accident in the first place. Secondly, if you do have an accident, recognise that it is often easiest to pay compensation for the animal involved and simply accept the fact of damage to your vehicle. Litigation is going to be costly, lengthy and the outcome uncertain, quite apart from the fact that the owner of the animal may not have the resources to meet your claim.

Veterinary fences

For an idea of the extent of these, refer to the map on page 299. Among the country's top earners of foreign exchange are its beef exports, the bulk of which go to the European Union. In order to do everything possible to control outbreaks of foot-and-mouth disease, Botswana's Veterinary Department has erected fences to divide the country into a number of huge 'paddocks'. Movement of stock (and pets) across fences is strictly controlled.

These barriers are popularly referred to as 'vet fences'. I mention them here because they provide an entire highway system that gives wide access to remoter areas. For example, the cut-line which demarcates the boundary of the Central Kalahari Game Reserve can be accessed *from main roads* via the Kuke Fence, the Makalamabedi Fence and the Makoba Fence.

The fences are almost always in pairs, roughly 100 m apart. They are four- or five-stranded and nearly 1.5 m in height. For the most part there is a track on the outer sides of both fences, and although infrequently maintained, the track is usually of a perfectly adequate standard.

When I last counted, there were over 2 500 km of fences in Botswana: a considerable highway system indeed, well over half of it covering remote wilderness areas! Gates are infrequent but they are all in sensibly strategic places. It is important to know where the gates are. The map included with this edition (page 299) is too small to show the detail, so before venturing forth I strongly recommend you purchase the latest map of *Botswana Foot and Mouth Veterinary Control Fences* from the Department of Surveys and Mapping, P/Bag 0037, Gaborone, tel 395-3251.

For those of you with a penchant for exploring the unusual and the little known, I do heartily recommend that you use the vet fence system. But caution! Remember that moving pets or large quantities of raw meat through these fences requires a permit (see page 49).

Navigation

Global Positioning System (GPS)

The Global Positioning System (GPS) is a satellite-based navigation system that pinpoints a position on the earth's surface with remarkable accuracy. There is a Russian as well as an American GPS; the latter is the one mostly used in the West and in southern Africa.

A GPS involves (usually) a hand-held instrument that makes contact with orbiting satellites and, within minutes, displays a geographical position. Developed for military purposes, it can be accurate to within metres (though civilian channels are not as precise). Despite this, most GPS applications today will give a 'fix' to within 50–100 m. Five years ago GPSs were extremely expensive; today the price is but a small fraction of what it was and is still falling. More and more, travellers will own a GPS and use it routinely for their wilderness travel. It is for this reason that GPS references have been included in this new edition of the book.

At the time of writing, the deliberate error initially introduced into the GPS system – allegedly to prevent it being used by terrorists, for example – has been removed. This should reduce reading errors from tens and hundreds of metres down to just a few. Be warned, however: many of the readings used in this text were taken before the improved accuracy. Expect small errors, therefore. Incidentally, if you should have any new routes, roads or points of interest to report to the author, information and GPS references will be very much appreciated (see

'Feedback', below and on page 15); when supplied, please notify what datum was used; see next paragraph).

It is important to note that different countries use different datums, or standard 'baselines' on which all their maps are constructed. Most GPSs allow the user to select the datum of the country in which they will be travelling. The manufacturer's 'standard' or 'default' datum is known as WGS 84. The datum for southern Africa (including Botswana) is Clark 1880. The differences in final position between these two datums – WGS and Clarke 1880 – can be considerable. For this reason, it is important to know which datum was used for the GPS reading. If it is Clark 1880, the fix, when transposed to a map, will be as accurate as the technology allows. If the datum is WGS 84, an error of up to 300 m may occur.

However, such errors are minuscule compared to the distances involved in Botswana, and therefore hardly relevant. Nevertheless, the user needs to be aware of them and to be a little more forgiving if small discrepancies do occur.

Note: All GPS positions given in this book are followed by the bracketed words (1880), (WGS 84) or (u/k – meaning the datum is 'unknown').

Cut-lines

This term describes straight swathes, cut through and cleared of vegetation, that sometimes run for hundreds of kilometres. They have usually been created by prospectors and survey departments who (before the advent of the GPS, presumably) used cut-lines to carve vast tracts of wilderness into manageable portions, sections within which it was possible to find one's way without getting lost. Almost invariably, cut-lines carried the prospector's or surveyor's vehicular traffic.

Once their purpose is served, cut-lines are left to fall victim to encroaching bush, but the process takes many years and it often happens that other people find a use for the make-shift 'road'.

Old cut-lines have opened up huge portions of Botswana to the casual traveller. An excellent example is the Central Kalahari Game Reserve, where extensive travel would still be impossible without them. There are, though, many, many others.

Cut-lines do not always appear on Government Survey maps, however, and this is the difficulty. In the past the seekers of oil, gold, diamonds and other minerals have all, in their turn, cut these long, straight tracks through the bush but a centralised recording system has never been prepared.

Cut-lines are invaluable aids to getting around Botswana. Those that I know of, and that are useful, will be found within these pages. Many others exist (and I would like to know of them; see Feedback, page 15), and adventurous travellers will want to explore them to find new magic in the country's wilderness areas.

The following are basic facts about cut-lines:

• Cut-lines are always absolutely straight (they are 'cut' with the help of a compass and follow a compass bearing).
• They do not necessarily go to any particular destination, and sometimes come to an abrupt end.
• Cut-lines in current use will have well-worn vehicle tracks down the middle. If the tracks are grown over it, it may be risky to follow the route.
• A sure indication of a cut-line is the distant, vertical notch you'll see in the tree-line on the horizon (the Kalahari-traverse cut-line viewed from Deception Pan is an excellent example of this).
• Cut-lines invariably (but not always) run east–west or north–south, and mostly on magnetic as opposed to true bearings.

Vehicle spares

While many readers will be travelling to safari lodges, others will be doing their own thing, and it is to the latter, independent travellers who will be driving their own vehicles, that the following is largely addressed.

Always carry at least one spare wheel, together with a jack and wheel brace. This may sound self-evident, but it's surprising how many motorists buy or borrow a high-lift jack without checking that they can actually use it on their vehicle. A puncture repair outfit is of no use without tyre levers. Take valve keys along, too. Essential spares include fuses, a tyre pump and pressure gauge, light bulbs, points, condensers, spark plugs, a regulator, radiator hoses (top and bottom), a fan belt, warning triangles (a legal requirement in Botswana), engine oil, a small coil of soft baling-wire, jump-leads, brake and clutch fluid and a full set of tools.

Carry a spare set of keys and, ideally, find a place on the outside of the vehicle where they can be secured, hidden yet relatively easy to get at. Never leave the spare set in the vehicle! A towrope and shovel are useful; so too is a hand-held spotlight.

A useful tip is to keep, under or near your seat, two different-size screwdrivers, an adjusting spanner and a pair of good pliers wrapped up in a cloth. It is surprising how many little things can be attended to, with just these tools, without having to haul the whole toolbox out of the depths somewhere in the back.

In this book, one can offer only general guidelines on the availability of vehicle spares in Botswana, since much depends on the make of vehicle and the particular problem. All the main centres – Gaborone,

Francistown, Maun, Mahalapye, Kasane, Ghanzi, and Lobatse – will stock the commonest spares for the most popular vehicles. Smaller towns, especially along the railway line, will be able to get them very quickly.

In the more remote areas, garages are few and far between and proper spares almost non-existent. This is sometimes offset, however, by the increasing levels of ingenuity and self-reliance that people in these areas have developed. In an emergency these are the folk in whom your trust must be placed and, while you may not get a very professional job, the chances of your being able to drive on are very good.

Maps

The main source of official maps of the country is the Department of Surveys and Mapping, P/Bag 0037, Gaborone; tel 395-3251. An excellent catalogue, which can be obtained on request, gives detailed information on exactly what is available. Maps can also be purchased from the Department's offices in Selebi-Phikwe, Maun and Francistown but stocks are limited (they carry only the large, general maps of the country, and the 1:50 000 of their immediate areas). The offices in Maun do sell maps, although the range is also very limited. Special arrangements can be made to order them for collection in town.

A number of commercial enterprises, such as curio and bookshops, sell a limited range of the more popular maps.

Residents of or travellers passing through South Africa can obtain Botswana maps from, among other outlets, the Map Office (Pty), Ground Floor, Standard House, 40 De Korte Street, Braamfontein, Johannesburg, tel (011) 339-4941/49, fax 339-4951. I have always found the people there unusually helpful and efficient. If all else fails, ask for Jean Oxley, who can apparently work miracles when necessary!

For those considering close and detailed study or work in just a small area of Botswana, especially in the more remote and featureless regions, aerial photographs are recommended. The 230 x 230 mm black-and-white prints are available only from the Department in Gaborone and will take a week to process from receipt of order. There is medium-scale cover of the entire country at 1:50 000, of varying ages, none more than ten years old.

Available are conventional six-colour maps, in scales from 1:1 500 000 to the very popular 1:350 000 editions, for the Okavango and for the Chobe areas. Also a mixture of monochrome and full-colour maps for the whole country in scales 1: 500 000 and 1:250 000, together with a series of 1:100 000 and 1:50 000 maps covering the east and the southeast and the northern half of Botswana. Certain shops stock street maps, showing plot numbers and street names of Gaborone, Francistown, Selebi-Phikwe and Lobatse. A touring map, produced on behalf of Shell Oil, can be obtained from the author, who is Shell's distribution agent in the country (see page 16).

Self-drive: what you'll need

Packing your vehicle

Some Botswana roads are rough and facilities limited. Assuming that you've planned a lengthy trip, you will have to carry a lot of equipment with you, and space is at a premium. It makes sense, therefore, to give thought to the way in which you pack your vehicle – and very careful thought, too: cornflakes soaked in petrol doesn't go down very well!

There are three basic rules to follow when planning your packing:
1. Wrap hard objects with sharp edges in a cover (an old piece of underfelt or something equally substantial).
2. Pack heavy objects at the bottom of the pile.
3. Strap everything down or pack things inside boxes and strap the boxes down.

Remember that the constant bumping and shaking, together with a copious layer of dust, will create abrasion that can rub through paint or canvas during a long journey.

You will be dealing with five types of gear:
1. Food and drink.
2. Camping and cooking equipment.
3. Clothing.
4. Photographic equipment.
5. Vehicle spares and fuel.

Divide each of these into two categories: those you need immediately to hand, and your bulk supplies.

Food and drink

You can get most basic foodstuffs within Botswana. It does, however, pay to plan your menus well in advance so that you have some idea of what you need to buy and at what point.

It is worth carrying a large cooler-box and planning for fresh produce for the day you arrive and for 24 hours after you leave main towns. Botswana is very hot, and although ice is easily available in the main centres (except on or immediately before public holidays when supplies may be sold out), food will go off quickly. In addition, the way your vehicle bounces around will rapidly pulp soft vegetables and fruit, so tomatoes and peaches, for instance, don't last long. Onions and carrots do, however, and add flavour to canned meals. Oranges are always refreshing.

Avoid pop-top plastic bottles, the type containing oil or vinegar. Pressure can pop them open at very much the wrong time. Choose screw-top containers instead. Decant paper-packeted foodstuffs (for example, sugar, dried milk) into screw-top containers and plan to have a '48-hour tin' ready to hand together with a bulk supply that gets buried.

The following foodstuffs will provide the basics: Bannock mixture (flour and baking powder to make a pan bread); lemon juice, instant potato powder, stock cubes for stews and the like, rusks, glucose sweets, chewing gum, dried fruit, milk powder, coffee, tea bags, Oxo cubes or similar, peanuts, raisins, rice, butter/margarine, muesli mix, bread (when available), cheese portions, sugar, salt, pepper, oil, vinegar.

Fresh vegetables and fruit that last well include potatoes (plus tinfoil to cook them in), cabbage; onions, carrots, oranges and lemons. Be warned that elephants are partial to oranges and will do anything to get at them. Celery and tomatoes are refreshing but don't plan to keep them too long.

Useful canned food includes corned beef (an excellent base for stew), pilchards, potatoes, tomato purée (for adding flavour to cooked foods), baked beans, peas, pickled fish, tomatoes, cream (for treats), luncheon meat, sweetcorn.

Work out your general menus in advance. You'll probably find it best to pull out the food for the next 24 hours while in camp and pack it in a small box so that it's easy to get at. Then, if you are delayed the next day and encamp late, a meal can be prepared quickly. There is nothing guaranteed to raise blood pressure more than getting to a destination after dark and not being able to get a meal going until the whole vehicle has been unpacked. Everybody will be tired and probably fed up, particularly if it's raining, but a hot meal, quickly prepared, works wonders for morale.

Camping gear

No experienced camper will need to be told what to carry but, for those who are a little uncertain, some guidelines are offered here. They are drawn from personal experience.

Camping equipment in Botswana needs to fulfil a number of functions. You must be able to provide shade during the day and protection from dust and thorns on the ground. A large canvas sheet is ideal for both functions. It can also be used to help vehicles out of sand, to lie under when it rains and to catch rainwater for drinking or bathing. It will also keep you warm when wrapped around your sleeping bag.

Where there are likely to be predators in the vicinity, your gear must make provision for a totally enclosed area in which to sleep. There have been several recorded incidents of lion or hyaena taking a bite out of a sleeping person. And if you do have to sleep in the open, it really doesn't make sense to do so without some kind of all-round cover – a lightweight tent with a built-in ground sheet, for example.

You don't, though, really need a camp-bed: one can sleep perfectly comfortably on the ground, or on a foam or inflatable mattress. A small pillow is a good idea (unless you are practised, sleeping without a pillow can be very uncomfortable). In Botswana, nights can be very cold during winter, when the clear skies cause rapid heat loss from the earth. Warm sleeping gear is recommended. During the summer months mosquitoes and biting insects can be a nuisance, and a tent with a fly-screen or some kind of mosquito net is essential.

Pack your camping gear where it comes readily to hand – preferably on a roof rack – and strap it down well before moving. Make extra sure that tent poles are firmly held in place. It is very useful to be able to set up camp quickly, particularly after a long day when you may have to do things in the dark. Practise a few times at home: it's amazing how what sounded like a simple exercise when somebody explained it to you becomes complex and nerve-racking when you try to do it in the bush, in the dark!

Cooking utensils and other basics

Keep cooking equipment simple and sturdy. Glass tends to become a casualty on safari. A small (3-kg) gas cooker with a single ring is useful. Take a spare cylinder too. (*Handy tip:* jets get easily blocked, so either carry cheap replacements and a spanner or use one of the aerosol sprays, like Q20, for example, to blow the wrong way through the jet. This clears it. It's the blast of propellant that does the job; the agent itself is not so important). This size cooker is ample for three people. You can also, usually, build a fire if you want to, but remember to collect wood before you arrive at a campsite as the surrounding area will, invariably, already have been stripped.

A *potjie* (cast-iron pot), flat bottomed or three-legged, is a worthwhile investment for fire cooking. Watch those three pointed legs: they can inflict lethal damage on surrounding luggage!

A suggested checklist for cooking and other useful equipment comprises a gas cylinder plus ring, kettle, wooden platters, small jug (for ladling water/soup), tin-opener, braai (barbecue) grid, with clip to hold it closed, plates (melamine), mugs, knives, forks, spoons, chopping knife, thermos flask, small spade (for, among other things, toilet use), plastic basin (for washing dishes, clothes and self), washing powder (in screw-top container), flat-bottomed *potjie*, bowls, chopping board, small pan which can double as frying or cooking pan, plastic glasses, matches and/or lighter (water proofed), paper towels, toilet paper (in a waterproof plastic bag or container), two 10-litre containers of water (preferably black plastic to avoid growth of algae), short length of washing line and pegs, dish-washing liquid (in screw-top container).

Divide all these items, except the cooker and potjie, between a 'day' box and a 'kitchen' box. The 'day' box contains those things likely to be used while travelling (mugs, knives, forks, spoons, wooden platters, tin opener, for example). This enables you to stop and have lunch, invariably cold, without involving a major unpacking exercise.

It is very useful to be able to lift the box out, collect the cooker and dispatch the cook to one side to get on with the meal while everybody else prepares camp. This is not as easily done if the various components are scattered around all over the vehicle.

Clothing

Big suitcases tend to be a nuisance. Several canvas hold-alls are better than one large container: because they are soft they can be packed more tightly and they don't rub against other things. You can also separate your clothing into different uses with smaller containers – warm, night-time gear in one bag, daytime clothes in another and so on. Plan to carry as little as is compatible with personal hygiene and comfort. Clothing can be very bulky and you'll be surprised how little you really need. Remember also that clothes get crumpled in the bags, so if you have a special outfit for, say, a sociable drink in town, it must be fairly crease-resistant.

Photographic equipment

Part of the enjoyment of the trip for me is taking photographs. That means that camera equipment – at least the camera you habitually use – must be handy. Because there's so much dust around it also means that it will probably travel with you in the passenger cab rather than behind, in the vehicle's open back or other severe dust zone. Don't assume you'll be able to buy your particular film in Botswana; bring plenty with you.

As I often reproduce some of my shots professionally, I use a tripod whenever I can. A 35-mm colour slide going to an A4 page is enlarged more than 50 times and so every blurring caused by movement will be exaggerated. A tripod steadies the camera. For the same reason I use a low ASA; one thing there is plenty of in Botswana is light! (See also page 31.)

Fuel

Carrying and storing fuel needs special thought and planning. In making your decision assume the worst: fuel fumes will leak and so will the liquid. Given this, where and in what would you store it? The roof is a favoured place (but watch the high centre of gravity). So is a 200-litre long-range tank, which I use. Plastic drums are a third option. I often hear conflicting arguments about plastic drums and static, and have also been told that the black drums are suitable. As I don't generally use either I suggest you take advice on this one.

On the road

Vehicle breakdowns

When travelling in a four-wheel-drive vehicle in Botswana's remoter areas, you should be aware of the host of things that can go wrong. It is not possible, in one book, to pre-empt all possible problems but one or two hints may help in a time of crisis.

Whatever else you remember, don't forget one golden rule: *Keep calm*. This is of critical importance. No matter how much of a hurry you are in, if you've broken down, you're going to be late. Take a break while you regain control; make a cup of tea if you want. Above all, think about your situation before you act. Many problems are caused by very small and sometimes unlikely items coming adrift. Electrics are the most common source of engine failure or poor performance. Only as a last resort consider taking the carburettor apart!

Jacking up a vehicle

If you're stuck in mud, clay or deep sand, jack up the vehicle and put branches, planks or stones under the wheels. Sometimes, though, instead of the vehicle going up, the jack goes down, sinking into the ground! To avoid this, take the spare wheel off and use it as a base for the jack. Otherwise try a short length of planking, a board or a thick pad of folded canvas. Inflatable jacks are another option but a bit over the top for someone, like me, who relies on a high-lift jack.

Here's a tip for the uninitiated: if the vehicle is new to you and you have a high-lift jack, *try it out* before you have to use it in earnest. These jacks require bull-bars or special lifting points, and without them they are useless because there is nowhere on the body of the vehicle for them to be positioned for lift.

Flat battery

If your battery is flat and you can't push-start because of sand or mud, and assuming there isn't a spare battery and you have a generator fitted (as opposed to an alternator), try this:

- Jack up and remove one of the driving wheels. Wind a long length of cord around the hub. Ask one or two of your companions to pull on the cord, thus rotating the wheel. With the ignition on and the vehicle in gear, start the engine in the normal 'push-start' way (foot on the clutch as the hub builds up speed; foot off the clutch when maximum speed is reached). If you're in a forward gear, make sure the hub is being rotated in the right direction! The procedure won't work, though, if you have an alternator.
- If there is a second battery handy (that is, if there's a second or passing vehicle), then use jump leads. It's usual to connect red to red and black to black, but this only works if the 'dead' battery still has some life in it. It's much more effective to connect red to red and the sound battery's black to an *earth* (engine block or body-work) on the stricken vehicle, especially if it is fitted with an alternator. If you have only one piece of lead or wire, you can make an adequate earth connection by putting the two vehicles together, metal to metal (usually bumper).

A tip received from P.H.N. Holmes of Paarden Eiland (Cape Town) sounds useful for starting a petrol engine if you have a weak battery. He says: 'Remove every *other* spark plug (in the firing order) from the engine. The load on the starter is greatly reduced and the higher cranking speed can be enough to get the engine going. Thereafter, the spark plugs can be replaced and the HT leads fitted with the engine running. The noise is awful, so plug the ears!'

Clutch and brake fluid

You should never travel without a supply of this fluid. However, if you are caught without it, there are alternatives in an emergency. Almost any liquid will do – water, urine, vegetable and cooking oils. However, *never use mineral oils* as they will rot the rubbers. Whatever foreign substance is used must be flushed out as soon as possible.

Slave or master cylinder

Once you are on the move again, you can change gears without the clutch. With a bit of practice and experience this can be done smoothly and does not harm the gearbox. The problem lies, however, in getting the vehicle moving in the first place. Warm the engine and then switch it off. Engage first gear, depress the accelerator and turn on the starter. This won't be kind to the starter, but it will get you going – unless you are stuck in very deep sand, in which case you have a very long wait, or a very long walk, ahead!

Bush etiquette

When you see a headline that tells of yet another death, you might feel that the wisest way to behave in the bush is not to go there in the first place! Not so. All that's needed is discipline, and attention to some basic guidelines. Good behaviour in the bush is like good behaviour in any other circumstances – simple courtesy and consideration, and aware-ness of others' needs, are the keynotes – but with one major difference. Thoughtlessness in the bush can be extremely dangerous, even fatal.

There are travellers' tales aplenty about close shaves with wild ani-mals. After all, a holiday in the wilds of Botswana is all about getting back to unspoilt Africa with all its challenges. It may be very tempting to get so close to the elephant that its eye fills the viewfinder of your telephoto lens. Resist the temptation. The risk isn't worth it, not only from the point of view of your own safety, but also because the greater the number of unfortunate incidents, the more necessary and likely it will become for the authorities to create stringent regulations and make efforts to enforce them. This will only end up curbing *your* freedom, which is one of the special features of a visit to the wildlife areas of Botswana.

Etiquette when driving

• Keep a respectful distance from wild animals. We humans do not relish invasion of our personal space; how much less comfortable must a wild animal feel about close contact with humans and vehicles. If you do find yourself in close proximity, some anticipatory planning is required; work out an escape route in case of need.
• Be extremely wary of animals with young.
• Do not move any distance from your vehicle unless you are accompa nied by a guide who knows the area.

Etiquette when camping

• Never feed wild animals, whatever the temptation. Remember that if you do so, you're probably signing its death warrant. One of Savute's inhabitants was a young elephant, an affable bull who discovered, early on, that one of the delights of being around tourists was that he was fed. Oranges, particularly, were an ecstatic and addictive new experience. With his very fine sense of smell he found that he couldtrack down oranges in tents and vehicles, and he started helping himself. Sometimes helping himself required flattening a tent or breakinginto a vehicle and the fact that humans were around was no deterrent. Needless to say this brought a flood of complaints to the Department of Wildlife and National Parks, and the elephant was eventually shot as a nuisance animal. Many would say that the wrong animal got the bullet.

- Where there are game animals around, sleep in a tent or vehicle but never in the open. Use a tent with a built-in fly-sheet that closes firmly so that no part of your body sticks outside. An arm or a leg protruding from a tent is, for a carnivore, nothing more than effortless food.
- Take all your rubbish with you out of the park. After all, you managed to bring it all in. I know this can be difficult, and that bags break. Double-bag it, and leave it where there is an obviously functional removal system – in a town or perhaps at the park gate. Many campers make a great effort to ensure that no rubbish is left lying around, some times burying it, leaving an immaculate campsite behind. Do not bury your rubbish: unless you dig a monumental pit, it won't be too long before the monkeys, baboons and hyaenas locate the burial place, unearth it and systematically scatter the detritus.
- Don't camp on a hippo track; keep a watch out for game tracks generally, and respect other creatures' right of way. This also applies to places like bridges. One party decided to sleep on the wooden bridge in the Moremi Game Reserve because they had heard that lion used it to cross the river and they were keen to see the animals. They did! They also found out how difficult it was to move when you're in a sleeping bag, and how not to get six people through two Land Rover doors in a hurry. They were lucky – the lions were not hungry and didn't strike out.
- Beware of crocodiles. When you're hot and dusty and arrive at a great pool of water, there is an understandable temptation to plunge in. The Okavango has a very healthy crocodile population that includes some very large beasts. Many stretches of water will have a resident crocodile. They move very quietly and incredibly swiftly. In one recorded incident a girl bathing at the edge of a pool was taken by a crocodile. The rest of the party heard a scream, ran to the water and found a cake of soap and a swirl of muddy water. The girl's body was never found. Bathe only after you've thoroughly inspected the area. Look for eyes and nostrils protruding just above the water; check along the nearby banks. Bathe with somebody keeping watch. Again the basic principle: don't be afraid, but do be aware that you are in wild Africa.

Driving in the bush

This is one of those things that's easy when you know how. Newcomers seem to approach it, though, in one of two extreme ways: they regard it as a 'piece of cake', no different from any other kind of driving, or they become over-anxious, as if they are about to plunge into the maw of the unknown. Both approaches are wrong: it's by no means a piece of cake, but over-anxiety often sets up a self-fulfilling prophecy and something usually *does* go awry. This is not a book about 4x4 driving. A few helpful tips are included here but, for really expert advice, I recommend you have a look at *The Complete Guide to Four-Wheel Drive in Southern Africa* by Andrew St Pierre White (ISBN 0-620-24184-5) and his excellent videos on the subject. Enquiries to Cape Town (27 21) 785-5752.

Gears

The first rule is to anticipate the hazards ahead. You will soon learn to diagnose those dry, sandy patches. Slow down and change into the gear in which you can negotiate the sticky patch *before* you reach it. Once you're in it, keep up your revs. If you have a rev-counter, don't allow the engine to drop below 1000 rpm. If this does happen, change down as quickly and smoothly as you can. Beware of 'snatching' – that is, accelerating too quickly – because this can shear a half-shaft or cause a wheel to spin and dig in. Find a balance between swiftness and smoothness.

Sand and mud

As most of Botswana is rather like a vast beach with sand hundreds of metres deep, your biggest challenge is likely to be sand driving. But these tips also apply to mud driving. Beware of the 'black-cotton' mud that occurs in some areas. If it has rained and you see a very black surface ahead of you, take especial care. The mud that forms in the black soils is sticky, tenacious and will thoroughly bog you down. Travel with a high-lift jack (see page 80); it will save a lot of time and effort if you do get stuck.

A general rule, I'm told, is to have hard tyres in wet mud – the idea being that they will 'cut down' through the soft material to a harder surface beneath; and soft tyres – which will spread the load – over soft sand or a surface like a beach, or in the Makgadikgadi. Despite this advice, many drivers use very hard tyres in sandy country in the hope that they will reduce the risk of punctures. My experience indicates a sensible compromise: soft tyres on deep sandy roads, hard tyres when there's no road and its real 'through the bush' driving.

Once stuck in either sand or mud, lift the wheel(s) clear, place sticks and branches under it/them (watch out for sharp pieces that will go straight through the tyre, adding to your problems!), and clear burdensome sand or mud away from the sides (insides and outsides) of each of the wheels.

When the vehicle is stuck down to the chassis, a good trick is to lift the whole of the back (a big advantage of a high-lift jack) and push sideways so that it slips off the jack and falls into a new set of tracks. Doing this alternately front and back allows you to 'crab walk' in a chosen direction. Beware, though: high-lifts are dangerous, totally unforgiving – and I have a scar to prove it. Do not be frightened of them but be very careful. Make sure everybody is clear of the vehicle, especially children and dogs.

Sometimes you miss a gear change in really soft sand and have to attempt a standing start. This usually happens in low-ratio country so conditions will in any case be bad. The trick is to reverse a metre or two, which will give you enough run to keep moving. If you start forward straightaway you could easily dig yourself in and make matters much worse.

Much of Botswana is blessed (or cursed) with challenges called sand ridges, part of the old shoreline or relics of an ancient desert. This sand is particularly tenacious and the ridges have turned back more than one party of travellers. Understanding the characteristics of sand will help you cope with the problem. As the temperature rises the tiny pockets of air between the particles of sand expand, and when a heavy wheel drives over it there is a large volume of air to displace, so the vehicle sinks in deep. In contrast, when it is cooler there is a smaller volume of air to displace, the sand is more compact and will support a greater weight. If you can do your sand ridge driving, therefore, in the cool of the morning, you'll have fewer problems than in the heat of the day. The sand is also more compact when wet.

Knowing your vehicle

Before setting off on your journey, do make sure that you really know your vehicle, especially if you've hired or borrowed one. Did you know that free-wheeling hubs have to be engaged by hand before your 4x4 drive works? Have you checked that a high-lift jack can be used? The lifting shaft must be clear so it's usually placed under the bush-bars front or back. No bars or equivalent? Can't use the jack!

Lessons from Makgadikgadi

Having been stuck in the Makgadikgadi wastelands more times than I want to remember, I consider myself an expert (on getting stuck, that is!). Maybe I've learnt some lessons. Here's what to do:

• Be very cautious if you drive across the surface of the pans. It generally looks like caked, grey, cold gravy, which may seem ideal for high speed driving. But it's not all the same under the surface and, without any change in outward appearance, you can suddenly find yourself axle-deep in mud.

Driving on pans. Never drive on Makgadikgadi without the 'hubs in'. Be ready to engage four-wheel drive at the slightest provocation. Be very wary of driving off into the blue, across the open pan, where there are no tracks. Stay on the existing tracks or, if you do move away, stay close to shorelines. Keep your speed up (80 km/h plus). If you feel the surface give, or mud starts flying up from the wheels, *do not brake*. If the condition continues, curve gently away towards the nearest shore. *Do not swerve away suddenly.*

If you get stuck and have friends and vehicles with you but no winch:

Step One. When you feel yourself going in, and you know it's too late, let the vehicle come to a stop on its own. Do *not* brake, and do *not* try to drive out.

Step Two. With the help of friends – one pushing at each wheel and, more importantly, reporting wheel spin – try gently to drive out. Stop instantly if a wheel spins, or you 'll only dig yourself further in. (**Note:** allocate your least-favoured friends as the pushers immediately behind the rear wheels!)

Step Three. Lower tyre pressure to between 1.0 and 0.8 bars and repeat step two. Keep them this soft while you stay on the pan. Note: put the valve caps back. The valves will fill with mud if you don't and you'll have a major problem re-inflating the tyres. If this strategy doesn't work, you now have to roll up your sleeves and tackle the problem seriously!

Step Four. Remove all weight from the vehicle and repeat step three.

Step Five. If this does not work, you are in for the long run and need the help of your high-lift jack (if you haven't already used it). This is going to be your salvation:

Using the base-plate you brought with you, or preferably, a spare tyre, place a firm base beneath the high-lift jack and raise the whole rear of the vehicle. Place stones, dry soil, branches, firewood – you may have to do a lot of walking for these materials, which is why you try to avoid leaving the edge too far away! – anything suitable you can find, before lowering the wheels onto this new, firm base. Do the same at the front and then drive out!

Getting out from a bad 'stick' can be a long, tedious job – but one always does get out (after all, I'm here to write this). Just be prepared, and have someone brew up some tea while you're working. The latter is in fact a serious point: it's important to keep the crew hydrated; they're losing moisture much faster than they think under that scorching sun and on that highly reflective surface. Keep pouring in the liquid!

On the other hand, if you do have a winch there will be a problem because there won't be anything to attach it to. Take the spare wheel off and dig a trench the exact width and depth of the wheel, at right angles to the front of your vehicle and within easy reach of the winch cable. Attach the cable to the wheel and sink the wheel deeply into the trench. This will give you something firm to pull against.

Since first writing this I've got into the habit of carrying two short aluminium ladders around with me for serious pan-driving. With tyres dropped to 0.8 bars, I've been experiencing extraordinary freedom to drive the pan surface. This does not mean that I now no longer get stuck. I still do, but I've found that jacking up the whole of the rear of the vehicle (basing the foot of the jack in the spare wheel), and placing a 2-m ladder under each back wheel, is an absolute winner.

Wheel balance

Once, after completing the Hunter's Road in appalling conditions, I found that driving my truck on tar produced an incredibly bad 'wobbling and shaking' experience. In fact, the truck was barely driveable at normal speeds. The problem? Mud sticking to the prop-shaft and to the wheel rims. When the mud is distributed unevenly and it is hard and dry (it had become so after several hot and sunny days) it completely upsets the balance of wheels and rotating shafts. This causes a most uncomfortable drive and, more particularly, unnecessary wear on bearings. Stop, and carefully dig off all the dried mud from both the outside and inside of the wheels.

Steering

There's often a temptation to 'fight' the steering wheel, try to make it go where you think it should. If you are on an existing track in Botswana, the vehicle will more or less steer itself, so all you really need to do is keep your hands lightly on the wheel. One of the hardest lessons to learn is that, in sand, a vehicle's wheels behave quite differently from anything that you will have experienced on normal roads.

When it feels as though you've hauled and twisted the steering column so radically that the wheels must have been pulled right around, stick your head out of the window and have a look. The chances are they are not even straight yet! To get used to the phenomenon, it's worth the effort to find some 'tame sand' in which to practise (sand is 'tame' when there is someone around to help you!).

Tyre pressure

When you're stuck in sand, try dropping your tyre pressure (see also page 84). The degree to which you do so will depend on the load you are carrying and the nature of the vehicle, but you should aim for something in the region of 1.0 bar. This advice may also be valid when you're in mud but, again, it depends on how deep it is. Within reason, the softer the tyre the better the traction since the tyre spreads, giving you a bigger 'footprint'. At low speeds this will not significantly shorten tyre life. Remember, however, that when you do lower pressure the likelihood of a puncture is increased and the clearance of the vehicle is lowered. This can be a problem if there is a high ridge down the middle of the track.

Radiators and grass seeds

When driving through grass, check the radiator and keep a close watch on the temperature gauge. If the needle starts to move up, stop and check the state of the radiator. Often, in grass or on tracks with a grassed centre, the passage of the vehicle breaks off the seed heads which penetrate the very fine air gaps that pass through the radiator. As they accumulate, they insulate it, preventing the air from flowing through and the heat from dispersing. You'll have to remove as much of the seed material as possible and stop until the engine has cooled down. Whatever you do, though, do not open the radiator when it is very hot: always let it cool down first. Modern radiators are pressurised and the sudden drop in pressure means a rapid rise in engine temperature, and this can damage the engine. You also run the risk of a spurt of scalding steam, which can cause injury. If the radiator is seriously clogged, remove it (after draining and retaining the water) and clean the air spaces, one at a time, using stems of dry grass or the like.

You can avoid much (but not all) of this problem by fitting a fine gauze screen of some sort in front of the radiator to deny seeds access (you can contrive one yourself; there are some very expensive and sophisticated-looking grass screens on the market but I doubt they would be much better). The screen must not only be placed in front of the radiator but also extend the full width of the vehicle and reach down and round, well under the engine, to be fully effective. A method I have found inexpensive and apparently effective is a double thickness of 90 per cent shade cloth folded over a 1.5 m length of doweling rod fastened to the top of my front bush-guard. I let it reach to the ground and leave it long enough to stop just short of the front wheels. The end that drags on the ground soon becomes tatty, but it usually lasts for a few days and is quickly, cheaply and easily replaced. Grass seeds are very small and it is important, therefore, that the shade cloth be doubled over in order to give the best protection.

I only recently came to understand that a radiator is a surprisingly sophisticated piece of equipment and that radiator specialists have clever ways of measuring its efficiency. For peace of mind: once in 100 000 km or so, get an expert to look at this component.

Leaking radiators

When radiators leak they never do so quietly in the garage, over a weekend when it doesn't matter. They always pick the most inconvenient time. My friends and I have used the following emergency radiator repairs:

Pour in mealie meal (ground maize) for a quick fix to a small leak. Or the whites of two eggs, which worked when even commercial sealants failed (and continued working for the next 20 000 km, say Patrick and Veronica). And then, of course, there's the commercial sealant and, something else I've found useful, those two-mix steel putties. By the way, radiator professionals tell me that any of the foregoing will ruin the radiator: the materials can't be cleaned out, they reduce the effectiveness of the radiator and usually mean that the core will have to be replaced. Well, as they say: 'You pays your money and you makes your choice'.

Exhausts

Over the years I've been collecting photographs of burnt-out vehicles in the Kalahari. Without putting too much effort into it, I think I have personally seen eight, all destroyed by fire. In almost every case the fire starts either through a thoughtless design fault, or from dry grass that collects underneath the vehicle, close to a hot exhaust. If you are driving long distances off-road or through thick grass, you must stop and check thoroughly under the vehicle. Check to see if any grass has accumulated. Do the job thoroughly; the prospect of a successful insurance claim is not going to help you out in the Kalahari! Keep checking regularly.

Driving through water

Before negotiating a stretch of water, stop and examine it carefully. Walk through it to give you some idea of its depth and the nature of the bottom. If it looks even slightly risky, get into lowest range low gear, even if you don't think it necessary. It'll be a bit late to change down when you're sinking, so rather go in slowly, steadily and over-powered than fast and under-powered. Try to avoid submerging the exhaust. A slow passage creates less turbulence and less chance of getting the electrics wet.

In order to avoid excessive moisture in the engine, many experienced Delta travellers stop and remove the fan belt when faced with a long water-crossing. This dramatically reduces the spray inside the engine compartment. However, before doing this, check how high the bottom of your fan is. Often it's located above door-sill height. In this case the water won't come above the bottom of the door, so don't waste time with the fan belt.

Gravel roads

Botswana is actively upgrading its main routes but there are still significant stretches of gravel along some of them. On these, you will find yourself enveloped in thick, blinding dust when there's oncoming traffic, and this is *very* dangerous. Indeed there have been a number of horrific accidents on untarred main roads – most of which could have been avoided with thought, anticipation and care. When you first see the vehicle coming towards you, scan the rest of the road between for pedestrians and the ubiquitous livestock, and for any other oncoming vehicle that might be following the first one. Switch on your lights and slow down; stop altogether if you have any doubts about how clear the road ahead is.

Despite the frustration of trailing a heavy truck and the billowing clouds of dust it creates, be very cautious when you try to overtake. Better still, rather pull over, have a cup of tea and let the vehicle ahead pull right away. After all, you're on holiday, and there's really no good reason to risk an accident, even if it's the smallest of risks. This more relaxed approach is not only applicable to driving situations but to a wider context also. The indigestion that results from absorbing too much too quickly, whether of food, information, sightseeing or whatever, also applies to travelling. Don't be tempted into 'touring indigestion'. Plan to spend at least two nights in any one place every four days, especially if you are camping.

Driving after dark

A particular problem of driving in Botswana, as in many other remote rural regions of Africa, is that caused by livestock straying onto the road (see also page 70). This is especially dangerous after dark. The situation is taken so seriously that one company forbids its employees to drive after nightfall, even if it means that they will be late returning to their work.

Wherever possible, avoid night-time driving, but if you simply have to, do so slowly and carefully. Good spotlights will help, but they must be well set and, remember, even spotlights cannot penetrate dust. They may in fact reduce visibility through the 'bounce' of the glare on the dust.

Distance table in km

The distance of the most direct route is shown on the chart. Measurements have been taken from the best available sources and all are subject to 5% error.

Triangular distance chart. Each place lists distances (km) to the places that follow it; routing notes ("via …") are shown where the most direct route passes through an intermediate town.

From \ To	Francistown	Gaborone	Ghanzi	Jwaneng	Kang	Kanye	Kasane	Kazungula	Lobatse	Mahalapye	Mamuno	Maun	Nata	Orapa	Palapye	Ramatlabama	Ramokwebane	Selebi-Phikwe	Serowe	Serule	Tsabong	Werda
Bokspits	1229	792 (via Werda)	869 (via Tsabong)	629 (via Sekoma)	704 (via Sekoma)	705	1733 (via Gabs)	1719 (via Gabs)	755	992	993	1149 (via Tshane)	1419	1318	1064	1311	1196 (via Palapye)	1108	1136		246 (via Bots)	390
Francistown		437	519	272	247	323	14	1002	275	1006	494	307	430 (via Fin)	256	395	642	235	176	116	60	891	145
Gaborone			682 (via Kang)	163	410	91	941 (via Fin)	927 (via Maun)	75	200	806	934	627 (via Fin)	526	272	123	519	404	316	344	547	402
Ghanzi				272	519	595	1104 (via Fin)	1090 (via Fin)	645	882	214	280	587	840	435	164	682	567	479	507	384 (via Sekoma)	239
Jwaneng					247	76	1104 (via Fin)	1090 (via Fin)	126	363	643	799 (via Ghanzi)	790	840	435	164	682	567	479	507	384 (via Sekoma)	239
Kang						323	1351 (via Fin)	1337 (via Fin)	373	610	396	552 (via Ghanzi)	859	936	682	411	929	814	726	754	352 (via Tshane)	314
Kanye							1032 (via Fin)	1018 (via Fin)	50	291	719	875 (via Ghanzi)	617	363	88	610	495	407	435	460		315
Kasane								14	1016	741	1101 (via Maun/Nata)	621 (via Nata)	314	744 (via Fin)	669	1064	586	657	713	597	1488	1343
Kazungula									1002	727	1101	607 (via Nata)	300	730 (via Fin)	655	1050	572	643	699	583	1474	1329
Lobatse										275	1009 (via Fin)	702 (via Fin)	752	347		48	594	479	391	419	510	360
Mahalapye											1006	734	427	328	72	323	319	204	116	144	746	601
Mamuno												494	807	1483	1078	807	1028	1210	1112	1150	748	710
Maun													307	737 (via Fin)	657	1057 (via Fin)	579	649	706	590	904 (via Ghanzi)	866 (via Sekoma)
Nata														430 (via Fin)	355	750	272	343	399	283	1174	1029
Orapa															256	654	322	393	212	328	1073	928
Palapye																395	247	132	44	72	818	673
Ramatlabama																	642	527	439	467	548	403
Ramokwebane																		235	291	175	1066	921
Selebi-Phikwe																			176	60	951	806
Serowe																				116	863	718
Serule																					891	746
Tsabong																						145

PLACES TO VISIT: THE MAIN CENTRES

Gaborone

Originally, what was to become Gaborone was a siding on the railway line. It took its name from the chief of the Batlokwa group, whose village was some 3 km away on the east bank of the Notwane River. The place was selected as the site for the new capital city in 1964 and became the capital of the new republic of Botswana in September 1966.

Gaborone is not considered a prime tourist destination, since 90 per cent of leisure traffic goes to Ngamiland. But many people, mainly for business and diplomatic reasons, do come to Gaborone and there are things of interest to see. As yet the tourist infrastructure isn't very well organised so it is a matter of finding your own way around, and this is usually best done by hiring a car (see page 63).

The first local guidebook, *The Complete City Guide to Gaborone* by Patricia Farrow, is available in most bookshops. A more detailed guidebook is currently in press.

Gaborone has a population of approximately 200 000. The city centre is the main Mall, with the City Council offices at one end and government offices at the other. Nearby are two casinos, two cinemas and a number of restaurants. The streets are safe to walk in, theft does occur but it is not a serious problem. Be careful, however. The water is safe to drink.

Accommodation and restaurants

The main hotels (telephone numbers in brackets; remember the prefix if you're phoning from outside the country) are **Gaborone Sun** (395-1111), **Grand Palm** (391-2999), **Cresta Lodge**

(397-5375), **President** (395-3631), **Oasis Motel** (392-8396, 392-8501), **Gaborone Travel Inn** (392-2777) and, in Molepolole, **Mafenya-Tlala Hotel** (592-0522). See also hotel list, page 221.

Among the bed-and-breakfast establishments that have been in business for some time are **Lolwapa Lodge** (390-1200), **Brackendene Lodge** (391-2886), and **Morula Lodge** (392-8500). Others can be located from the roadside signs that are going up. All offer rates substantially below those of the hotels.

A new venture planned for 2001 is the **Swiss Connection**, a lodge which comprises up to ten spacious, luxurious chalets, a restaurant, bar, pool and lots of ambience. Located at Ruretse, about 6 km beyond Phakalane and 32 km from Gaborone (off the main Francistown road), it will serve lunches, dinners and 'spitbraais' (barbecues), and offer such extras as transfers from airport and town and, later on, drives to Khutse Game Reserve and other areas. Phone and fax 316-1425, email swisscon@it.bw.

There is one campsite in Gaborone: **Citi Camp** (tel 318-0285, PO Box 20222, Gaborone), located next to the well-known Bull and Bush bar and restaurant. It's a clean, well-run establishment with reasonable rates, plenty of camping space, rondavels for hire if required and neat and clean ablution facilities.

Apart from those in the hotels themselves, the better-known restaurants include **Sanitas** (near the dam): beautiful, shady setting; coffee and lunches only; a must if you have a vehicle, otherwise something of a walk; **The Moghul** (Pakistani; best chicken wings in Africa); **The China Restaurant** (Chinese; very good); **The Swiss Chalet** (Continental cuisine; upmarket); **The Maharaja** (Indian); **Mokolodi Game Reserve** (lovely sunset spot; see page 219); **Steers** (steaks); **Mike's Kitchen** (steaks), **The Jasmine Garden** (Chinese); **The Great Wall** (Chinese); **The Bull and Bush** (a great meeting place); **The Taj** (Indian), and **The Kgotla** (Continental restaurant and coffee shop).

What to see

If on foot around the Mall, it is worth taking in the **Parliament** buildings, and the **House of Chiefs**, both in the Government enclave. At the opposite end of the Mall are the **National Museum** and the **Art Gallery**. Both are in the same building and are definitely worth a visit. The museum, especially, offers a good overview of the country and its material culture. An especially interesting visit is that to the **Craft Centre** in

Broadhurst (Nakedi Road). In addition to its fascinating shops there's good food and coffee at several venues within the complex. Those with an interest in the Boer War will appreciate a visit to the **Military Cemetery** in Gaborone Village. Also worth a visit are the **National Botanical Garden** and the **Natural History Centre**. Still in its infancy, the 7-hectare grounds are being developed with the establishment of lawns and walking trails, and a separate display house for reptiles, insects, fish and amphibians. In pursuit of its vision, the national **university** has been improving in every aspect of its endeavour. It aims to become a leading centre of academic excellence in Africa and already has an enviable reputation in the wider region.

Somewhat further afield – and you'll need a car for this, plus a local guidebook for specific directions – are some nice walks around the **dam** and up **Kgale Hill**. The **Gaborone Game Reserve** is also worth a visit. It costs very little to enter and, while it is not very big, it is home to some interesting antelope (including eland, kudu, gemsbok and wildebeest), birds and, if you are lucky, a sight of the three resident rhino. A little further out of town, on the Lobatse road, is the **Mokolodi Game Reserve** (see page 219). This is a private sanctuary, much larger and with a wide range of animals, including elephant and giraffe. It also has a pleasant restaurant. Continuing on this road, you'll get to Ootse and the attractive **vulture-nesting colony** there. A trip to **Oodi Weavers** is worthwhile (but take your wallet!). This is a locally owned co-operative whose workers spin, dye and weave attractive mats and wall-hangings.

City Tours provides excellent guided tours of Gaborone and the surrounding areas. Bookings can be made through any hotel or travel agent, or directly (phone 391-9744). On offer are standard half- and full-day trips, both guided and chauffeured; more personalised packages can also be arranged.

A number of interesting **villages** around Gaborone include Gabane, Kolobeng, Thamaga, all on the Kanye road, Molepolole, and on the road north, Pilane, Rasesa and Mochudi.

Some 20 km from the city centre on the Lobatse road you will find the **St Clair Lion Park**. In addition to horseback riding (see further on), there are six somewhat overweight lions on view. The park encloses the city's only caravan park, which offers a restaurant, bar, camping and a **4x4 driving course**.

Kolobeng, 33 km from Gaborone on the Kanye road, is the site of Dr David Livingstone's third and last attempt at building a mission station. It was from Kolobeng that Livingstone set out on his journey of discovery, with William Cotton Oswell, to Lake Ngami. Later, it was from Kolobeng that he left on his last southern African journey to twice cross the continent and, on his way, to arrive at the lip of the Victoria Falls.

Thamaga village is well known for the good quality and attractive pottery that it intermittently produces. **Manyana village** has some interesting rock art – certainly the best preserved such work in this part of Botswana. Nearby is a large fig tree, said to have shaded Livingstone during some of his sermons.

Molepolole, 50 km from Gaborone on an excellent road, is the tribal capital of the Bakwena group. The small museum, the many stone walls, the various historical sites around and the pretty walks make this a good place for a day's outing. Also visit the **Kgosi Sechele I Museum**, the former Bakwena capital **Ntsweng** and, by appointment (phone 392-0815), the Schachter & Namdar **diamond cutting factory**, which is fascinating.

The same can be said of **Mochudi**, 45 km from Gaborone off the main road to Francistown, which also has a charming museum, known for its fine collection of 19th- and early 20th-century photographs and for the magnificent view across Mochudi from its dramatic hilltop position. The *kgotla* (traditional place for tribal administration), a **blacksmith** and the picturesque nature of the village guarantee an interesting day.

The countryside around Gaborone is ideal for **horseback riding** and both lessons and horses can be arranged with the following: Gaborone North Equestrian Centre (also a cattery and kennels; tel 390-9063), the Lion Park Equestrian Centre (contact Angela Tilney on cell/mobile phone 72116601, or on 391-2178), and Gaborone Stables (316-1539 or cell/mobile phone 71606330).

Arne's Horse Safaris takes riding a little further. Just under 40 km from the city, Arne offers cottage/chalet type accommodation, riding, lessons, walks and excellent views of the distant city. The hilly countryside around Arne's is full of Botswana's early history. The 19th-century road to the north passes close by and traces of the old wagon trail are still to be seen. For more details and to book, phone 71234567.

About 8 km beyond the turn-off to Mochudi, past the village of Rasesa, a signpost indicates **Matsieng's Footprints**. This national monument consists of petroglyphs – depictions of animals and footprints that have been cut into the exposed rock using natural tools. They are almost certainly the work of

Bushmen (San). But the engravings have become an important feature of Tswana lore, held to be the place where the First Man, Matsieng, emerged from the earth, to be followed by all the animals that fill the world.

Gaie Bushman Tours takes individuals or groups to a San community at **Phuduhudu**. Over a few days or a weekend, guests share life with the community, and in storytelling, hunt preparation and wild food gathering. Dances are also performed. Run on behalf of a community trust, this is a unique opportunity to see at close hand these remarkable people and participate at a one-to-one level in their daily lives. Contact Chris Toye on 397-3388, email toye@it.bw or any travel agency.

Francistown

Botswana's second city owes its existence to gold and to the railway. The area of lower Tati River, about 60 km away from Francistown, was the site of the first (1867) gold rush in southern Africa. The gold was difficult to work and the diggers eventually drifted away to South Africa. Mining became important again in the 1880s and 1890s and the town started life in 1897 after renewed interest in gold and the arrival of the railway.

Accommodation and restaurants

Francistown's main hotels are **Thapama Hotel and Casino** (241-3872; commercial; town centre), **Marang Hotel and Casino** (241-3991; all facilities, including camping; lovely setting), **Ann's Guesthouse and Guided Tours** (241-6936; on Tati River; secluded; tours), **Tati River Lodge** (240-6000; modern, all facilities, also camping/ caravan sites), **Shashe Lodge** (248-4800; pool, tennis, 33 km from town, Gaborone road). See hotel list, page 221.

Among the restaurants are **Barbara's Bistro** (situated in the Francistown Club; visitors are welcome), **Continental House of Pizza** (Haskins Street, behind Shell), **Ivory Grill** (Thapama Hotel and Casino), **Nando's** (Francistown Mall, Blue Jacket Street), **Tiona's Coffee Shop** (town centre, Blue Jacket Street).

What to see

There is much of interest around Francistown. As always, a vehicle is important. The region's archaeological remains are particularly interesting, with excellent representation of the Stone Age and both Early and Late Iron Age artifacts. Of special interest are the many beautiful stone-wall ruins that have survived from the time of the Great Zimbabwe state (AD 1250 to 1450) and its successors, which were initially centred on the Khami, or Butua, state (AD 1450 to 1830).

A good starting place is the **Supa-Ngwao Museum**, one of the outlets where you can buy Catrien van Waarden's informative, inexpensive *Exploring Tati*. The real interest of Francistown itself is the abundant evidence of its early mining history, notably at **Blue Sky**, **Monarch Mine** and **Todd's Creek**. Relics abound at these places and, reflecting an even earlier interest in the metal, the so-called **'Dolly Holes'**. It seems that a prehistoric way of extracting gold from the ore was to crush it, pestle-and-mortar style, in special holes in the rock. Many of these can be found with the aid of *Exploring Tati*.

Equally exotic are the amazing ruins that stand as reminders of empires past. Great Zimbabwe claimed hegemony and sanctioned the building of its characteristic **Zimbabwes** (Shona for 'houses of stone' or 'venerated houses') in an area that embraced much of present-day Zimbabwe, parts of Mozambique, South Africa and northeast Botswana. The Khami state, and those that followed, were no less impressive, bequeathing us, above all, the ceaseless search for greater quantities of gold.

Beneath the majesty and excitement of these stirring events, life for ordinary folk over the centuries may have remained unchanged, but they too leave their legacy, most easily seen in the numerous **rock art sites** that are found around Francistown.

Newly unearthed sites are a common occurrence. If you make a discovery, please inform the museum (see page 256). Tours of some places of historic interest in and near Francistown may be arranged. Contact Ann's Guesthouse and Guided Tours at 241-6939 (also see below). If you prefer to do things yourself, I would recommend visits to the following places. *Exploring Tati* is essential for detailed directions and can be obtained from most Botswana bookshops or by writing directly to Marope Research, PO Box 910, Francistown.

For **rock art**: Matenge, Irene Farm and Kalakamati. For **stone-wall ruins** of the Zimbabwe and Khami state periods: Majojo, Schermer's Ruin, Domboshaba and Vukwe. Other sites of interest include **Old Tati Town**, the remains of the original 19th-century mining centre about 60 km southeast of

Francistown; **Shashe Dam**, 30 km south on the Gaborone road; Thakadu Mine, a millennium-old copper mine 70 km from Francistown on the Orapa road (see map 28 Francistown–Orapa, page 288); and **Mukobilo Pan**, also on the Orapa road, 116 km from the Nata/Orapa road junction. This last is not only a very pretty pan but also an excellent camping site. You will find it on map 28 Francistown–Orapa.

Lobatse

In the days before independence, Lobatse was the country's principal town and retains many of the older style colonial buildings. For the most part, these are in a sad state of collapse. Of interest might be the **BMC Abattoir**, from where 19 000 tons of de-boned beef are exported annually for consumption in Europe. For a guided tour of BMC, phone 533-0589 or 533-2449. Most visitors stay at the **Cumberland Hotel** (see page 221).

Maun

Once very much a frontier town, Maun is now beginning to shed its 'wild west' image, and has developed into a major centre boasting satellite television, good eateries, and franchise take-away joints, supermarkets and gift, craft and curio shops. Here you can buy just about anything you might need for yourself or your vehicle. Extensive banking facilities are available.

Maun is the main administrative town for the northwestern districts and many government offices are situated here. Vestiges of the old remain but they are mostly hidden beneath a modern veneer. Maun has a large population of Herero, refugees from Namibia at the turn of the century. The stunningly dressed women in their long, colourful Victorian-style dresses will tempt the photographer to reach for their camera. Be warned though: unless you have previously negotiated both the photograph and the payment, you will not be popular!

Places to stay

Maun is both a base and a staging post for travellers bent on exploring the Okavango area, and is served by a number of excellent lodges and country hotels. Best known of them is Riley's, in town; individual profiles appear on page 206.

Restaurants

There are a number of eateries in Maun, among them **The Bull & Bush** (686-4250) which faces the runway on Mathiba 1 Road. The B&B (as it is commonly known) is open seven days a week for lunch and dinner (noon to midnight), is fully licensed, and specialises in steaks, pizzas and fish – and also caters for vegetarians. The B&B also boasts a big screen in an air-conditioned room to cater for all large sporting events. From the airport, turn right and drive 200 m along the road.

The Power Station (686-2037) is an imaginative and creative pub, disco and a place for a night out.

Julian's Café (686-2905), which is open Monday to Friday from 8 am to 5 pm and on Saturdays for breakfast and lunch, is currently (November 2000) awaiting its licence but customers are free to bring their own alcohol if they wish. Julian's offers the town's best value; the lunch menu is modern, eclectic, café-style. To get there from the airport, follow Mathiba 1 Road past the Bull & Bush, turn left on to Motshaba Road and turn right, and you'll find the Café opposite the Botswana Power Station.

Hilary's Coffee Shop (686-1610; at the top of the old Mall), which is open from 8 am to 4 pm Monday to Friday (and evenings on request), specialises in excellent home cooking, including breakfasts. It isn't licensed but does cater for take-aways and for vegetarians. Children are welcome.

La Sangria is to be found in the new Mall, opposite the police station. **The Sports Bar** (686-2676/686-0219), on the Shorobe road on the right just before the bridge, offers an extensive and delicious menu, and is open Tuesday to Sunday evenings only (from 6 pm, the kitchen closing for last orders at 10 pm). Take-aways can also be ordered between those times; the bar area is open from 5 pm. Closed on Mondays. There is also the **Spur** (steak house), **Steers** (also steak, and delicious bacon-and-egg sandwiches) and **Nando's** (take-aways).

What to see

Various places of interest lie within the Maun area, among them the **Nhabe Museum** in the centre of town and the small **game reserve** on the Thamalakane River. A bit further out but well worth a visit are **Okavango Ceramics** and the **Shorobe Basket Co-operative**, both on the Shorobe road. In town itself is **The

Craft Centre (at the power station near the airport; see further on), which produces, exhibits and sells the work of local artists. Original items includes handmade paper, pottery, sculptures, painted fabrics, wire work and paintings; there's also gallery space, often filled with art from as far off as Indonesia, plus photographs, Bushman paintings, sculptures and much else.

One of Maun's premier gift outlets is **African Art and Images**, just outside the airport entrance (turn left, its on your right). The shop specialises in top-quality paintings around three basic African themes: wildlife, landscapes and ethnic subjects. A fine print gallery contains an extraordinary collection of some of the finest prints produced by June and Tim Liversedge, wildlife photographers and film makers of international repute. Bronze sculptures from Britain and the USA, together with a wide selection of coffee-table books and artifacts from West, Central and East Africa, make for an interesting presentation. The shop claims it has the best selection of Botswana baskets in Maun. An extremely popular line is the exquisite ceramics that are produced by an extraordinarily gifted artist. Finally, there's a wide selection of gold and silver jewellery, together with African jewellery made from the finest materials.

African Affairs now has two shops in Maun, one located in Riley's Hotel and the second in the Maun Lodge. At both you'll find African souvenirs, postcards, books, videos, maps, casual safari clothing, jewellery, ethnic carvings and other beautiful objects. **Bushman's Craft Shop**, opposite the airport entrance, is ideal for last-minute gifts and mementoes. Further into town, **General Trading Company** (GTC) has a good range of clothing and curios. **Savannah Art**, in the Gunn's Camp office complex opposite the airport, sells beautiful objets d'art from around the world. **Quadrum Curio Shop** is on the first floor of the airport.

Parking in Maun

A perpetual problem for motorists needing to leave their cars in Maun is where to park the car safely? If you are lucky, the booking agency may let you park 'in the yard round the back'. There's also the airport parking, but, although there are generally no problems, this cannot be considered a high-security area. Additional parking is about 200 m from the airport building (turn left out of the entrance) and it is fenced and has a gate. I am told it is seldom used and never full but I cannot say that the gate is always locked at night. Most visitors use parking facilities provided by hotels and larger safari camps in the area.

Hiring wheels and wings in Maun

Among the recommended vehicle-hire companies in this town are **Avis Safari Hire** (tel 686-0039, after hours 686-0739 or 686-0535, fax 686-1596) and **Holiday Safari 4x4 Hire** (tel 686-2429, fax 686-2429, email van&truckhire@mega.bw).

Visitors who wish to charter an aircraft, to reach a camp or for game-viewing, should contact: **Aer-Kavango**, PO Box 169, Maun; tel 686-0393, fax 686-0623. **Air Xaxaba**, Gametrackers, P/Bag 100, Maun; tel 686-0302, fax 686-0153, email gtb.mngr@info.bw. **Bush-free Air**, tel 686-3599, fax 686-3599, email bushfree@global.bw. **Delta Air**, PO Box 39, Maun; tel 686-0044, fax 686-1703, email synergy@ info.bw. **Elgon Air**, P/Bag 198, Maun; tel 686-0654, fax 686-0037, email book@info.bw. **Mack Air**, tel 686-0675, fax 686-0675, email mack.air@info.bw. **Moremi Air Charter**, tel 686-2078, fax 686-2078, email moremi.air@info.bw. **Ngami Air**, PO Box 119, Maun; tel & fax 686-0530. **Northern Air**, PO Box 27, Maun; tel 686-0385, fax 686-1559, email nair@kerdowney.bw. **Sefofane Air Charter**, P/Bag 159, Maun; tel 686-0778, fax 686-1649, email garyk@sefofane.bw. **Swamp Air**, Tel 686-0569, fax 686-0040, email gunnscamp@info.bw. **Wildlife Helicopters**, P/Bag 161, Maun; tel & fax 686-0664, email wildheli@info.bw; or **Xugana Air**, tel 686-0921.

Serowe

This interesting town lies on the route from eastern Botswana into the Kalahari and on to Makgadikgadi, the Boteti River and to Maun and the game regions beyond. Most travellers pass it by, but it deserves more than a fleeting stop. Your first call should be to the **Khama III Memorial Museum**, located in the old 'Red House', a splendid Victorian building beautifully restored with the assistance of Danish aid. Next to it is the **Phineas McIntosh house**. McIntosh, a white man, was flogged at the command of the Regent, Tskedi Khama, in an incident that shocked the 1933 Bechuanaland establishment and brought marines from Cape Town by rail to 'apply discipline'. The **Royal Cemetery**, which contains the grave of the country's first president, Sir Seretse Khama, and the **Serowe kgotla**, are also well worth a visit. Thirty kilometres north of Serowe, on the road to Orapa, is the **Khama Rhino Sanctuary** (see page 218). There are two hotels in Serowe; see page 222.

Kasane/Kazungula

The Kasane area offers other attractions beyond Chobe National Park. Slightly downstream of Mowana Safari Lodge, on the Chobe River, are the **Chobe Rapids**. A footpath leads through the glorious riverine vegetation and giant trees, which you can reach by turning left along the river in front of Mowana or by locating the track to the east of Mowana's entrance gate.

Another place of interest is **Commissioner's Kop**; access is via a 4x4 vehicle track at the downstream end of the rapids, and which takes you to the top of the low eminence, and there are wonderful views from the summit. A path goes from the top to join that along the river by the rapids. Ask for Richard Randall at Mowana Safari Lodge; Richard knows everything there is to know about the flora and fauna of the area (he was President Bill Clinton's driver during the official visit) and one of the country's top **birding** experts. Ask him for advice about what unusual birds you might hope to see around the rapids area.

A little known (but worthy) venue in the Kasane area is the country's only remaining **Crocodile Farm**, in the village of Kazungula. It lies 200–300 m from the entrance to Kubu Lodge, and is open from 10.30 am –12.30 pm and 2.30–4 pm every afternoon. A modest entry fee is charged, and the visit includes a guided tour and drinks.

It is interesting to go down to where the **Zambezi ferry** is berthed and watch the activities. The place is on the main road linking Botswana and Zambia and, unfortunately, you have to go through border formalities, but usually these involve just leaving your passport, and it's worth the trouble. A hundred metres or so downstream is the spot where David Livingstone crossed the river. A 'sausage' tree used to mark the exact crossing, but this was burnt down about 15 years ago. A bridge may be built across the river at this point within the next two years.

Where to stay

The Kasane/Kasungula area is well served by lodges and country hotels; see Chapter 9, page 206.

7

PLACES TO VISIT: THE WILDERNESS

Botswana offers the visitor some remarkable and fascinating destinations. Some are scenically beautiful, others of cultural or historical interest; many are well known, others much less so. But whatever your reason for visiting the country, whether it be to view the game or the bird life, to explore the great spaces of the Kalahari or to experience the freedom of total isolation, you can be sure that your trip will be memorable and worthwhile.

The focus in this chapter is on the wilderness, on areas that lack, most of them, even a rudimentary tourist infrastructure, and they are for the independent, self-sufficient and experienced traveller. In short, they are little enough known for you to make your own discoveries – which adds to their attraction.

Aha Hills

Of all the places of interest in Botswana, the Aha Hills are probably the most remote and difficult to access. But their isolation and their incongruous location in the centre of a vast dunefield, lend a certain fascination to them. Straddling the border with Namibia, the Hills form a low plateau some 245 km^2 in extent and consist almost entirely of limestone, dolomite and marble. The rocks are some 700 million years old. It is said that their name comes from the onomatopoeic Bushman word for the barking gecko that is so abundant in the area.

In addition to magnificent views of real Kalahari country, the Hills offer the excitement of a largely unexplored area. Although only 50 km from Drotsky's Cave in the Gcwihabe Hills (see page 111), and formed of the same material, it is not known to what extent similar **cave formations** exist at Aha.

However, recent research strongly reinforces the belief that there are more caves to be discovered in and around these hills.

What exploration there's been has revealed two **sinkholes**, only about 15 km apart but apparently unrelated to each other. Both holes are vertical, dangerous and have been fully examined. One is about 45 m deep and the other about 75 m deep; neither leads to caves, although there is a small chamber at the bottom of the shallower one. Persons without experience or proper equipment are strongly advised not to investigate them.

The village of **Caecae** lies some 15 km to the south, the villages of **Dobe** and **Qangwa** about 60 km to the south, all three inhabited mostly by San (Bushmen) together with a small number of Herero folk. Early, Middle and Late Stone Age sites have been located in the Qangwadum Valley and, as at Drotsky's Cave, there is abundant evidence of previous climatic regimes.

Only the most limited range of food and supplies is available at the stores in Caecae and other villages along the way. There's no standing water at Aha, although one can rely on the wells and boreholes of the villagers. The nearest petrol after Maun is at Etsha-6 or at Andara in the Caprivi region. Visitors must be self-sufficient. Some traffic does use the main roads, but it's very infrequent, so be prepared for any eventuality.

Further information regarding the location of Aha's sinkholes can be obtained from the Botswana Society, Gaborone (tel 391-9673, fax 391-9745, email botsoc@botsnet.bw), in their publication, *Botswana Notes and Records*, Vol. 6, 1974.

Bokspits

The unusual name of this small village, set in the most southwesterly corner of Botswana, is derived from the place where a man called Bok once sank a well. It stands at the confluence of two great sand rivers: the Molopo, which runs mostly westward along Botswana's southern border and here turns south, and the Nossob, which drains from the north and northwest through the famous, and now newly named, Kgalagadi Transfrontier Park. Neither river commonly flows today, even after rain, but major floods have been recorded in both and may occur again – a most incredible sight. Today Bokspits is a struggling little centre whose residents once made a handy living from **karakul wool** ('Persian lamb') production. Petrol and diesel are available, and there is a police station, clinic and a well-stocked store.

Few would deny unofficial mayor Klaas van der Westhuizen's status as 'Mr Bokspits', and if anybody needs help or assistance, Klaas (or his son Franz) is the man to see. He will introduce you to local farmers if you would like to know more about the area, and also demonstrate his remarkable powers as a water-diviner!

Large, red, mobile **sand dunes** occur in the vicinity of Bokspits – fascinating subjects for photographers. About 20 km to the east is Rappel's Pan, which provides an excellent opportunity to investigate these curious features of the southern Kalahari. Provided one stays on the main roads there is no need to use a four-wheel-drive vehicle.

Among many interesting features of the area are the remarkable nests of the **sociable weavers**. These massive structures of woven grass stems may be home to several hundreds of the small communal birds. They also provide shelter for other creatures such as snakes, scorpions, a great array of parasites, and for other birds, including owls and falcons.

A magnificent sight, common along the Kuruman and Molopo rivers, are the striking groves of *Acacia erioloba* or camelthorn acacia. These are large trees, specially adapted for this difficult environment, and their seed pods are a vital source of protein for stock and wild animals, especially at that time of year when other food is more difficult to come by.

The road that leads to the northwest, along the Botswana side of the Nossob River, takes you to the Botswana entrance of the Kgalagadi Transfrontier Park (KTP). The entrance is known as Two Rivers (not Twee Rivieren). The latter name has been retained for the original South African gate which still exists. It is also possible to enter South Africa from Bokspits.

Cattle Trek Route

From the early 1900s there was a small but steady movement of cattle out of north-central and western Bechuanaland, across the game-filled wilderness to the Zambezi River and beyond. Tough, hardy men led these treks, and the stories of their encounters with the wild are legion. One of the main routes to the north was known simply as the Cattle Trek Route and so it remains to this day. With the advent of the motor vehicle the route quickly became a track, which it still is. Parts of it have disappeared and both ends are difficult to find, but the experience of utter wilderness is immensely rewarding.

A feature of the drive is the extraordinarily beautiful **land-scape**. Notable for its vegetation, it changes from grasslands to mopane woodland and, occasionally, to 'cathedral' mopane. Most memorable, especially towards the north end of the journey (which is a good day's drive that definitely demands a 4x4) are the magnificent mongongo nut trees (*Phytodendron rautaneii*), known as 'manketti' to many South Africans. These trees are distinctive and characteristic of the north. The straight, heavy boles are unmistakable and in the hot season, after the rains have fallen, they appear like giant umbrellas. Beneath them stand small groups (or pods) of elephant, the larger herd broken into smaller fragments so that all can benefit from the midday pools of deep shadow these trees create.

The south end of the journey involves entry or exit through **Nxai Pan National Park** (see page 124) and this, because of the high fee, is something of a disadvantage. The entire countryside to the east, west and north of the park (except the forest reserve in the extreme northeast) is concession area. The road through is a public one, but leaving the road or camping alongside it may infringe on the rights of the concessionaires, so some tact and diplomacy may be needed (on both sides).

For me, this road was high adventure. It is little known, it held the delights of exploration, it demanded good navigational skills, and there was the added element – plenty of wildlife, especially elephant. Coming round a corner to find 20-odd elephant standing in the shade of a mongongo tree less than 20 m from the road was a tad breath-holding, to say the least. For a detailed itinerary, see Recommended Routes, page 146.

Central Kalahari Game Reserve (CKGR)

Established in 1961 as both a wildlife reserve and a sanctuary for Botswana's San (Bushman) population, the CKGR was, until some years ago, closed to the general public. This has changed and a remarkable tract of Africa is now open to those who have the resources to make the journey – which definitely requires a 4x4! At the moment there are three entrances to the reserve. One is through Old Xade (the 'x' is a click sound so the word is pronounced 'click-r-day') in the west, some 190-odd kilometres from Ghanzi on a direct route (if you're approaching from the north) and 210 km from the trans-Kalahari highway. A second entrance is in the southeast at

Khutse, and the third is approached through Matswere Gate in the northeast via the village Rakops. Each offers a different experience of the Kalahari (but note my comments on veterinary fences and cut-lines on page 71). New entrances are planned and when established, they will facilitate entry into the southwest corner of Khutse and the southwest and northwest corners of the CKGR.

Khutse is described elsewhere (see page 120). The challenging drive from Khutse to Xade is for those who want to see the Kalahari in all its forms. Game is infrequent, pans are few, the real attraction is the immense visual variety and changing nature of the vegetation. Even in its drab winter dress, the late afternoon or morning sun brightens the dark greens of the *Boscia* and the bright yellows of the stunted *Lonchocarpus*, merging with reds, fawns and gold to make a memorable picture. In the wet, the range of greens is staggering, and against the blue-black storm clouds of the rainy season they give a meaning to the word wilderness.

It is on this route that one passes through or near a number of **San villages**, including Metsiamanong, Mothomelo and Kukama (see Map 2, page 262). I urge you to spend some time in them. You are meeting people who live closer to a true hunting and gathering existence than almost anyone on earth. They are fascinating people, worthy of your respect and interest.

The drive from Khutse to Xade is long (about 270 km) and tiring, especially if the sand tracks have been heavily used. But there are compensations, not the least of which are the challenge, adventure and, at journey's end, the sense of achievement. Approaching from the south and nearing Xade, you will have the Okwa on your right. This ephemeral river has its headwaters in Namibia. It once carried waters to the great lake, to which Makgadikgadi now stands as a dry, dusty memorial.

There is the special interest of a visit to Xade, a place that used to be a large, formal and growing formal San settlement. But the San have been moved to New Xade (officially known as Khweesakweni, outside the CKGR's western boundary and near the road leading to Ghanzi).

The journey northeastward from Xade is one of the most fascinating in Botswana. To someone accustomed to the variety of the CKGR's Kalahari, very little appears to change in the first 50-km stretch north from the settlement, but then you come to the first of a seemingly unending series of **pans**. As elsewhere in the Kalahari, game tends to congregate around these pans and so one discovers a whole sequence of spectacular views set among a multitude of game. You can expect to see ostrich, hartebeest, eland, wildebeest and kudu. You might also spot giraffe, although they are not common here. Jackal shelter under the tiniest shrubs on the open plains, and there are birds in profusion. Evocative names such as Piper's Pan,

Letiahau and Deception Valley grace the maps. Plenty of waterholes are in the area; campsites are located in enticing groups of acacia that stand like green islands on the open plain.

Mark and Delia Owens brought this place to public notice with their book *Cry of the Kalahari*. In my 19 years in Botswana (and a dedicated Makgadikgadi man myself!) I must admit that I have not seen the equal of the pan-country of northern CKGR.

What makes a visit all the more fascinating is that these pans, which, on a 1:250 000 scale map, clearly follow continuous lines, are not wind-formed, as are their cousins in the south and southwest Kalahari. Rather, they are the remnants of a once-vast river system that drained into the former paleo-lake Makgadikgadi, which lies further to the east. In other words, you stand in the now-dry bed of an ancient Okavango Delta!

Some 14 000 to 17 000 years ago the climate was very different from that today; rainfall was higher, evaporation lower and surface water common in this region. At least two major rivers brought water from the then moist west and southwest (the present day semi-arid Ghanzi region and beyond) and delivered it to the dying super-lake. Modern maps show these fossil river systems as the Letiahau (of which Deception Valley is a lower part) and the Passarge Valley. The drainage lines between Deception Pan and Makgadikgadi are blurred and impossible to follow further, but somewhere in this vicinity there must once have been a massive delta. This caused the great rivers to back up and fill the wide valleys we see today.

At that time it must have been a paradise of wild animals, brimming with life of every kind. For a sense of what it must have been like, stand on the track at Letiahau and look at the prominent but distant riverbanks to the left and right of the road. Imagine how much water that vast system must once have held. Is it any wonder that, even in the present arid conditions, this remains one of Botswana's most beautiful places?

Not only is there evidence of much wetter times in northeast CKGR, but the land also reveals abundant clues to the era of dryness and a great desert. The journey from Deception Pan to Sunday Pan crosses a north–south **fossil dune-field** before the track turns off to the northwest. The regular pattern of dune-crest and inter-dune valley speaks eloquently of ancient sand dunes now trapped beneath a mantle of trees, grass and shrubs. The Department of Wildlife and National Parks have recently opened up new areas in this region. These include the Passarge Valley and Tau Pan; both are definitely worth visiting.

Booking is essential, and one may overnight only at *designated* campsites (they are merely designated; there are no facilities at all and you must be totally self-sufficient). Thirteen such campsites have been created, allowing space for 162 people.

Chobe: river front and Nogatsha

Served by the tarred road from Francistown, the Kasane/Chobe area is becoming increasingly popular with the motorist. It is easier to get there – the whole journey can be completed in a standard vehicle – but the Chobe National Park's facilities (see page 213) are often overcrowded, especially in school holidays, and the area cannot easily be enjoyed except in a 4x4.

The overcrowding is being addressed by introducing a booking system (see page 207), and hopefully an effort will also be made to upgrade the roads for normal cars. For those without a 4x4, the only option at the moment is to take a place on one of the many game drives or boat rides organised by local safari operators (**note:** the entrance fee covers all your visits during a single day). The second effort to reduce overcrowding is the closure of Serondela camp and the construction of a replacement at Ihaha, still on the river but about 15 km further west. Lastly, the entrance to the park has been relocated and this, hopefully, will disperse visitors over a wider area.

Perhaps the greatest attraction of the Chobe River area are the **elephant**, which are almost always present. Their late-afternoon visits to the water's edge offer hours of fascinating viewing and wonderful photographic opportunities. But please be extremely cautious around them: the herds often consist mainly of females with young; the cows are sensitive to interference, and more than one incident has been recorded where a vehicle has been damaged after an imprudent approach.

Best times to visit Chobe are in the drier months, when the animals are driven back to the river through scarcity of water in the hinterland. Huge numbers gather in the area, particularly of elephant and buffalo. You will also see tsessebe, waterbuck, roan, eland, kudu, sable, giraffe, lion and, if you are lucky, the rare puku. The river's floodplain, with its mixed patches of open grassland, thickets of bush and riverine forest, makes an ideal viewing area. In the river itself you should see hippo, crocodile and, with patient watching, the wonderful otters.

The drier months and the floodplains are, however, not the only parts of Chobe worth visiting. Old water-points are being upgraded, repaired and properly maintained and new ones are being constructed. As a result, with water readily available, the Noghatsa region is now a must at any time of year. Boreholes and watering points at Savute have also kept game in that area, even though the famous Channel itself is dry (see page 134).

Birders will find the river-front particularly rewarding, but a still richer area for birds is the **Kasane Rapids**, a beautiful stretch of rock-filled river (for which formal protection status is being sought) immediately downstream of Mowana Safari Lodge. Here, with luck, you'll find the African finfoot, whitebacked night heron and rock pratincoles nesting out on the rocks during times of low water. Richard Randall, a birder of note, lives and works at Mowana Lodge. He is an official recorder for the area and is building up a vital data-bank of 'new' sightings and species. In this, he will appreciate your help.

Deception Valley

See Central Kalahari Game Reserve, page 106, and Routes 1A and 1B, Maps 1, 2, 3, 7, 8 and 28.

Drotsky's Cave (Gcwihaba Caverns)

This remarkable series of caves in western Botswana, not far from the Namibian border, was first shown by the Bushmen to Martinus Drotsky in 1934. Perhaps not as extensive as South Africa's Cango Caves, Drotsky's stalagmites, stalactites, flowstones, caverns and passages can nevertheless match any cave complex for truly breathtaking splendour. It has, for some, an additional attraction in that it is quite unspoilt and undeveloped. Apart from their scenic attraction, the caves are of great interest to geomorphologists and palaeo-climatologists, providing abundant evidence of former climates.

The caves are set in an apparently endless dune-field of rolling, arid country, and appear as a low outcrop of dolomite that barely protrudes above the ubiquitous sand on the banks of the now dry Gcwihaba River. Yet this river once flowed, and flowed strongly. There was sufficient water to dissolve the rock itself, to carve out the winding passages and caverns. At slightly drier times, falling rain percolated through the dolomite, forming striking displays of white flowstone or 'cave sinter'.

The age of the caves is not known, but there is evidence of a very wet period between 17 000 and 14 000 years ago – wet enough to flood and re-excavate the old passages. Drier times returned and some of the flowstones were deposited, to be partly eroded during a later wet period about 4 500 years ago. A succession of wet and dry times followed, including at least one especially wet one, between 2 000 and 1 500 years ago, when the most recent of the cave sinters were deposited.

There are two entrances to the caves. The track will lead you to one, on the slopes of a low hill, that is 300 m from the right-hand bank of the river. Beside it is a large information board erected by the National Museum. The second entrance is 200 m away from the first, in a direction at right angles to the river valley and further from it.

There are no facilities at Drotsky's, no water, not even in the cave complex itself, and no-one lives in the immediate vicinity. The nearest village (Caecae; see page 104) is 36 km and 1.5 hours' drive away. You *must* be entirely self-sufficient. The nearest reliable fuel sources are at Maun and Etsha-6. You'll need a minimum of two full days to explore the area properly. Because of the lack of water, game animals are rare and the chance of encountering any large predators is remote. Bats are present but, in drier times, they will have to be looked for rather than avoided.

Within the past few years enthusiastic explorers have discovered four new systems, one at **Gcwihaba** itself and three at **Koanaka Hills** (some 20 km distant, to the southwest and close to the Namibian border fence). In all four cases, these remarkable caves contain material of vital importance to palaeontological (fossil) studies and so for the moment, information about their exact location is not being disclosed to the general public. In order to prevent bats from entering one of the new caves through an entrance way which had to be created, a steel door has been fixed in place. The caves can be dangerous.

ere is no lighting, natural or artificial, so you must take your
wn. Torches are essential, gas lamps useful, and both will be
constant use so make sure that you have plenty of spare gas
and batteries. *Never* enter the caves without a secondary, emergency light supply on your person – matches or a small torch.
This precaution is absolutely vital; if there's no backup and your
light is put down and goes out, you could find yourself in a very
serious situation indeed. *Never* enter the caves alone.

But back to Drotsky's: previous explorers have left strings
marking the main routes. Some sections have been removed
but the remainder serve as a guide. It is possible to go in one
entrance and out the other but a good knowledge of the system is required in order to do this. Plans of complex are available from the Botswana Society, Gaborone; tel 391-9673, fax
391-9745, email botsoc@botsnet.bw. They also appear in the
Society's journal *Botswana Notes and Records*, Vol. 6, 1974.

Photographers are advised to equip themselves with more
than one flash, preferably slave units mounted on tripods. Three
standard flashes will provide sufficient light. Dust in the caves
is a big problem – care should be taken to protect equipment.

Ghanzi

The town of Ghanzi, in the west of Botswana, consists of a
small and thriving community and the centre of a substantial
cattle and game ranching industry. Deep in the Kalahari, it
owes its unlikely success to the limestone ridge on which it is
situated, a feature that provides an abundant supply of groundwater for most of the surrounding 190 farms.

Originally home to the San (Bushmen), Ghanzi's first white
inhabitant was the extraordinary **Hendrick van Zyl**, who took
up permanent residence in 1874 on what is today Ghanzi
Farm Number One. What information has come down to us
has been distorted and re-shaped in the telling so it is difficult
to sort fact from fancy. Known as 'The Laird of Ghanzi', Van Zyl
was member of the South African Republic (Transvaal) volksraad or parliament; slaver; hunter, and built himself a doublestorey house complete with coloured glass windows and French
furniture. His hunting prowess is legendary: in a single afternoon in 1878 he and his two sons slaughtered 103 elephants.
He also provided succour to the ill-fated Dorsland Trekkers –
and is reputed to have been a ruthless murderer of Bushmen.

Among the tales associated with him is one that speaks of 'Van Zyl's Cutting'. Most accounts tell of a 'cheese wedge' shape carved by Van Zyl from solid rock to form a sloping feature some 30 m long, 10 m wide and 4–5 m deep at the deep end. Apparently its purpose was to provide a source of near-permanent water far to the southeast of his home, thus allowing him to extend his hunting activities over a greater area.

The ill-fated Dorsland Trekkers reached Ghanzi in late 1875 but soon moved on to their sad future in Namibia and Angola. Next to arrive were the Rhodes' Trekkers, the first of whom reached the area in October 1898. Ten years later all but one family had left. The descendants of that family, and of others who drifted into the struggling settlement in those early years, remain in Ghanzi today, where they form the core of the Afrikaans- and English-speaking communities.

Today Ghanzi is prosperous. Land prices have improved, as have management practices and the quality of the herd. The town is a busy administrative centre and a pleasing testimony to the ability of widely disparate and strongly independent peoples to live together equably and in harmony. The ruins of Van Zyl's house can still be seen – on Dick Eaton's farm, Ghanzi One, 19 km north of town on the Maun road. Interested persons are asked to contact the owner for permission to enter the farm (tel 659-6505 or 659-6157). The management at the Kalahari Arms Hotel in Ghanzi will assist in organising the visit. Ghanzi can provide all your basic needs. It has a hospital, and is in telephone contact with the rest of the country.

An interesting place to visit is the San (Bushman) settlement at **D'kar**, 38 km northeast of Ghanzi on the Maun road (and 245 km from Maun). Initiated by the Dutch Reformed Church, D'Kar is on a 3 000-hectare farm owned and run by the San community, who call themselves N'coahkoe, or 'the red people'. Here, under the initial, determined and courageous leadership of Braam le Roux and assisted by Case Otto and others, the Kuru Development Trust (tel 659-6285) has helped establish a community of artists and crafters. There is an excellent craft and leather shop and a small art gallery, and several exhibitions of local work have been mounted at the National Art Gallery and Museum in Gaborone and a number of international venues. The project and its artistic output have been nurtured for many years by Peter and Maude Brown, who have helped the artists achieve remarkable levels of international recognition.

D'Kar is an inspiring venture, and merits your interest and support. Equally worth a visit is the cultural centre, which includes a museum and library. Camping facilities are available at D'Kar and are being constantly upgraded. A 7 500-hectare game farm, known as **Dqãe Qare**, has been purchased by the people of D'Kar, an exciting venue where you can spend a day or two walking among the animals in the company of a Bushman guide. The farm, which has both a guest-house and campsite, is part of an effort by the people of D'Kar to create employment, preserve indigenous knowledge and skills, and to generate income through tourism. On offer are guided walks, traditional dancing and storytelling. It is not expensive, is a quite unique experience, and is something not to be missed.

Hunter's Road

This is the name given to a wagon road used extensively, in the latter half of the 19th century, to move supplies and trade goods over the northern part of what is now Botswana – from South Africa's Witwatersrand to the banks of the Zambezi at Kazungula. It is part of a network of routes that early explorers and travellers in this part of Africa developed to help them penetrate the hinterland. Shoshong, the Ngwato capital, was a major centre and it was from there that the road to the north departed. On the way it passed through Tati Town to Marula.

Livingstone's early explorations had created interest in the Zambezi and, by the 1860s, traders and explorers were visiting the river in greater numbers. Usually, they took the road to Bulawayo and turned northwest at Ramokgwebane to follow the watershed. In 1870 or 1871 an English trader by the name of George Westbeech began trading with the Lozi in Barotseland, and found it convenient to follow the route from Ramokgwebane to the northwest. Eventually, he established a residence and trading store at Mpandamatenga, and two more stores at Leshomo and Kazungula, and began to improve the wagon trail from the southeast. The trail was extensively used in the next 20 years and became known as **the Hunter's Road**.

The Hunter's Road (see also page 199) was both a vital trade artery to the heart of Central Africa and the first major tourist route. Mpandamatenga was situated in a cool, well-watered area at the southern limit of the tsetse fly's range. Visitors to the Victoria Falls, who came in ever-increasing numbers as the years passed, typically left their horses and oxen in Westbeech's care at Mpandamatenga before setting off on foot to visit that remarkable site. Eventually, when early 20th-century politics dictated the need for defined international borders, the commissioners responsible could find no more expedient method for deciding the demarcation line than to declare the wagon trail itself to be the boundary between Rhodesia and Bechuanaland. And so it has been to this day.

Inevitably, a short-cut from Shoshong developed. Instead of passing through Tati and Ramokgwebane, some travellers went directly north, through Tlhabala and along the eastern edge of Sowa Pan to Nata. From here the trail led northwest and then north to the watershed, intersecting the Hunter's Road at Ngwahla Pan. This short-cut came to be known as the Western Old Lake Route: modern roads and fences have made the route from Shoshong and Tlhabala to Nata difficult to find (although we recently located a baobab tree, on the eastern shore of Sowa Pan, with the cryptic legend 'Ker 1875' carved into it, suggesting a possible resting place; see also page 174) and so the route I am describing begins at Nata and uses existing roads to get you to the border and Ngwahla Pan.

The route along the watershed follows the border tracks (one on each side of the actual border line; there is no fence, except along a few kilometres when you reach Ngwahla). The attraction here is that you pass by a series of pans which often hold water for three or four months after the rains, attracting game ranging from elephant, leopard and lion downwards – a not surprising proliferation when you consider the game reserves or hunting concessions that lie on either side of the route.

As you make the journey to the Zambezi, you can hear the pages of history turn. It was along this stretch, after having spent a year as the 'guest' of the Lozi king of Barotseland, that George Westbeech returned with a wagon-load of ivory in 1872 – a cargo worth, it is said, more than £12 000! It was this successful expedition that prompted Westbeech to set himself up at Mpandamatenga.

The pan names themselves – Stoffel's Pan, for example – are full of history. Christoffel Schinderhutte, or 'Stoffel' as he was known, was an employee of Westbeech. He left for the south from Mpandamatenga in July 1875, but his wagon broke down, he got drunk on 'Cape smoke' (home-made brandy), set off again while still out of his senses, knocked a servant off the wagon and crushed him to death beneath the wheels. Running amok, Stoffel then shot some of his oxen and one of his teamsters before rushing off into the bush, never to be seen again. The only trace ever found were his *veldskoens* (boots) and part of his beard, which were taken to Shoshong and there identified. How he met his death has never been established. Hendrick's Vlei is named after a servant who killed a giraffe there; Jolley's Pan for another of Westbeech's men who died from the fever at Mpandamatenga. Cream of Tartar Pan was known for the cross carved into its bark by Jesuit priests. The cross was still visible in the 1970s but the tree itself is no more.

Scenically, the route is quite incredible. The first part of the journey north from Ngwahla is somewhat trying, with much stunted mopane countryside to negotiate, but then follows stretches of beautiful broad-leaved woodland and pans and plenty of game. As you approach the Deka River and Mpandamatenga you reach the high basalt terrain, where you enjoy majestic views over vast tracts of country. Here there are well-wooded hilltops and wide, meandering valleys lined with swathes of tall grass through which streams make their way. This is Africa much as it must have appeared to those who travelled this way 150 years ago. Just south of Mpandamatenga is an astonishing grove of giant acacia (*Acacia polyacantha*), so tall that it looks like a hilltop looming on the distant horizon.

North of Mpandamatenga, straddling the border, is the extraordinary **Kazuma Pan**, a virtual sea of golden grass and an exhilarating sight not to be missed. There are water points within sight of the track, and I have never travelled this stretch without seeing animals on the great plain.

I can write only enough to entice the reader to try the route, but there is a lot more to be seen – Stone Age sites, mislaid 19th-century merchandise, strange initials carved on isolated trees, wagon-wheel scars on rocks, game animals, birds, the odd hippo at Mpandamatenga, and much else.

Kgalagadi Transfrontier Park (KTP)

This park recently underwent a dramatic change in status. Two adjoining sanctuaries – the Kalahari Gemsbok National Park (South Africa) and the Gemsbok National Park (Botswana), which had independent identities for the whole of their more than 50-year lifespans – have merged to create Africa's first transfrontier conservation project. The two parks are now effectively one. If nothing else, the Kgalagadi is a monument to the vision, the goodwill and the spirit of co-operation between two nations. It should, however, prove to be a great deal more, for it is unique, and it now offers sights and experiences far beyond the usual (see also pages 152 and 153).

There are now four entrances: the original one at Twee Rivieren, on the South African side; a second, at the same vicinity but on the Botswana side of the border and called Two Rivers; a third in the far north, at Kar Pan, also on the Botswana side (this is the distal end of the Gemsbok 4x4 Wilderness Trail; see page 119); the fourth at Mabuasehube in the east. At some time in the next few years a single gate will replace the pair at Two Rivers. Each of these entrances has (or shortly will have) Immigration and other facilities.

The South African National Parks amenities are all well developed and Botswana is rapidly coming up to speed. A shop at Twee Rivieren stocks a wide range of essentials and non-essentials as well as fuel, and the rest-camp offers both permanent accommodation and campsites. Visitors entering from Botswana may make use of these facilities once entry formalities are complete. There are no chalets yet on the Botswana side but campsites are available at each entrance and ablution facilities at all but Kar. There is also a camping site – six sites each with fireplace, showers, shade structures and pit latrine – on the Botswana side of the Nossob River, at Rooiputs, about 25 km along the river road (see Chapter 9, page 206). Entry into the Botswana part of the park differs from those of other parks.

There are three main sand roads in the park, all in first-rate condition. One extends 157 km up the Nossob River to Nossob Camp, and continues for a further 128 km (along the river) to Union's End. Note that there is no exit here into Namibia. A second road runs beside the Aoub River for 118 km to the camp at Mata Mata. A link road of 68 km joins the two river roads and affords excellent views of the drier Kalahari countryside with its typical, stabilised, red dunes. Fuel and basic essentials are available at both Mata Mata and Nossob rest-camps.

The park has a fluctuating complement of game but a visit is always well rewarded, though perhaps the best time is probably between January and April. At least two days is recommended, during which you can expect to see, among others, gemsbok, eland, hartebeest and springbok, as well as lion, cheetah and jackal. A fairly new attraction is the organised night drive – with a good chance of sighting brown hyaena, bat-eared fox and possibly leopard. Another appealing development is the **Gemsbok Wilderness (4x4) Trail** (see page 119).

Pans on the north side of the Nossob tend to have a linear, parallel arrangement, possibly reflecting ancient north–south drainage lines emptying into the river. Opalescent and elongated, they nestle between long, low dunes and almost always

host game animals, who sample the salt and trace elements that these features so conveniently collect and concentrate. With lower and more erratic rainfall, this part of Botswana's Kalahari is markedly different from the desert elsewhere. The sands are redder and the vegetation more sparse and stark. The parallel lines of sharply defined dunes provide endless variety to the scenery and, being so utterly remote, a sense of wilderness.

For all its remoteness, however, this vast wilderness has its place in history. On 16 March 1908, German and Hottentot forces, the latter led by Simon Cooper (aka Kopper), met in circumstances that were a blend of tragedy, excitement, adventure and mystery. Small patrols of men were ambushed and annihilated. Flashing heliographs sent front-line news to Berlin from the depths of the Kalahari. A specially trained force comprising

23 officers, 373 riflemen, four Maxim machine guns and 710 camels, set out to hunt down the marauding band numbering, it is thought, some 80 individuals. There were whispers of mutiny, and the German commander was suspiciously killed by the first shot fired. Sixty-six others died in the battle that followed. The actual battlefield has yet to be discovered: clues to the site are steadily being produced but the precise location of the encounter has yet to be found. More details of this fascinating incident can be found in *Botswana Notes and Records*, Vol. 24, 1992, pp 1–11 (obtainable from the Botswana Society, tel 391-9673, or email botsoc@botsnet.bw).

The present 4x4 trail starts at Grootbrak, just over 220 km west along the Nossob. Near this point is the Polentswa campsite, sited in a beautiful stand of trees. Like Rooiputs, it too has pit latrines, rustic showers (for which you need to bring your own water!) and shade shelters. From Grootbrak, the trail follows a route along that taken by the German forces in 1908. It circles through such exotic places as Red Rambuka, Twee Rambuka, Kaa Pan and Setachwe Pan, close to which the battle is thought to have been fought. A minimum of two vehicles must travel together, and they must have four-wheel drive. Travellers may return to their starting point or leave via the Kaa Gate at the north end. In the latter case they continue along the road through Zutshwa via two spectacular pans to Hukuntsi (see Map 26, page 286). There's an airstrip at Kaa Gate.

Apart from a trip along the wilderness trail, a visit to the KTP does not necessarily require a 4x4 vehicle: an ordinary saloon car can negotiate the three main roads and get to any of the camp sites. The park is open all year round.

The Gemsbok Wilderness Trail: Do's and Dont's

• Make your bookings for the trail in advance.
• All relevant fees for full period of your stay within the park are payable before you start the trail.
• Check in at Two Rivers before starting off. This is essential for safety tracking. Collect a trail baton to carry with you: the baton signifies that your use of the trail has been authorised.
• The time allocated for the trail is three days and two nights. You may not take a shorter or longer time.
• Travel in an anti-clockwise direction, starting at Polentswa (turn off from the Nossob road at Grootbrak) and finishing north of Lijersdraai, also on the Nossob road.
• Because the start of the trail is so far from the entrance gate, it is recommended that you spend the night before and the night after the trail at different campsites, for which separate bookings should be made.
• Remember: you are totally responsible for your own safety.
• You must be completely self-contained for the whole trip, carrying your own water (minimum 10 litres per person per day), food, fuel, vehicle fluids, tools, firewood, spade, two spare tyres or tyre repair kit and other essential and recommended items (see page 76 for a checklist).
• The trail itself is about 257 km long; timing: allow for an average speed of 20 km/h.
• Vehicles: a 4x4 is essential; maximum 3 500 kg unladen weight; mini-mum of two and maximum of five vehicles in any one party; trailers are not permitted.
• Campsites: sites are designated, for the first night at **Setatswe** and the second night at **Lang Rambuka**. No other areas may be used. Note that sleeping outside without a tent is extremely dangerous (see page 77); keep tent flaps zipped up.

- The group leader is responsible for the actions and conduct of the group, and to observe a few basic bush rules to ensure that the trail will remain unspoilt for those that follow:

Rule 1 Stick to the track (see map supplied by park). There must be *no* off-track driving.

Rule 2 Take special care not to start a grass fire.

Rule 3 Campfires should be lit on the sites of previous fires; fire slabs and ash pits are provided.

Rule 4 Dig holes, *at least* 40 cm deep, for toilet purposes, and burn all toilet paper.

Rule 5 Leave no litter whatsoever, not even cigarette ends. Any litter left by previous users should be collected, and any other obvious breach of the rules by previous users be reported. The culprits will be traced and appropriate action taken.

Rule 6 Cause no harm or harassment to wildlife.

- Check out at Two Rivers (which will complete safety tracking), and hand in the trail baton.

Khutse Game Reserve

This relatively small (2 500 km²) game reserve is the closest of Botswana's sanctuaries to Gaborone (excluding the small reserves in or near the city; see page 94). Set in typical pan country of undulating savannah, it abuts the Central Kalahari Game Reserve to the north. A four-wheel-drive is essential.

Most of the arid-adapted herbivores can be found in Khutse, together with the more common predators, including leopard, lion and cheetah. Game is usually seen on or near the pans (of which there are a great many), but it is a seasonal wildlife area. The presence of animals is difficult to predict: much depends on luck and on where and when the rain last fell. January to March are generally thought to be the best months to visit. If there has been a drought, game may be scarce, if not absent, but in the latter event there is an abundance of smaller creatures; thousands of barking geckos fill the night with their calls. These beautiful little creatures sing from their burrows during the first hours of darkness, adding to an unforgettable African experience. Khutse is also renowned for its bird life. The Kalahari is unique and Khutse allows visitors to savour it to the full.

Entrance to the reserve involves a fee for vehicle and passengers. Campsites (see page 209) are laid out. Although water is available at the gate, it is fairly salty and visitors should bring their own. The road layout comprises a circular drive (see Map 1, page 261). Starting at the gate, it forks after 13.6 km at Khutse II Pan. The road to the left extends 53 km to the Mabuakolobe and Moreswe pans; that to the right continues for 12 km, where it forks again. The south fork completes the circle to Moreswe Pan; the right one continues to what used to be the Bushman settlement of Xade and is now a base for the Department of Wildlife and National Parks. Maps are sometimes available at the gate but you should receive one with your booking confirmation. If not, make a hand-drawn copy of the one on display.

Lake Ngami

Although a four-wheel-drive vehicle is not essential for a visit to Lake Ngami, it is strongly recommended. There are no sources of supply in the area beyond the occasional small general dealer's store and its limited range of goods.

Lake Ngami has spawned a host of myths, and even to this day it remains something of an enigma. This was the mysterious inland lake, rumours of which infiltrated the lore of Africa. It's the lake that called David Livingstone across the Kalahari and launched him on his great journeys of discovery.

Today Ngami is a lake that has no outflow exit, and merits its name only after one of the infrequent overflows from the Okavango Delta via the Kunyere and the Nchabe (Boteti or Lake) rivers. There hasn't been such a flood for 15 years or more, and Ngami is now completely dry. In the past, water also entered from both the Nchabe (northeast) and the Thaoge (northwest) rivers, and thus it was that the Nchabe played the unusual role of both supply and exit, depending on the flow from the Thaoge and relative water levels in the Delta itself. There is evidence that lake levels were once much higher, and enclosed a huge area of 1 800 km^2. When Livingstone reached it on 1 August 1849, Ngami had already lost much of its former glory and it is unlikely to have been more than 810 km^2 in extent. He estimated the circumference at 120 km. As the years passed, the supply of water diminished. Often it was quite dry for long periods. In the last hundred years Ngami has been but a ghost of its former self, barely exceeding 250 km^2 in area.

The dynamics of Ngami's inflows are now better understood and it seems clear that the gradual drying up of the

Thaoge River is the main reason for its decline in size since Livingstone's day. The reasons for the Thaoge's demise are more speculative, but opinion now seems to favour a change in the levels of the tectonically unstable Okavango Delta.

Lake Ngami remains the centre of an important cattle-raising area for the Tawana and Herero peoples. Estimates of the number of cattle supported by the lake flats and surrounding areas vary from 30 000 to 70 000 head; invariably dramatic collapses occur in the livestock population in time of drought.

Mabuasehube area

Across the southern third of Botswana, from east to west, runs a ridge of land marginally higher than the surrounding countryside. Characteristically, it is dotted with many thousands of pans, and typically there is a high sand dune, or series of dunes, on the south or southwest side of each pan. Some dunes are as much as 20 or 30 m high. The pans, most of which (if rain has fallen) will hold water for several months, range from bare, salty clay to surfaces lightly covered with grass. They have a vital role in the ecology of the area and have also played an important part in humankind's invasion of the Kalahari, providing people (by means of shallow, hand-dug wells, usually near the edge of the pan) with access to water and grazing for their animals. It was partly in recognition of these facts that what was originally called Mabuasehube Game Reserve (now part of the Kgalagadi Transfrontier Park, or KTP) was established.

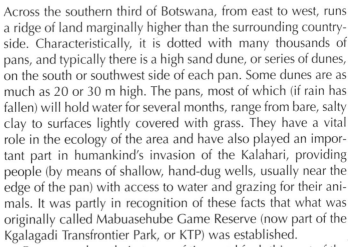

Remote and costly in terms of time and fuel, this part of the KTP is nevertheless well worth a visit. The simple beauty of the stark pans, the extraordinary colour changes that occur as the day progresses, and the often abundant game (it's a good place for seeing the rare brown hyaena) will make it a unique visit.

There are six major pans or pan clusters in this part of the park, and many smaller ones. During the rainy season, from October to April, wildebeest, springbok, gemsbok, hartebeest and eland, with their associated predators (especially lion) usually abound. The three watering points, at Lesholoago, Mabuasehube and Mpaathutlwa pans, do much to retain the game in the area throughout the long dry months.

Mabuasehube offers only basic facilities (water, toilets and fixed campsites) and the visitor must be entirely self-sufficient. The nearest fuel is at Tsabong, a district headquarters 110 km away. On the approach, the last fuel stops are at Jwaneng Werda. Both centres have limited shopping facilities. There is also a small store at Khakhea. Mabuasehube is not fenced, but there's an entrance fee and bookings must be made for overnight camping. Telephone the Department of Wildlife, Parks and Reserves Reservations Office (Parro) on 580774 before proceeding. At least two full days should be allowed in this part of the KTP in order to appreciate all it has to offer.

Makgadikgadi-Nxai Pan National Park

Note: Formerly there were two separate preserves, one on each side of the Nata–Maun road. To the north was Nxai Pan National Park and to the south Makgadikgadi Game Reserve. These two areas have been amalgamated and are collectively known as Makgadikgadi-Nxai Pan National Park. But the two components are very different from one another and for that reason are described separately below.

Makgadikgadi Route

This reserve is a vast (3 900 km^2) unfenced area of open plain and bush country to the south of the main Francistown–Maun road, about halfway between the two centres. It is informally serviced by a series of tracks, mapped on the notice boards at the north and northwest entrances but otherwise not sign-posted. A four-wheel-drive vehicle is not necessary during most of the year, but is becoming increasingly advisable.

From November or December, after the first rains, to about May, innumerable game will be encountered – herds of zebra, springbok and wildebeest that seem to stretch from horizon to horizon. Each draws in its wake lion and other predators.

However, the area itself has a simple beauty. The rolling grasslands seem endless. Early-morning mirages build clear and distant 'mountain ranges' which dissipate as the sun edges higher. Over the centuries shallow depressions in the plain have accumulated deep deposits of clay and detritus and, in these reservoirs of richer soil, trees have taken root so that the plain is dotted with widely separated islands of vegetation. If you are prepared to sit quietly for an hour or so on one of them, you'll soon be accepted by the fauna and can enjoy the rare privilege of watching the wildlife go about its daily business, undisturbed and at close quarters.

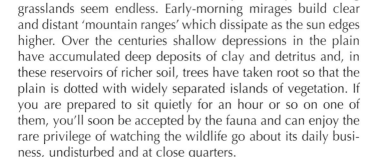

Two localities in the game reserve are particularly worth visiting as they both make memorable campsites. One is **Njuga Hills**, the other is **Xhumaga** on the Boteti River.

Njuga is an ancient dune of especially large proportions. A track leads up to two good campsites, each with magnificent views, each equipped with basic toilets. To spend an evening or two here is to sample the real magic of the Kalahari. One can watch the endless grasslands turn to gold and listen to the call of barking geckoes as the sun takes its leave of another day, while (at one of the sites) a resident mongoose noses through your belongings for cheese, which it has come to adore.

On the east or left bank of the Boteti River, opposite a village called Xhumaga, game scouts have established a second camp and nearby, under a group of shady acacias in a large sandy area overlooking the river, a new public campsite has been built. Here (with luck) you will find cold showers and flush toilets. There is an adjacent stand-pipe that delivers fresh water, and also a convenient pit for dumping rubbish. A new, medium-priced safari lodge, **Leroo-La-Ta**, has made its appearance in the area, on the same side of the river, under the trees and overlooking pools of hippo and crocodile.

The Xhumaga campsite itself is remarkable for its position in the ecotone between riverine woodland and the grasslands of Makgadikgadi. The bird life is prolific and the scenery unusual, for the Boteti has been a river flowing to nowhere: its waters simply soak away into the sand. But in recent years it has not always flowed, and it's wise to check beforehand, with the Department of Wildlife (tel 397-1405), that there is water there.

Visitors to the Makgadikgadi park must be self-sufficient in food and fuel, and must bring firewood – which is singularly scarce at Njuga (the remaining trees are suffering accordingly) although supplies may be available at the Xhumaga campsite.

Nxai Pan Route

A four-wheel-drive vehicle is necessary to get to this sanctuary; the entrance lies 36 km north of the Francistown–Maun road.

Nxai Pan National Park now extends southwards to include Baines' Baobabs and the Kudiakam pans, and links up directly with Makgadikgadi grasslands to the south. It is set on the northern fringe of the Makgadikgadi basin, and includes Nxai Pan itself, part of an ancient lake-bed. There is a manned entrance gate (a fee is charged for vehicles and passengers; booking and payment is required in advance) but has no facilities other than two campsites with ablution blocks. Visitors must be entirely self-sufficient although there is usually a reliable water supply. Game scouts will direct you to the two main campsites, both of which are within 10 km of the gate.

About 15 km to the east of the entrance, inside the park, is a large, unnamed pan complex. Kgama-Kgama Pan lies a further 9 km to the northeast. The pans themselves are the only parts of the park to which there is ready access. A road map is sometimes displayed at the entrance gate.

At certain times of the year (December to early April, if rains have fallen), game can be prolific and the viewing spectacular. The area is a breeding ground for herds of gemsbok, zebra, wildebeest, springbok and eland, and is one of the few places in Botswana where impala and springbok occur together.

In the south of the national park is another complex of pans, the largest of which is **Kudiakam**. On a site overlooking the latter is a group of very large baobab trees, a picture of which was painted by Thomas Baines on 22 May 1862. Photos taken in July 1987 show scarcely any discernible changes. These trees are known today as **Baines' Baobabs** (and also as the Seven Sisters and the Sleeping Sisters) and provide a very popular camping spot. Here there are three informal, undeveloped campsites, each accommodating a maximum of 12 persons and three vehicles. Bring your own water. Game scouts do visit the trees and may ask you for your permit.

Moremi Game Reserve

The Moremi was declared by the Tawana people in 1963, an act which was described at the time as a shining moment in African tribal history. Administered today by the Department of Wildlife and National Parks, it is a rich, fascinating area located on an extensive sandveld area, which includes Chief's Island, in the northeastern part of the Okavango Delta, and it encompasses several different types of ecological zones.

Entry is controlled by two gates, one in the north and one in the south. There's an entrance fee, and booking for campsites is essential (see page 207). A system of roads provides what is essentially a circular drive, which enables you to experience the ecological diversity of the reserve. The drive passes through dense mopane woodland, forests of giant acacia trees and, in places, skirts the edge of the Okavango, and there are magnificent views of floodplains, reed banks and open lagoons. Animal and bird life are prolific throughout the year but the drier months, from May to November, are best for viewing. At both entrances, and at various locations along the road, there are designated campsites. It is worth spending at least one night in this reserve but again, note that campsites must be booked and paid for in advance (see page 207). Mekoro (traditional canoes; singular: mokoro) are not available for hire in Moremi.

You will see most game animals within the reserve, including lion, leopard, elephant, zebra, buffalo, lechwe and impala.

Ntwetwe Pan

This enormous, fascinating area, the twin in many ways of its easterly neighbour, Sowa Pan (see page 135), has been receiving more and more attention from independent visitors, for it is a gloriously free and open part of the country, and almost completely unspoilt. The region is full of places of interest and I encourage you to explore it. Innumerable ways lead to the area and it would be impractical to try and list them all – apart from the fact that this would spoil the fun for intrepid explorers! In Chapter 8, page 146, is a description of a major north–south track, and another that enters the area from the southeast and establishes a link with Sowa Pan and the island of Kubu.

The **north–south track** links Orapa mine with the village of Gweta. It is highly probable that this was the track that David Livingstone travelled on his journeys to Linyanti and the Caprivi. By means of it, one can visit two famous baobab trees. The first, known as **Green's Baobab** (see Map 10, page 270), lies immediately beside the route and is scarred with initials from a century or more ago, that of trader and explorer Frederick Joseph Green. Green had been hunting along the Boteti River as early as 1851, but in 1858/9, when his initials were carved into the bark of the tree, he and his brother were exploring the vicinity of Makgadikgadi while on their way to western Matabeleland. The initials of H. van Zyl, the notorious explorer, hunter and murderer (see page 112), is also among those to be found on the tree. You will also see those of P. Viljoen, son of Jan Viljoen, a well-known hunter and trader and an early visitor to Lake Ngami (getting there about 18 months after Livingstone). He was accused by the missionary of 'buying several African boys'.

Within 300 m of the tree, to its southwest, you will find **Gutsa Pan**, which is mostly dry now but does hold water for some months after rain. Over 100 years ago there were reports of hippo in the area. More amazing, I know for certain it has hosted hippo within the past ten years. The mystery is: where do they come from? The Boteti River is 75 km away! When full, the pan is particularly beautiful with its waving palm trees and its bird life. Even when it's dry there's a lot to see; Stone Age artifacts abound and the hunting blinds (used initially by San to ambush their quarry) are still visible. Look for an especially well preserved one under a tree on the west side.

An equally famous though less visited tree, **Chapman's Baobab**, lies to the southeast of Green's Tree (see Map 10, page 270). This tree is visible from great distances across the pan and is worth seeing if only for its size and photogenic qualities (the colossal, six-stemmed specimen measures 24.8 m in girth at about 1.5 m above ground level). It was certainly a landmark for early explorers of the region, and a casual examination will reveal the signatures of James Chapman, members of the ill-fated Helmore-Price expedition and other well-known explorers. The cavity between the main trunks is reported to have been used as a postbox by travellers from both north and south.

To the west of the north–south road is what I call the 'land of a thousand islands'. Reflecting a chaotic climatic past, these numerous 'islands' are in fact sand dunes stranded on the surface of the ancient lake-bed, and they are one of the most fascinating features of the Botswana wilderness. They are evidence of much more arid times when the lake temporarily dried and barchan dunes (crescent-shaped shifting dunes), steep and concave on their leeward sides, convex on their windward sides, began to advance across its baked and bare surface. Eventually there was a wetter period, the lake flooded again and the dunes were trapped. The climate continued to change and the lake level fell once more, but incrementally this time, almost as if the water was struggling against the elemental forces that wished to banish it forever. Many of the island profiles show distinct steps and lines of vegetation, revealing clearly where the fall in lake levels was momentarily arrested long enough to leave permanent evidence in the shape of ancient shorelines.

To drive through this area is a unique experience. The pan surface is hard and unyielding and, in my experience, very much safer than elsewhere on Makgadikgadi. A good map is essential (see page 75). With its help, and if you sit on the roof of your vehicle for a good view, the experience is very much like sailing a galleon of old through unknown seas, with islands beckoning from all around. It's an exhilarating experience.

Careful navigation will lead you to a waterhole known as **Mgobe wa Takhu**, in the northwest of the area, which contains water for much of the year. To the north of the waterhole you'll find a little-known track (an old cut-line) that will deliver you to a group of palm trees known as Makolwane a ga Wateka, 10.6 km east of Njuga Hills (see page 124).

To the west of the **south–north** (Orapa-to-Gweta) **track** that crosses Ntwetwe Pan, and about midway between the opposing shores, is the island of Gabasadi. An unusually large barchan dune, it is bare of vegetation but you'll find it worth climbing to the (low) crest for the wonderful view of Ntwetwe that it yields, especially in early or late light. Here, if you look carefully, you will find pottery shards and Late Stone Age tools; and it was here that Prince Charles, on a visit to Botswana, sat and painted his last picture before returning to England. He remarked that it was so hot that his watercolours kept drying before he could spread them onto the paper!

Along the west shore of Ntwetwe, which you reach from the Nata–Maun road, there are, as elsewhere on this pan, numerous Stone Age sites. Among them, in a hidden cleft, is a secret waterhole that seldom dries. You'll find cattle at the waterhole, and sometimes game animals as well. Around it are hunting blinds built of calcrete blocks, used by the San of old who hid there to ambush the game as it came down to drink. Along the access route are stands of glorious aloes (*A. littoralis*) that bloom in winter and add a splash of colour to the landscape.

This whole region is one that can fill days of pleasure for those with a penchant for 'beach walking', exploring and encountering the 'non-game' wilderness at its unexploited best.

Okavango Delta

The Delta must truly be one of Africa's most enchanted places: a swirl of lushness in a desert of Kalahari sand; a remarkable phenomenon. It owes its origins to the emergence of a rift valley across the course of the Okavango River. When exactly this occurred is not certain but, geologically speaking, it is likely to have been a relatively recent event, possibly between two and four million years ago. Certainly, the process is still developing, and constant movement in the earth's crust may well explain the shifts in water distribution which are so much a feature of this incredible area. In the aeons that have followed since the rift valley was formed, windblown sand and sediment delivered by the river have filled it and its original floor now lies as much as 300 m below the fan-shaped Delta that we see today.

A characteristic of the Delta is its annual flood. The Okavango, which rises in Angola, brings its bounty of heavy rains to Botswana's border. The swollen river breaches its low-water banks and begins the annual inundation of its flood-plains. No two floods are ever the same, but one can say that the permanent Delta is some 6 000 km^2 in extent, while a big flood may cover as much as 13 000 km^2. At Mohembo, where the Okavango enters Botswana, the flood begins from November as water levels rise. Peak flood levels are not reached until the following February or March, and it can take six months for the flood to work its way through the labyrinth of channels and lagoons to reach Maun. There, it refills the Thamalakane River, which drains the area and takes the remainder to the Boteti and Lake rivers. More than 95 per cent of the Okavango's water evaporates before it reaches Maun.

Flooding in the Okavango is not a violent process. The waters spread gently down the channels and across the plains. The total fall in height from one end of the Delta to the other is only 62 m, and that over a distance of some 250 km! The slow movement means a low sediment load, hence the clarity and purity of the Okavango's water, for which it is renowned.

One of the world's few inland deltas, the Okavango adds enormously to the variety of experiences open to the visitor. Fishing is an obvious attraction, but there's also **game-viewing**, if not always on the same scale as in Chobe and Savute. One can take to the waters of this magic world of islands and lagoons by traditional canoe (mokoro) or powerboat. Aircraft can be hired, and a flight across the Delta is a memorable experience. So too is a helicopter trip – but it's an expensive one. Speaking of expense, I am told that the most fantastic way to view the Delta and its game is from the back of one of Randall Moore's trained African elephants at Abu Camp (see page 234). I don't doubt this; I have spoken to too many with stars in their eyes after they have been on an elephant safari.

It is, however, difficult to enjoy the Okavango to the full without using the services of professional safari people. The most important reason is something I've already referred to (see page 24): so-called photographic and hunting concessions now blanket the whole area and concession owners will not welcome casual visitors. Moreover, although the Delta is mapped, no practical map can hope to show the intricacies of the myriad, ever-changing channels. Indeed, many channels cannot be seen easily at all as they are overgrown with reeds.

In order to find your way around successfully you will need a guide and some kind of craft. All the services that you require can be arranged by any of the numerous safari camps and businesses operating in Maun and elsewhere in the Delta, and it is best to make the necessary arrangements through them. You'll find a list of recommended operators on page 60.

But there is a way of enjoying the Okavango without actually going there! Tim Liversedge, formerly with the Wildlife Department, has lived in Maun for many years, combining his interests in wildlife with photography, and has produced a series of outstanding videos of which perhaps the best known are 'Haunt of the Fishing Owl' and 'Year of the Flame Bird'.

Okwa River (east and west)

The river rises in eastern Namibia and runs west into Botswana. 'River' is in fact something of a misnomer, for few have seen it flowing strongly (although, in times of heavy rainfall, it does exactly that – but briefly). The attraction of the Okwa is the opportunity it affords the adventurous traveller for sampling almost untouched wilderness. There's little underground water so even cattlemen have not reached some parts of the system, thus remaining beyond the aspirations of human settlement.

Because of their very different natures, I always think of the Okwa in two portions: that to the east of the Kang-Ghanzi road, and that to the west. Both are worthy of a two- or three-day trip.

The **eastern side** is my favourite, for there is little to be seen but landscape and occasional wildlife. The Okwa was once a very large river. During wetter times, millennia ago, it carried huge volumes of water east through the Kalahari and north, eventually to help fill the great paleo-lake of Makgadikgadi (see page 123). Despite the total absence of any water today, the evidence of its former size is seen everywhere – a wide valley, water-worn rocks where they protrude through the surface, wave-cut platforms, pebble shelves and low cliffs in the calcrete sides. It is this same system that, joined by other northern rivers, once formed a delta at the edge of the great lake, one which would have been not unlike the Okavango today. Traces of this delta can be seen in the chain of so-called pans running from Letiahau through to Deception Valley in the north of the Central Kalahari Game Reserve (CKGR).

The journey east to the cut-line demarcating the border of the CKGR is some 150 km. A well-worn vehicle track covers the first 50 km east of the old Ghanzi road. After about 10 km, the track winds between some impressive low cliffs on the south bank. Opposite, on the north side of the river, you'll see a slab of rock above the bank. Stone Age tools have been found here, and on the sloping slab you will notice 42 elongated grooves, each worn into the rock and each about 10–12 cm long. It is neither known how these grooves were made nor what purpose they served.

At about 50 km from the old Ghanzi road, the track terminates and the next 100-odd kilometres are travelled without the benefit of a track – you have to make your own road down the valley. The going is sandy and, obviously, slow, but the open woodlands that line the banks and the towering sand dunes that overlook them are quintessential wilderness, and you'll find some glorious campsites with commanding views over the river. Once the CKGR cut-line is reached, you turn north to reach the main Ghanzi–Xade access road.

To travel the **western Okwa** is an unusual experience. Unlike the eastern portion, there are river tracks along almost the whole of the 200-odd kilometres. Initially, the scenery is more dramatic than in the east. Tree cover isn't thick – indeed it seems to consist almost exclusively of *Acacia mellifera* – and the short grass allows one wide views of the landscape. The high banks, the sweeping curves and the dramatic size of the valley itself all add to the remarkable experience.

After a few hours' drive one begins to move into cattle country, and large cattle posts have been established along the valley floor – they represent big investments in stock, and herds of 500 cattle or more are not uncommon. Cattle posts are also useful to the traveller, for they provide abundant water (though at times a little salty!). Good maps, good navigational skills and good luck are all-important elements in negotiating this route.

As with the eastern side, the variety of vegetation, the frequent outcrops of rock with their associated stone tools and other Stone Age remains, and the sheer beauty of the landscape, make this a fascinating trip. Because of the cattle posts – which become more numerous as one progresses further west – it is not quite the same wilderness experience as the east: but, all the same, it's fun and well worth doing.

Orapa Pans

The focus of this section is on a chain of very large pans immediately to the south of the Makgadikgadi complex (the Ntwetwe and Sowa pans), but north of the road from Francistown to Orapa and westwards to Mopipi. The attraction of the area is the ease of access (though it still demands a 4x4), the extraordinary landscapes and vistas, the varied nature of each pan, and the fun of navigating and map-reading one's way around. I mention only the larger ones in the area, but each offers seclusion, privacy, adventure and interest. Starting from the west is **Tsokotsa Pan**, then **Rysana**, **Guguaga**, **Nkokwane** and, finally, **Ntsokotsa**. There are splendid places to camp at all of them.

My favourite spot is the northeast corner of **Ntsokotsa**, where a grove of African star chestnuts (*Sterculia africana*) stand in an outcrop of granite to provide a spectacular campsite. Immediately to the east is a low rise, set about with baobab trees, and beyond, in a vlei about a kilometre away, a semi-permanent pool at which cattle drink and birds in their thousands gather. The campsite is also on the very edge of the grassland west of Sowa Pan, and from it a north-bound track leads, eventually, to the pan's west shore. The track also leads past a single, extremely large baobab that is the site of an old cattle post. Here you can still see a hand-dug well, just to the north of the tree, that contains water at a depth of about 7 m. The water is a little salty but it would serve thirsty travellers in an emergency and I always remember it for this reason. As far as I can establish, David Livingstone may have crossed this pan on his journeys north to Linyanti and beyond.

Nkokwane is also a spectacular pan. I particularly like the southwest end where the escarpment rises abruptly. An easy climb up to the heights above offers stunning views north over the pan. Each of the other pans has a special charm of its own and points of interest. There are said to be rock engravings on

Rysana. **Guguaga** has low but remarkable calcrete cliffs and amazing shorelines, while on **Tsokotsa** we found piles of freshwater mollusc shells in such huge quantities that they were nearly a metre high and represented what must once have been millions upon millions of tiny creatures.

Savute and Mababe

Set in the north of Botswana, well within the Chobe National Park (see page 213), Savute is perhaps one of the best-known game-viewing areas in the country. Under ideal conditions the number and variety of animals to be seen can be staggering.

Savute is especially known for its elephant, and particularly as an area preferred by lone bulls. More docile than the cows, these gentle giants are quite at home among the parked cars and campsites (they have been observed stepping delicately between guy-ropes without touching them or damaging the tents!). Be warned, though. Docility does not prevent these animals from seeking a little variety in their diet. One person had the boot of his car destroyed when a bull used his tusks as a tin-opener to get at the oranges he could smell inside. Under no circumstances feel tempted to feed the elephants.

Game-viewing is at its best from November to May, but the provision of artificial waterholes has helped keep a wide variety of animals in the area and improved year-round viewing.

The **Mababe Depression** (that immense ancient lake-bed to the east of the Gubatsha Hills) stretches endlessly to the horizon as a flat and apparently featureless plain but, when it has received its first rain and turned to a carpet of green, hundreds of thousands of animals are drawn to it. Zebra, impala, hartebeest, wildebeest, kudu, warthog, buffalo, lion, leopard, hyaena, wild dog and jackal are but a few of the bewildering variety of wildlife to be seen. It's the experience of a lifetime.

As you drive into Savute from the south you will see, on your left, a low sandy rise, the **Magwikhwe Sand Ridge**. More than 100 km long, it is an old barrier beach that may once have defined the western boundary of the great lake. Beyond it, to the west, is a chaotic pattern of ancient sand dunes which may have been lagoons and mud flats lying beyond the ridge.

It is still a matter for speculation how this once massive lake received its waters. The most popular explanation is that, in the distant past, the Upper Zambezi, the Chobe and the Okavango rivers flowed together, across the north of Botswana and down to the sea via the Motloutse and Limpopo. Then a gentle warping of the earth's crust dammed this flow to create a vast lake. In time further crustal movement caused the rivers to find a new route to the sea. Their direction changed by faulting, the Upper Zambezi and the Chobe turned to the northeast and, after plunging over the Victoria Falls, joined what is now the Middle Zambezi. Trapped by an emerging rift valley, the Okavango bled its waters into vast accumulations of sand to create today's Delta. Condemned by a changing climate, which reduced rainfall and brought a return of almost desert-like conditions, the super-lake, cut off from its sources of water, dried up, leaving only the evidence in the shape of Makgadikgadi pans.

Reminders of the lake's existence are still abundant. Apart from the sand ridge, you will notice the nearly sheer northeastern faces of the **Gubatsha Hills**. These were cut into cliffs by the crashing force of the waves which once pounded against them. In the lee of the hills there are accumulations of rounded gravel – pebbles that have been ground to their oval shape by ceaseless rolling on the shores of the lake.

One of the great mysteries, and fascinations, of Savute is the **Channel** itself. It stretches over a distance of 100 km, from the Chobe River through a gap in the sand ridge to the Mababe Depression. Falling only 20 cm in each kilometre of distance covered, it can bring water from the Chobe to Mababe, creating a small marsh at the entrance to the Depression. It is this channel and its water which explains the fantastic abundance of game that has been seen at Savute. However, it hasn't flowed since 1981, and, even before that, flow regimes were erratic and unpredictable. Therein lies the great mystery of Savute.

We know from the accounts of early explorers that the Channel was flowing in the 1850s, and until about 1880. At that time the flow ceased, and the Channel remained dry until the mid-1950s when, without explanation, it began to flow again. Since then, it has 'switched' on and off several times. It is this quixotic pattern that explains the dead trees you will see in the Channel. No convincing explanation for this paradoxical flow pattern has been proved. For me, the most likely candidates are tectonic instability, which may be tilting surfaces first in one direction and then in another, and the coincidence of high flood levels in *both* the Chobe River and the Zambezi (which backs up along the Chobe).

You'll find San rock art at several places within Gubatsha Hills; national park staff will be able to show you where.

Even without water from the Chobe, Savute remains a place of enchantment, of singular beauty, and it still boasts one of the greatest concentrations of animals in southern Africa. It certainly is a place not to be missed.

Sowa Pan

Sowa Pan can be explored, with care, experience and common sense in an ordinary vehicle, but a 4x4 is recommended. It will have to carry a heavy load as the whole area is quite isolated and offers no facilities whatsoever. You will need to provide your own water, food and fuel. Sowa and its companion pan to the west, Ntwetwe (see page 126), together form the great Makgadikgadi pans, which are all that is left today of a once great lake that covered most of northern Botswana.

The history of the lake is not yet completely known. It is unlikely to be older than two or three million years, and it may have held substantial quantities of water up to quite recent times. The most prolonged wet period for which there is good evidence was from 17 000 to 14 000 years ago. There were other such periods between 4 000 and 2 000 years before the present. The most recent evidence suggests that the old lake-bed might have been substantially flooded as recently as 1 500 years ago. It is certain, however, that, at some time in the geological past, levels have been as high as 40 m above the present lake-bed. Even today good rains will bring floods of water. I was told by an old man, who lived next to Ntwetwe Pan, of fish he caught near his house there in 1944 and, even today, it is common for water to flood into the northeast and southwest of Sowa. When this happens, numerous waterbirds congregate in their millions, and flamingos breed in the shallow waters.

There are places of indescribable beauty along the shores of these pans. Perhaps only a poet could really convey the feeling of tranquillity, space and freedom engendered by the immensity of these silvered pans and adjacent grasslands. Many such places remain to be discovered in this remote and enchanting wilderness, but those that are known are well worth visiting. One is Lekhubu Island, more popularly known as **Kubu**.

This small rocky island, whose name is derived from the Setswana word 'Lekhubung', meaning a rocky ridge, is studded with baobabs, and it has a very special atmosphere of its own. Its isolation, the starkness of its setting against the blinding infinity of the featureless pan, makes for a totally unique experience. Few who visit Kubu leave untouched by its magic.

Near the survey beacon which marks its low summit, lies a ring of rolled pebbles that define an old lake shoreline. At 919 m above sea level, it is one of the lower and probably more recent shorelines, created almost certainly within the past 20 000 years. Stone-wall ruins, the origins and secrets of which remain to be disclosed, add further mystery to the island.

To reach Kubu, find the turn-off described in Route 8, Part 2 (page 177). From that point, the island is 19 km away. The track heads roughly northeast. Most of the way you will be guided by previous vehicle tracks. Some travellers claim to have found the island easily, and that often there's a 'highway' of tracks to follow. This may be true, but the tracks do get washed away during the rains. In their absence, you will have to thread your way through the tussocked grass. Place a lookout on the roof to watch for the low hillock that is Kubu. When sighted, don't drive directly towards it across the open pan unless you are following vehicle tracks: the surface can be treacherous, especially during or after the rainy season, and it is difficult to extricate a vehicle that has sunk in deeply. Instead, work your way around the edge of open spaces, staying close to the grass. It will take a little longer but you will at least arrive! On the open pan, it is safest to keep your vehicle in four-wheel drive.

Kubu is also noted for its **archaeological remains**. Most obvious of these is a semi-circular stone wall on the south end of the island. The wall, with its deliberately constructed 'loopholes', is associated with the former 'Khami state' (an early African society based on Khami near Bulawayo that, in one form or another, existed from about 1450 through to the 1830s). The wall may date to the late 17th or 18th century.

Also on the island are more than 400 distinct circular stone cairns, each a metre or so across and up to 30 or 40 cm high, constructed of easily-lifted stones. What these signify is unknown but present thinking suggests that they mark places for initiation ceremonies. To the north end of Kubu, among the giant boulders of a granite outcrop, are the remains of an Early Iron Age village. The pottery and ostrich egg-shell beads are still abundant (as all such artifacts are the property of the government, I hope you'll assist in making sure they remain that way!). I have seen evidence, on Kubu, that local people use the site as a rain shrine. If you should see handfuls of broken pottery, beads (of both glass and ostrich shell) and small coins, collected into piles in prominent places, please do not touch them. Respect other people's rights.

Note that Kubu Island is now controlled by the local community. There are staff on duty, a small fee is payable, and you are requested to respect what you see and hear: camp where you are asked to camp and, if the island is too full (there is no booking system), move elsewhere.

About 10 km on the horizon to the south of Kubu, and within sight, are two **smaller islands** which suggest, even more eloquently than Kubu, the splendour and isolation of Sowa Pan. It would be unwise to approach these islands directly unless you're certain of the surface conditions. Again, work your way along the periphery. Still, large expanses of bare pan must be crossed to reach them. I've sometimes noted that there are large areas of a darker colour in the pan surface, which may indicate patches of dampness lethal to vehicles. But this is not a reliable indicator; indeed, I know of no way of pre-guessing what the surface ahead may be. Prayer (of the fervent kind!) and faith are the only two supports I am aware of.

If at any stage of your drive on the pan surface you feel the vehicle sinking, these are steps may help. First, as mentioned, pray! Second, do not do anything sudden. Don't swing the steering wheel wildly, brake violently or accelerate. A soft patch will create a distinct drag on the wheels; collapse is heralded by the drag increasing to the point where the surface suddenly gives. Try and move away from the softer areas when drag is felt. Two tips are offered for driving on this pan: don't try to negotiate it in a 4x4 (you'll have no time to change if you really need it!), and, before setting forth, drop tyre pressure down to about 0.8 or 1.0 bars. It's a nuisance to inflate them again afterwards but less trouble than a four-hour digging job!

In the southeast of Sowa is the lesser known island of Kokonje, or **Kokoro**. Detailed directions can be found in Route 8, Part 1 (see page 173). From the turn-off indicated you will see the island about 3 km from the shore. It is possible to drive across to it by following the fence out from the eastern shore, but the shortest approach is from the north, where the island is much closer to the mainland. You can drive around to this point, either by crossing the grassland or by wokring your way round the edge. There is a shelf-beach in the area, which you can drive up to to reach a campsite with a magnificent view. Kokoro is a beautiful island, also set about with fossil beaches and, at more than one locality, with Late Stone Age sites. Like Kubu, Kokoro is still used as a rain-making shrine. If you should approach either of these islands from the south to pass Mosu, it's worth turning into the village. Here there's a spring, set among palm trees, from which gushes clear, fresh water. Behind Mosu rises a towering escarpment, once the precipitous southern shore of the great lake. Now eddies of hot, dry wind swirl dust against its flanks where once cool waves washed.

In recent years, important Iron Age **archaeological sites** have been found in many places along the escarpment crest, and it is slowly becoming clear that, although arid now, this region supported large numbers of villages and, probably, a higher population about 1 000 years ago than it does today.

There are signs that goods from over the ocean, from India, from Persia and the Far East, found their way, through a network of villages and from hand to hand, to these ancient village sites at the south end of Sowa Pan. By the same token, local goods travelled to Zaire and the west coast and down the old trade routes to the Indian Ocean and the Orient beyond. Evidence of this trade includes the exotic sea shells and tiny blue or green glass beads recovered from the sites, each recounting a compelling story of oriental influence.

The **east shore** of Sowa is the most thrilling area to explore. There are few roads and one simply follows (with very great care) the very edge of the shore. It is best to travel in company, at least in pairs, both for safety and for the pleasure of having friends to share the magnificent vistas. The sweeping bays, the mirages, the towering whirlwinds and the extraordinary, grass-covered peninsulas that jut far out into the pan are something rare and inspiring to see. Bereft or all familiar landmarks it is at once moving and exhilarating. As far as your eye can see, to your left, to your right, there is nothing except a blemishless infinity of grey that blends indistinguishably with the sky.

My good friend Alec Campbell, who has lived in the country since its Bechuanaland days and who once ran the Wildlife Department, tells me that the area was well known as prime elephant country and much sought after when hunting licences were being issued. Today there are no elephants and little game. The broad stretches of mopane woodland are now cattle country. But evidence of elephants may still be seen: on the many large and prominent baobab trees, you will see the scars where elephants once tusked their way through the bark.

As one works one's way north you will navigate around three great grassy peninsulas, each more beautiful than the one before. You'll pass an old military target-practice range with the rusty wrecks of old Bedfords lying half buried in the clay, surrounded by a million shell fragments and spent cartridges.

More evidence of the extensiveness of Iron Age trade comes from the eastern shore of Sowa Pan and the **ruins of Toranju**, which you can visit. Toranju itself is set back some distance from the pan. It is a ruin closely associated with the Great Zimbabwe state and an excavation has disclosed clear evidence of trade with the east coast. It is the most westerly of its type so far discovered and probably marks the western extent of influence exercised by Great Zimbabwe between AD 1275 and 1475. There seems little doubt that this lonely ruin was probably the main local collecting centre for that precious commodity, salt. It's interesting to learn that modern man is not the first to think of mining the mineral from the pan: historic Bushman and Kalanga salt extraction pits exist in Nata Sanctuary which, I'm told, were still in use up to 1990!

Near Toranju is a place known as **Tshwaane**, a U-shaped pit roughly 12 by 30 m wide and now some 30–40 cm deep. It is the only surviving example, in Botswana, of what early travellers described as a 'game trap'. Nineteen-century hunters used lines of brushwood, several kilometres long, to 'funnel' game towards the pit, which was obviously very much deeper then. Once entrapped, spearmen struck down at the animals.

The lights you will see from the shore as you look to the northwest at night are those of the Sua Pan Soda Ash project.

In the northeast of Sowa Pan is the **Nata River delta**. The river flows down from Zimbabwe, and in a good wet season it may flood large areas to a shallow depth. Bird life at this time is breathtaking and canoeing, boating and board-sailing become the sports of the moment! In the dry part of the year the grasslands invite you to explore. There is no game here; it is cattle country, as are all the grasslands around Sowa, but the presence of livestock detracts not at all from the feeling of openness and freedom. And to the west lies the limitless expanse of Sowa with its kaleidoscope of muted pastel colours, ever changing to reflect the passage of the sun through its day.

Near the delta is **Nata Sanctuary** (see also page 220), an area of grassland abutting the shore, and the product, largely, of the dedicated efforts of Nigel and Liz Ashby, formerly of Nata Lodge and the Kalahari Conservation Society. Created in 1988, it is fenced to keep cattle out, and was given over to tourism by the local tribesmen. Representatives from four nearby villages, including Nata, are members of a board of trustees, which directs surplus revenues from the project to fund capital expenditure in the villages. There are toilet, ablution and camping facilities, and rates are reasonable. The sanctuary is 230 km² in extent, of which 55 per cent is grassland and the remainder, pan surface. This part of the pan is filled only when the Nata River is in flood but, when that happens, the huge sheet of water attracts thousands of birds, including summer migrants, to nest and breed here. The concept behind the sanctuary is, in my opinion, the only one through which wildlife of any kind will survive in the long term. Local residents have to be part of the scheme, and they have to benefit from it. I hope, with your support, that the sanctuary will continue to prove viable.

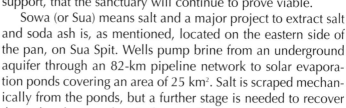

Sowa (or Sua) means salt and a major project to extract salt and soda ash is, as mentioned, located on the eastern side of the pan, on Sua Spit. Wells pump brine from an underground aquifer through an 82-km pipeline network to solar evaporation ponds covering an area of 25 km². Salt is scraped mechanically from the ponds, but a further stage is needed to recover the soda ash via a chemical extraction process.

Tshane/Hukuntsi Village Cluster

Almost in the centre of Botswana's Kalahari, and over 100 km from the nearest town, four villages cluster together. Remote though they are, they're of interest because so much of the country's early history is represented in the area, which may be reached via the Kang–Tsabong routes (see page 158).

Tshane is located on high ground overlooking the magnificent Tshane Pan, on whose southern and southwestern sides are wind-created dunes. Animals are still watered from hand-dug wells at the pan's edge, giving insight into traditional ways.

Lokhwabe (which means 'stony pan' in Setswana), 11 km from Tshane to the southwest, is the home of, among others, the Hottentot descendants of Simon Cooper who fought the Germans of South West Africa during the 1906–8 rebellion (see page 118). It was also he who confronted German forces after their epic campaign through what is now the Kgalagadi Transfrontier Park (the old Kalahari Gemsbok National Park, see page 26). After that battle, Cooper and his followers sought the protection of Britain and were allowed to settle at Lokhwabe. Cooper is buried in the village.

About the same distance north from Tshane is the settlement of **Lehututu**. Those who are familiar with early explorers of the Kalahari will have heard of this village. Indeed, it was once a busy commercial centre and, although times have passed it by, the old store is still standing and remains open for business. When the inventive Mr Farini traversed this portion of the Kalahari in 1885 (on his way to reveal to the rest of us his wondrous stories about the Lost City) he reported on, and his son photographed, 'King Mampaar and his wife'. This is a clear allusion to the Moapare family, chiefs of the area, who live there still (though now they have moved to Hukuntsi). Lehututu is an onomatopoeic Setswana name for the ground hornbill.

Hukuntsi, the fourth village in the group, is the administrative headquarters for the area and the one to which the main road leads. Interestingly, perhaps because the four villages are close to each other and, as a group, remote, the name Hukuntsi means, roughly, 'four points of the compass'! Petrol and diesel are sold here, and there are several well-stocked stores.

Tsodilo Hills

Tsodilo Hills, located in Botswana's remote northwest, are among the most rewarding of destinations for adventurous visitors (see also page 194). Brought to world attention by Laurens van der Post in *The Lost World of the Kalahari*, they do indeed speak of myth and mystery, and the magic of the place is almost tangible. The Hills, of micaceous quartzite schists, rise abruptly from rolling sand-dune country. The dunes, long since stabilised and now held in place by abundant vegetation, might at first escape your eye from a distance, but, as you approach over the sandy track you will gradually become accustomed to the gentle climb to the 20-m wooded crest, and the descent to the flat, grass-covered valley before the next crest.

Four hills, set roughly in a line, make up the group. The most southerly, and the largest, is bare rock rising 400 m above the plain. Immediately to the north is a group of scattered summits and beyond that two small, separate hills. The San (Bushmen) call the largest the Male, his companion the Female and the nearest of the small hills, the Child. There is no name for the fourth and smallest hill. It is the Male that is first seen, its summit looming above the trees, suggesting by its very incongruity and size the mystery and enigma that is Tsodilo.

As one approaches, the road will take you to a permanent settlement of **Hambukushu**, a Bantu-speaking people, near the Male hill. Also in this vicinity but about 1.5 km away is a small Zhu Bushman village. There has been Bantu occupation in and around Tsodilo for at least 1 200 years, and the Bushmen are known to have been in residence for very much longer. Indeed ongoing archaeological studies have revealed occupation by humans for at least 100 000 years. That Tsodilo is a place of special significance to the Bushmen is suggested not only by the existence of a number of secret and permanent springs among the hills but by the **rock art** in the area. There are over 5 000 individual depictions at more than 400 separate sites. The majority are on the Female hill, mostly around the base on the west and along the side of major drainage lines.

The National Museum and Art Galley has undertaken and completed the task of photographing every known painting. This exercise, in addition to its vital archival importance, has also helped locate more sites and a further 500-odd depictions. Other workers have identified shorelines of a small lake that once stood to the west of the Male and Female hills. It may have been in this lake, or in an extension of the Okavango, that former inhabitants, used bone fishhooks to catch their meals. Either way, the hooks found in one of the Tsodilo digs date back at least 20 000 years, and are rare and precious artifacts.

Perhaps the most dramatic and exciting of recent discoveries have been those of more than 20 ancient mines among the Tsodilo Hills. Some of these were known in the past but were not recognised for what they were. Nevertheless it is clear that, between about AD 800 and AD 1100, people at Tsodilo were mining black haematite, and possibly mica, and trading the minerals through the extensive trade networks of Africa. Their technique appears to have involved the use of fire to heat the rock, causing the minerals, on cooling, to spall off the face.

With all these discoveries, and an ever-growing interest in the Tsodilo Hills, visitor impact inevitably increases and steps to control the human presence must, sadly, be put in place.

The Hills are a national monument and belong in the custody of the National Museum. The Museum maintains an airstrip, near the Male hill, which is suitable for single-engined aircraft only. In an effort to keep cattle away from the vicinity, a fence has been built westward from the south end of the Male. All roads leading to the Hills now lead to the fence gate, which is close to the Hambukushu village. Visitors will be met there and directed to the Museum's field offices, about 5 km away on the west side of the Female hill and within sight of the Van der Post plaque and then, at the office and small display centre, directed to one of four campsites in the immediate area or to one of three more distant ones. The latter offer no facilities except a fireplace. Campsites near the office have access to piped fresh water, showers and toilets. The site museum is complete and gives a wider understanding of the Hills and their precious art. When all the new facilities are in place and working, an entrance fee will be charged.

In place are six **trails**, of varying length, that wind their way through and among the Hills. Three are clearly cut paths, the other three will require local guides, who are available through the Museum office. Those that are cut are marked with coloured signs; brochures describing each numbered viewing point will be produced. Since these brochures are written by Alec Campbell, the man who has done so much work to explore and understand these hills, they are the best possible source of information and also make quite fascinating reading.

Apart from water and campsites, there are no facilities at Tsodilo. Bring food and fuel with you. The nearest fuel points are Etsha-6 village to the south and at Andara in the Caprivi to the north. The airstrip at Tsodilo is maintained by the Museum but is not manned. A minimum of two nights is recommended to explore the Hills fully.

Tswapong Hills

Moody, misty, moulded a million millennia in the past, the Tswapong Hills are one of Botswana's undiscovered treasures, known only to a handful of explorers and those whose traditional villages skirt the base of this mountain island. More than a thousand million years old and covering some 1200 km², they stand in their own microclimate about 300–400 m above the surrounding plain. They consist of ironstone, quartzite and a conglomerate of rounded, water-worn pebbles, and they are capped by hard, resistant rock that makes them flat-topped and sheer-sided with many striking, vertical cliffs.

 Higher rainfall and geology make Tswapong a place of mist and running streams, unique in Botswana where evaporation exceeds rainfall in all months of the year. On the heights, rain-water forms a small lake, an almost permanent feature. Surplus water, unable to penetrate the hard capping rock, follows fractures and lines of weaknesses eventually to carve deep gashes, and massive gorges that are the hallmark of these hills. Through these flow streams whose age-old water has filtered through the rocks above and seeped in fingered catchments into tumbling rivulets, some ephemeral, others permanent. Those that escape the mountain's grip sink into the talus slope that lies beneath the surrounding skirt of Kalahari sand. The gorges provide micro-niches exploited by plants and animals, and by man.

 In the skies above soar bateleur, black eagle and other raptors. Deep within the hills are nesting sites of the **Cape vulture**, this their most northerly breeding colony. So far, 345 species of birds have been identified here, and floral surveys point to a wealth of unique plant species (including over 100 edible plants). In valleys and gorges, beautiful orchids blossom, falling in magnificent cascades from high up in the branches of riverine trees. Wildlife, however, is scarce: kudu, leopard, baboon and impala are found only in remote and isolated pockets. The huge herds of elephant, buffalo, giraffe and antelope that once gathered are now 100 years in the past.

 In the long and winding gorges are to be found some of the earliest traces of the Bantu-speaking people in southern Africa, those who reached the subcontinent during the first Christian millennium. Gorge after gorge is littered with pot sherds. Finely made and exquisitely decorated, the clay pottery spans almost two millennia. Below occasional rock-art sites, collapsed and buried iron smelters lie in ruins by the hundred. Carbon dates extend from AD 350 to modern times – a testament to the continuity of human occupation and the abundant ironstone.

Perhaps because of their misty and brooding nature, or because of the dark gorges or the long span of human occupation, local people strongly associate the hills with their ancestral and spirit world. Still, today, rain shrines are seen and occasional fires, laid on hilltops, await a kindling flame to take rain prayers skyward in their spiralling smoke.

Western Woodlands (Masetlheng Pan)

This incredibly beautiful part of Botswana was shown to me by that grand adventurer and man of the bush, Izak Barnard. If you want a first-class tour of the area, travel with him. Failing that, I thoroughly recommend an independent visit.

The pan of **Masetlheng** lies just 90 km west of Hukuntsi (see page 140). The journey there takes you through a series of striking pans and gives a very good feel of what these features look like (notice the build-up of wind-created dunes on their south or southwest). On the way you pass through, and have the opportunity of visiting, relatively new (Bushman) villages.

Some years ago, Botswana allowed the drilling of a deep exploratory **borehole** within a kilometre or two of Masetlheng Pan. This hole, which was part of the search for oil (an unsuccessful one), penetrated to the remarkable depth of 4.2 km! However, the project also spawned a maze of still-existing tracks and cut-lines that one can explore. No published maps of these are available as they were created relatively recently and the information, the private property of a now-defunct exploration company, is difficult to retrieve. However, many of the tracks survive since local cattle owners, hunters and explorers find them convenient ways of getting about.

The deep hole lies beside the main north–south cut-line. Southwards one can travel towards the Kgalagadi Transfrontier Park boundary, Kaa Pan and the new northern entrance (see page 117). From that point on you can explore west to the Namibia border, southeast along it to Mabuasehube or return to Hukuntsi via Zutshwa. Alternatively, drive north to rejoin the road from Hukuntsi and travel northwest towards the Ncojane arms and, ultimately, the border with Namibia at Mamuno. Along the way lies **Ukwi Pan**, interesting for the wave-cut platforms that are exposed there.

By far the greatest attraction of Masetlheng, however, is the acacia **woodland** just a few kilometres north of the pan. This vast stand of large trees, growing in a countryside of close-cropped grass, varies from 3 to 5 km in width and stretches for some 40 km (according to Izak). The dominant species are *Acacia luderitzii* and *A. erioloba*. There are no young trees and no scrub, so the impression of a carefully manicured and maintained parkland is quite overwhelming. It is, I think, one of the most beautiful places I have seen in Botswana. Do go there.

RECOMMENDED ROUTES

You'll find more than two dozen suggested itineraries in the pages that follow, between them covering most of Botswana – or at least those parts of the country that are especially well worth exploring. They promise interest, exhilaration, and adventure. The profiles are detailed, highly specific in terms of distances, GPS references and maps, and they should be read in conjunction with the Map Section that appears between pages 260 and 299. For more general road-travel information, turn to the sections on Getting around (pages 60-93) and Driving in Botswana and On the road (pages 66 and 81), and, for profiles of some of the more rewarding regions and places, to Chapter 7 (page 103).

 ## ROUTE 1
Gaborone to Khutse Game Reserve

TOTAL DISTANCE: 220 km. **TIME**: 3.5–4.5 hours. **VEHICLE**: 4x4. **MAPS**: Map 1 (page 261), which includes GPS waypoints. Also Republic of Botswana, 1:500 000 series, sheet 7; 1:250 000 series, sheet SF.35.13 'Khutse'; Shell Tourist Map of Botswana. These maps are not essential but the enthusiast will appreciate them. **KHUTSE PROFILE**: page 120.

To reach the Khutse Game Reserve from Gaborone, take the tarmac road via Molepolole, continue straight on, right through the centre of Molepolole, find the signposted turn-off at (58.6 km) to Letlhakeng (a further 61.5 km and end of tar). About 46 km from Molepolole it's worth looking to the northern side of the road for a deep, striking river gorge. Today the river no longer flows but the incised nature of the valley and its precipitous cliffs indicate the huge volumes of water it must once have carried. Petrol is available at Letlhakeng, from a pump 100 m on your right after you turn left at the traffic circle. To continue to Khutse, return to the traffic circle and turn left (thus remaining in your original direction).

From Letlhakeng the road is signposted. It is 24 km to Khudumelapye on a reasonable sand surface. Signs in this village turn you left along a shallow riverbed and in front of the small Farouk Trading Store. The track is often difficult to follow but pass to the right of the store (as you face it) and you'll soon find the main road again. The road deteriorates from here onwards and becomes extremely sandy, but upgrading has been done recently and it is steadily improving. It is 32.6 km to Salajwe and, beyond that, a further 43 km to the Khutse Gate.

ROUTE 1A

Central Kalahari Game Reserve (CKGR): Khutse–Xade–Deception Valley–Rakops – an adventure!

TOTAL DISTANCES AND TIMES: Gaborone–Khutse Gate: 220 km, time: 3.5–4.5 hours; Khutse Gate–Xade: 272 km, time: one day (if you're lucky!); Xade–Deception Valley: 172 km, time: 4 hours minimum; Deception Valley–Rakops: 86 km, time: 2 hours. **VEHICLE:** 4x4. **MAPS:** Map 1 (page 261) and Map 2 (page 262), which include GPS waypoints. Also the following Republic of Botswana maps: 1:500 000 series, sheets 3, 4, 6 and 7; 1:250 000 series, sheets SF.34.4 'Toteng', 34.8 'Letiahau', 34.12 'Okwa', 34.16 'Kang' and SF35.1 'Bushman Pits', 35.5 'Lake Xau', 35.9 'Metseamonong', 35.13 'Khutse'. **CENTRAL KALAHARI PROFILE**: page 106. **DECEPTION VALLEY PROFILE:** page 110.

At the time of writing, there are three official ways into this game reserve, namely through Xade in the west, Khutse in the southeast and Matswere Camp in the northeast. The Khutse entrance is reached from Gaborone (see Route 1, above). Xade can be reached from the Trans-Kalahari Highway or from Ghanzi.

From Ghanzi, seek the *old road* south (I have not travelled this route recently but Veronica Roodt's Shell Map of Botswana shows it departing from the newly built tarmac link to the Trans-Kalahari Highway some 9 km from the town). Follow this to the southeast for 27 km and turn east for 160 km to Old Xade and the Department of Wildlife and National Parks office.

To reach Xade from the Trans-Kalahari Highway get yourself to the point on that road where it crosses the Okwa River (see Route 13, page 187). This point is 45 km south of what we can call the Ghanzi junction (GPS 22.03.39.8S/21.32.04.1N) or 183 km north of Kang. You will see a good gravel track turning east on the north bank of the Okwa and a sign indicating Xade after 209 km. At 10–12 km on the gravel track you will reach a T-junction with the old Ghanzi road. Here too there's a sign giving directions to East and West Hanahai and Xade and you turn left (north) onto the old road. Follow the signs. Be prepared to turn right (east) for the last 140-odd kilometres.

Word of warning: Neither approach to Xade is suitable for saloon cars. The approach to Matswere Camp is from the new tarmac road between Rakops and Motopi. Rakops is to the west of Orapa and Mopipi and is found on any map of the country.

The northern half of the CKGR is well served by good tracks and is frequently visited. Although a number of tracks can be driven in an ordinary car (at least in the dry season) and, in the event of a breakdown, help is not likely to be too far away, I do not personally recommend the use of saloons or light trucks here. Even if you can drive in this area in these kinds of vehicle, the approaches are such that you are not likely to arrive. Stick to a four-wheel-drive!

The southern part of the CKGR is quite another matter. The tracks are very *sandy* – some of the worst sand I have seen in 19 years of travel in Botswana. Although not always obvious, there are many remote cut-lines along which vehicles can travel. Be warned, breakdowns can occur and people do get lost. Travellers are infrequent.

I do not intend to deter individuals from visiting this part; I wish only to sound a strong warning. Do *not* venture into the southern CKGR unless you have adequate supplies of food and water, a map, a good vehicle and are a competent 'bush' mechanic, are in the company of a second vehicle and have ensured that friends and the game reserve staff know where you have gone and when you expect to be out again. Do *not* treat this area lightly; unprepared travellers have died in the remoteness of the Central Kalahari. I believe it is foolhardy to venture into the more remote areas without being properly prepared; and this includes an investment in good maps. This route is covered in two parts: Khutse to Xade and Rakops to Xade.

Route 1A
Part 1: Khutse to Xade

TOTAL DISTANCE: 272 km. **TIME**: About a day or two!
VEHICLE: 4x4 essential. **MAPS**: Map 1 (page 261) and Map 2 (page 262).

A hundred metres or so west of Khutse Gate you will see a well-used track leading to the north. It is marked 'Gope'. Although you can drive to Xade via Gope, this route is longer and, I am told, adds little to the experience.

Turning right after 13.6 km and right again after an additional 12 km, you will – after a total of 46.8 km and while travelling a little west of north – cross an east–west cut-line. This links with the Gope road. Ignore it and continue northwest. After 7 km you'll reach the village of Kukamma, which may or may not be occupied at the time of your visit. It may be difficult to find the track out of this village but you will eventually locate it if you continue northwest and keep your eyes open.

A critical junction occurs after 10.5 km beyond the village. At that place, the track you are on turns due north onto a clear north–south cut-line that is as well used to the south as it is to the north. A track also continues to the west. It leads to Kikao village. Turn *right* (north) here.

At 87 km from the gate is a sign that reads 'Xade 184'. From the 91-km point on for the next 3 km you'll pass a series of San settlements culminating at the borehole at Mothomelo. You may experience some difficulty in locating the road out of this village (the settlements may or may not be occupied). The road along this section is extremely sandy and the going heavy.

At 113 km on the east side you may notice the abandoned De Beers base camp, named Bape. Four kilometres further on is a second crucial turning point: a T-junction to the west. Two clear confirmers indicate it. Firstly, if you look to the west you will see, within a few kilometres, the shape of a valley cut by a northeast-flowing river. Secondly, if you continue north for 400 m you will see a cut-line joining your original route from the east. The east and west lines appear to have 'missed' each other by this 400 m. Turn west here. The track improves, and you can shift into high ratio drive and cruise up to 30 km/h.

Your route turns abruptly north after 33.5 km although you'll observe a faint track continuing west. Still, the track is good, and hi-range can be enjoyed. The final westward turn occurs after another 31.8 km, and the last 35 km is easy driving. At 33.3 km you cross a tributary of the Okwa and, a little further on, a turning north to Molapo settlement. For Xade, of course, you continue west. After 34 km along from the Molapo turn-off, the track splits. The cut-line continues west, but a new track angles off to the northwest. Follow this for 20 km to Xade. The Department of Wildlife office is on your right as you enter; the deserted clinic and primary school are on your left.

Route 1A
Part 2: Rakops to Xade, via Deception Valley

TOTAL DISTANCES AND RECOMMENDED SPEEDS: Mopipi–Rakops 68 km: tarmac; Rakops–Deception Valley 85.5 km: average speed 45 km/h; Rakops–Xade 257.6 km: average speed 35 km/h. **VEHICLE:** 4x4 essential. **MAPS:** Map 3 (page 263), including GPS waypoints, Map 7 (page 267), Map 8 (page 268), Map 28 (page 288) and also the following Republic of Botswana maps: 1:500 000 series, sheets 3,4,6 and 7;1:250 000 series, sheets SF.34.4 'Toteng', 34.8 'Letiahau', 34.12 'Okwa', 34.16 'Kang' and SF35.1 'Bushman Pits', 35.5 'Lake Xau', 35.9 'Metseamonong', 35.13 'Khutse'.

Route 7 (see page 160) takes one from Serowe to Orapa Mine and Route 7A from Orapa to Rakops. To get to Mopipi, follow the tarmac road west of Orapa, drive around the south side of the Mine Concession and a further 46 km, from the point at which you rejoin the main road, westward to Mopipi. From the petrol station at Mopipi village, continue to follow the tar and the road signs west to Xhumo (38 km), then 30 km northwest to Rakops. Follow the main (now tarred) road out of Rakops for 3 km north. There you will see the sign to **Matswere Camp** and the CKGR. The road onwards to Motopi is excellent.

Twelve kilometres from the turn-off you will notice a perceptible rise in the road as it goes up successive, sandy levels. This is the old lake shore and speaks of times when the great lake of **Makgadikgadi** filled the vast spaces around you. Stop and look back at the view: it's worth it. Imagine an immense sea filling the land to far horizons!

Forty-seven kilometres from Rakops brings you to the border of the CKGR and Mananga Gate. 'Kuke Corner' is 22 km to the northwest along the boundary cut-line; the opposite direction is nowhere in particular. A further 8.8 km to the west is Matswere Camp and the current (November 2000) permit office. From here, a 27.5-km drive finds you on a prominent, well-used east–west cut-line, cut as part of a geological survey in 1973 and known as the Kalahari Traverse (KT cut-line).

After hitting the KT cut-line, you turn west for 2.2 km and enter **Deception Valley**. From this point it is possible to drive further west along the KT cut-line to gain access to Sunday Pans (very pretty and about 20 km on) or even further to Passarge waterhole (just under 60 km; try to have the sun behind you when you travel these sections – it enhances the sights and colours in spectacular fashion).

Immediately north of Passarge waterhole, there begins a well-defined drainage line, the remnant of a large river system that flows to the northeast. There is now a new track along the line, and to explore it is a must – it's a very beautiful drive. Again, one is in an ephemeral river system and, although little water ever flows in it today, it too was part of the great lake that once covered much of northern Botswana. To tempt you, there are good views of the **Passarge Valley** from spot height BPS 507, approximately 1 km east of Passarge waterhole, just off the KT cut-line (see Map 3, page 263). The road northwest to Motopi is only worth following if game scouts have confirmed that the borehole there is working and that there is water (it was out of order in November 2000). Despite what is sometimes said, the KT cut-line does not continue westward to Ghanzi.

The main route to Xade turns south, along Deception Valley and, at 45 km, passes Letiahau waterhole. At 18.7 km beyond that, the track turns out of the **Letiahau Valley** (which you entered at Deception). This whole 64-km drive is over hard pan surface between great islands of acacia trees standing shoulder to shoulder, as if for shelter and protection against the silent immensity of the northern Kalahari. It is a stunning drive, usually with some sort of game always in sight!

After leaving the Letiahau Valley, a 37-km drive brings you to the complex known as **Piper Pans**. Pan formations are encountered again a further 20 km to the south and continue in a spasmodic sort of way for another 30 km. After that, for the last 20.5 km into Xade, there is only the vastness, the colours and the fascination of the Central Kalahari to be enjoyed.

Almost all of this road offers easy and relaxed driving.

ROUTE 2A
Gaborone to Mabuasehube in the Kgalagadi Transfrontier Park

TOTAL DISTANCE: 450 km. **TIME:** 7–8 hours. **VEHICLE:** 4x4. **MAPS:** Map 4 (page 264), Map 5 (page 265), Map 6 (page 266) and Map 32 (page 292). **KGALAGADI TRANSFRONTIER PARK PROFILE:** page 116.

There are three approaches to these pans at Mabuasehube. One is from the south, through Tsabong. A second route is from the north, via Kang and Tshane. (For details of these routes see Route 6, Kang to Tsabong; page 158). The third route, which approaches from the east, is considered to be the best and is recommended – the road is better and the distance shorter.

To travel by this route, drive from Gaborone to Khakhea, via Thamaga and Moshupa, Jwaneng and Sekoma (Map 4, page 264). After passing through Kumakwane (27 km from Gaborone), one crosses the Kolobeng River. A National Museum signpost on the south side of the road, beyond the bridge, directs you to

the remains of **David Livingstone's** last mission station at Kolobeng. It was from here that he left to discover Lake Ngami and, ultimately, for his great trans-Africa journey. One of his daughters is buried here.

From Khakhea, drive south on the main road for 40 km to the village of Kokotsa (63 km north of Werda), distinguished by a prominent pan on the east side of the road and a microwave tower on the west. Up to this point, the road's been tarred all the way from Gaborone. Leading to the west for about 200 m past the base of the tower is a short length of tarmac. Take this and, where it turns sharp left, continue straight on, due west along the cut-line for about 100 km. The first part of the track is not anything to get too excited about but, after 20 or so kilometres, it opens out and much improves. It takes you to the main road from Tshabong to Tshane. Turn left and go south for about 16 km, at which point you will arrive at the new (and impressive) entrance to the **Kgalagadi Transfrontier Park**.

You can also reach the park from Gaborone by driving to Tshabong and taking the main (currently) gravel road north for 120 km towards Tshane. This route is longer in both distance and time and has little to recommend it other than that you see more of Botswana. You also need to be sure you have spare fuel or long-range tanks, otherwise you are likely to run out of fuel. Tshabong is the closest fuel source. I don't know of any plans to tar the gravel road; I do think it would be accurate to say that it is of 'varying quality'.

ROUTE 2B

Hukuntsi to the Kaa (north) entrance of the Kgalagadi Transfrontier Park

TOTAL DISTANCE: 171 km. **TIME**: 4–5 hours. **VEHICLE**: 4x4.
MAPS: Maps 5 (page 265), 26 (page 286) and 27 (page 287).
KGALAGADI TRANSFRONTIER PARK PROFILE: page 116.

I have not travelled this route myself. It has been newly cut and I am beholden to the Department of Wildlife and National Parks (DWNP) – in particular to Phil Marshall – for details of this section. The route is new, for DWNP only recently opened a northern entry gate into the Kgalagadi Transfrontier Park. Start at Hukuntsi and look for the DWNP signs pointing to Zutshwa and Kaa. On this sand track, it is 64 km to Zutshwa and, beyond, a further 107 km to Kaa Gate. Co-ordinates for this trip are on Map 27 (page 287). I am told the route is very pretty with lovely woodlands, big dunes and several very attractive pans.

ROUTE 3
Gaborone to Ghanzi and Mamuno

DISTANCES: Gaborone–Ghanzi 682 km. Gaborone–Mamuno 806 km. **TIMES**: Gaborone–Ghanzi 7–8 hours; Gaborone–Mamuno 8–9 hours. **VEHICLE**: All roads are tarred. **MAPS**: Map 5 (page 265); also Shell Tourist Map of Botswana. **GHANZI PROFILE**: page 112.

The road to Mamuno and Ghanzi from eastern Botswana is now tarred, providing a top-quality link from east coast to west coast (Maputo to Walvis Bay). It is known as the Trans-Kalahari Highway. There are two inherent dangers on this route. First: *the road is not fenced* and there have already been tragic encounters with both wildlife and cattle. Be careful driving at night. Second: the road is a major cross-countries highway and used by *many heavy vehicles*. These are mostly extremely well driven but you'll come across the occasional lunatic and there are often breakdowns, with vehicles stranded on the roadside. Again, *be careful, especially at night*.

At 227 km north of Kang is Ghanzi junction. Turning north will lead 45.4 km to Ghanzi. Continuing west, you will join up with the line of the original road at Tsootsha (the old Kalkfontein, at 72.4 km) and on through Karakubis, Xanagas and Charleshill to the border post at Mamuno. There is a first-class Engen filling station at Charleshill, beside the main road. It has a well-stocked shop and is open 24 hours a day.

It is also worth noting that there are **rock engravings** (petro-glyphs) at three sites at or near Mamuno. One site is very close to the main road. The National Museum sign can be seen on the north side of the road, just a few hundred metres before the border post; GPS 22.16.42S/20.01.02E (Clark 1880 datum); see *Botswana Notes and Records*, Vol. 7, 1975, page 19 for details.

Starting from Gaborone, follow the tar through Thamaga and Moshupa to Jwaneng, the site of one of Botswana's dia-mond mines, and pass directly over the first traffic circle you come to. This is 86 km to Sekoma. Have a look at **Sekoma Pan**, just after you have passed the town; observe the three-peaked dune on the southwest side. Continue straight on after Sekoma and you'll arrive at **Kang** – after passing through Mabutsane and Morwamosu. Both villages have small general dealers and bottle (liquor) stores. Water and telephones are also available there. From Sekoma to Kang is 161 km.

Kang (off the road on the north side) is one of the largest villages on the route. There are several stores here, including a butchery and a bottle store. Fuel is also available at all hours from a filling station on the main road. Just before Kang village, on the south side of the road, are tracks leading to a large and striking pan, which is well worth seeing. The main road forks at Kang, the left branch turning southwest to Tshane and Tsabong. Continue straight on.

There are many boreholes along this route, although they're set back from the road. They are part of the chain that was established for watering cattle that, years ago, were trekked from Ghanzi to the abattoir at Lobatse. None is signposted.

Bere (110.6 km) and Takatshwaane (142 km) northwest of Kang are both San (Bushman) settlements. They are signposted, and neither is far from the road. A further 40 km beyond Takatshwaane brings you to the crossing of the **Okwa River** (183 km from Kang). Flowing only in years of exceptional flood, and then only for short periods, the river is still of interest. It was once a major tributary of a great lake that covered as much as 110 000 km^2 of northern Botswana. A glance at the high banks and great width of the river valley is enough to confirm the one-time size of this now ephemeral watercourse.

From the Okwa to the new Ghanzi junction is 44 km, and then there's an additional 45 km to **Ghanzi**, which offers a full range of facilities. Here you'll find a good hotel (which will make arrangements for campers), fuel, a hospital, and shops supplying most general goods. It is from Ghanzi that one can visit the famous **Bushman Centre** at D'Kar, 38 km north on the Maun road, 245 km south of Maun on the Ghanzi road. On the same road, 25 km north of Ghanzi, is **Dqãe Qare Game Farm**, with its guest-house and campsite, owned and staffed by San. It is also from Ghanzi that one can get to **Van Zyl's Cutting**.

Van Zyl's Cutting is not a regular tourist site, and is located on private land. However, if you're researching or have some other serious interest in it I am quite sure you'll be welcome. You are best advised to contact Thomas Tuahuku, the owner of the farm on which it lies (PO Box 65, Ghanzi, or enquire in Ghanzi for directions to Xaga Farm, Number 99 NL). The cutting is some 60 km from Ghanzi and one passes through several farms to get to it. Also see Republic of Botswana 1:250 000 monochrome map, sheet SF.34.6. The position of the cutting is 21.45.39.1S/22.10.04.2E (GPS Garmin, Clark 1880 datum).

ROUTE 4
Jwaneng–Sekoma–Khakhea–Werda

TOTAL DISTANCE: 239 km. **TIME**: 2.5 hours; tarred road (for directions to Sekoma, see Route 3, Gaborone–Ghanzi, page 54). **VEHICLE**: All roads are tarred; at the time of writing (November 2000), Jwaneng is the last fuelling station before Werda. **MAPS**: Map 4 (page 264), Map 5 (page 265); also Shell Tourist Map of Botswana.

At Sekoma, there is a tarmac turn-off to the south. For this sur-prising and welcome facility we must thank the people of Norway, who paid for 160 km of new road. The completed tar now runs from Sekoma through Khakhea to Werda and then turns southwestward, along the border to the village of Makopong and beyond, to the administrative centre of Tsabong.

Khakhea, which is notable for the very large pan to its immediate west, has an interesting story attached to it. In the 19th century, so the tale goes, two white men, exhausted, lost, waterless in the Kalahari and close to death were discovered by a group of Bushmen. These enterprising rescuers took advantage of a Bushman 'sip well' at the pan and used it until the two travellers had made a full recovery. Later the travellers returned, dug a well and opened a store at this place, which accounted for the founding of modern-day Khakhea.

From Khakhea it's 103 km to Werda, where you can pur-chase both petrol and diesel and where there is a general deal-er who stocks most items you are likely to need. It is possible to leave Botswana at this point; to do so, report to the Botswana Police who serve as Immigration authorities. There is no corresponding facility on the South African side, so you are required to travel to Bray, 58 km away, and report to the South African Police Services there. Border facilities are avail-able from 8 am to 4 pm only.

ROUTE 5
Werda to Bokspits

DISTANCES AND TIMES: Werda–Tsabong 145 km on tar, 1.5 hours; Tsabong–Bokspits (in Botswana): 245 km, on poor gravel, 3–4 hours; Tsabong–Bokspits (in South Africa): 325 km, on good gravel, about 4 hours. **VEHICLE**: A 4x4 is not required on this route. **MAPS**: Map 4 (page 264) and Map 6 (page 266); also Shell Tourist Map of Botswana. **BOKSPITS PROFILE**: Page 104.

To reach Werda, either enter Botswana from Bray, in the Republic of South Africa, or alternatively see Route 3, Gaborone–Ghanzi (Map 5; page 265) and Route 4, Jwaneng–Werda (Map 4; page 264).

The distance from Werda to Tsabong is 145 km, all of which is tarmac. Tsabong, which is the administrative centre for Kgalagadi District, has most of the basic facilities for the visitor, including fuel.

There are two ways to get to Bokspits from Tsabong, one within Botswana, the other in South Africa. Both are recommended. It is 110 km to Khuis and a further 135 km from there to Bokspits. The road is used daily but its state varies enormously, from quite good to poor. While corrugations are likely to be a problem and progress will be slow and uncomfortable, the route itself is interesting, different and worth the trouble – and the road is graded and the bush dragged occasionally. There is quite spectacular scenery by Botswana standards: rocky slopes, bright-red dunes that threaten to (and sometimes do) engulf the road, interesting villages with authentic local architecture and inhabited people of mixed descent. There is talk that this section will be tarred within the next few years.

To leave Botswana at this point, it is necessary to report to Customs and Immigration at the new South African border post at McCarthy's Rust, 25 km from Tsabong and open from 8 am to 4 pm. From McCarthy's Rust to Vanzylsrus is 132 km on excellent gravel roads. There are three different routes to Vanzylsrus; the shortest is to turn off at Elandsvlei and go through Prairie Glen farm. Watch for this turn-off, which is not signposted as a route to Vanzylsrus (see Map 6, page 266).

Vanzylsrus offers all the usual facilities. From there to Bokspits is a further 168 km on similarly good-quality roads.

The country in this region is fascinating. It is still Kalahari but much more arid. The dunes are more pronounced, the red sand more obvious and, in the changing light of day, it offers superb photographic opportunities. Among its features are the numerous and massive *Acacia eriolob* trees.

It is worth deviating 11 km west of Vanzylsrus, at a sign-posted turn-off to the north, which takes you to the new border post of Middelpits, 26 km away, and beyond it to a group of villages on the banks of the **Molopo River**. The Molopo, now dry except for the occasional and short-lived flood, was a great river in times gone by, as is evidenced by the massive valley and the eroded calcrete walls.

Worthy of a visit are the high cliffs just below the village of Khuis (they are within sight of the place but a little downstream) and the impressive gorge, carved through solid rock, at Kolonkwaneng (a little upstream). Both villages are within a radius of 10 km of Middelpits.

While travelling from Vanzylsrus to Bokspits, you'll be following the Kuruman River, which takes its name from the amazing spring at the town of Kuruman (Kudumane in Setswana). In this area, however, the river seldom flows.

Entry into Bokspits is well signposted. Shortly before the border, at Andriesvale, is a motel, close to which you will see the turning for South African Customs (open from 8 am until 4 pm). Visitors entering Botswana are required to report their arrival to the police at Bokspits. Fuel and basic supplies for the independent traveller can be purchased in Bokspits.

ROUTE 6
Kang to Tsabong

TOTAL DISTANCE: 355 km. **TIME**: 10–11 hours. **VEHICLE**: 4x4 essential. **MAPS**: Map 4 (page 264); also Shell Tourist Map of Botswana. For directions to Kang from Gaborone see Route 3, Gaborone to Ghanzi, Map 5 (page 265).

The first section consists of 111 km from Kang to Hukuntsi, all on tar. Fuel is obtainable at Kang and also at Hukuntsi, 11 km from Tshane (also tarred). Tshane is one of four villages that cluster together in the heart of the Kalahari (for more detail, see Tshane/Hukuntsi Village Cluster, page 140). It is 240 km from Tshane to Tsabong.

Whether the road to Tsabong can be reached directly from Hukuntsi, now that the tar goes directly there, or whether one still picks it up at Tshane, is uncertain (ask in the vicinity). But from whichever point you start you'll find that the sand road is very badly corrugated and traffic volume light. You will be obliged to drive slowly and the journey is uncomfortable, although the section from Mabuasehube south is rather better. The whole journey takes up to 6 hours in all – perhaps less. There are no towns, villages or facilities along the way, although water may be available past the new entrance to the Mabuasehube section of the Kgalagadi Transfrontier Park (KTP). The road no longer passes through the KTP but around the boundary, so you no longer see Mabuasehube Pan. Beyond this point there are a further 110 km of poor road (currently being gravelled northwards from Tshabong), which can take up to 2.5 hours, before you reach Tsabong.

ROUTE 6A

Hukuntsi to Western Woodlands (Masetlheng Pan)

TOTAL DISTANCE: 100 km. **TIME**: 4–6 hours. **VEHICLE**: 4x4 essential. **MAPS**: Map 5 (page 265) and Map 26 (page 286); also Shell Tourist Map of Botswana. For directions to Tshane and Hukuntsi, see Route 3 (page 154) and Route 6 (page 158). **WESTERN WOODLANDS PROFILE**: page 145.

When you reach Hukuntsi (see Route 6 above), ask the way to Masetlheng Pan. The village has been tarred throughout and there are signposts so it should not be too difficult to find. Make your enquiries at the store near Hukuntsi Pan.

Once you've ascertained the road, follow it out of the village, first to the west, later swinging to the northwest. The track will be sandy and difficult. It was along this cut-line that Petro-Canada dragged their massive drilling rigs when, in search of oil in 1989/90, they drilled a 4.1-km deep borehole at

Masetlheng Pan. The point just beyond this pan is noteworthy: here a cut-line heads due south from the main track. The borehole is on the west side of the cut-line a kilometre or two to the south at GPS 23, 41. 59S and 20, 51. 08E (datum unknown).

From Hukuntsi, the first feature encountered is a pan called Kwakai, which is just before the large **Zonye Pan**, 28–30 km from Hukuntsi. The road is of deep, soft sand and the going is extremely slow. Seven kilometres after **Zonye Pan** and some 33 to 35 km out of Hukuntsi you'll find Bohelabatho Pan;

Bohelabathwana Pan lies 3 km beyond. The scenery then reverts to that of the essential Kalahari until you've covered 73 km from the start. Here, cross **Ngwaatle Pan**, a kilometre or two on the far side of which is a **San village**.

There's still 28 km to go before you reach Masetlheng Pan. Once there, proceed a further 10 km along the track and take your pick of the wonderful campsites that abound in the woodlands to the northwest of the pan.

ROUTE 7
Serowe–Orapa–Mopipi

DISTANCES AND TIMES: Serowe–Orapa 212 km; time: 2 hours; Serowe–Mopipi 282 km; time: 3 hours. **VEHICLE**: The roads are tarred. **MAPS**: Map 7 (page 267); also Shell Tourist Map of Botswana. **SEROWE PROFILE**: page 101.

The turn-off to Orapa at Serowe is a few kilometres before the town centre but is well signposted. There is no petrol along the route, except at Letlhakane, at its northern end. On the journey north, there are several features of interest.

Between Serowe and Paje you will see an escarpment to the west. This is the eastern edge of the Kalahari. The flat-topped hills about you are sandstone outliers that have been left behind by the westward moving effects of erosion. Stretching to the east is the Lotsane River and, to the northeast, the Motloutse valley leading down to the great Limpopo.

After the sharp left-hand bend at Paje, the road begins to climb the escarpment and basalt boulders appear on both sides. This basalt is exactly the same system as that which creates South Africa's Drakensberg, and that underlies the Kalahari sands, that outcrops along the Hunter's Road (see page 201) and over which the Zambezi flows at Victoria Falls. On the edges of the road, as you reach the crest, you'll see the familiar red sand of the Kalahari for the first time.

After Paje – once over the crest and into the Kalahari – you will see, on the west side of the road, the **Khama Rhino Sanctuary**. The sanctuary, home to the remainder of Botswana's rhinos in addition to some recently acquired from South Africa, is developing at an amazing rate. Call in: you'll be most welcome. For more details see page 218.

The next village is Mmashoro, where you will see flat-topped hills on either side of the road. You might be surprised to learn that, on each summit, there is an extensive and important **Early Iron Age site** that has yielded gold fragments and clear evidence of trading across Africa and down to the coast. Evidently, the Kalahari has not always been as inhospitable.

Between Mmashoro and Letlhakane is the Makoba veterinary fence. (From this point, if you intended to travel up the east side of Sowa Pan, you would proceed north, along the east side of the fence on a good track to Tlalamabele on the Francistown–Orapa road; the journey involves 64 km and approximately 1.5 hours, and it's usually possible to complete it without a 4x4.) As you approach Letlhakane, you'll see the massive dump of the mine to the north. This is **DK1** (the mine itself, not the village, which you encounter from about 189 km onwards). The mine is said to be the world's richest source of gem-quality diamonds.

The handiest petrol point is at 191.5 km, among some shops on the left-hand side of the road. At this point there is also a T-junction there at which, if you turn right (north) eventually leads, after 12 km on gravel, to the main Francistown–Orapa road at a point exactly opposite the track to Kubu Island, one of the access routes for Sowa Pan. However, it is actually nicer to drive into Letlhakane and find the Shell service station. There, an able and enterprising Motswana businessman has opened a small restaurant called **Granny's Kitchen**. He also provides accommodation. The result is a perfect refreshment, meal or rest-over spot – entirely unexpected in so remote a place and always most satisfactory.

For Orapa, do not turn right into Letlhakane but rather continue straight on. The road leads you to the east gate of the mine at 215 km. The diamond-mining town of **Orapa** is contained within a large security fence. It is private property and permission is needed to enter. While the town has all facilities, they are not automatically available to the travelling public. A permit may be applied for, in advance, from the head office of Debswana in Gaborone (PO Box 329, Gaborone; tel 395-1131, fax 395-2941). Or you could try to persuade the security personnel at the guarded gates to let you in, but you may not be successful. Emergencies will, of course, be treated sympathetically. The main road by-passes Orapa to the south (21 km) and leads on from there to Mopipi Reservoir and the Boteti River.

Route 7A
Part 1: Mopipi to Maun

DISTANCES, TIMES AND ROADS: Mopipi–Rakops: 69.3 km; time: 50 minutes; tarred road. Mopipi–Motopi 199 km; time: plus-minus 2.5 hours; tarred road under construction in 2001: 54 untarred kilometres only remaining; Motopi–Maun: 87 km; time: 1 hour; tarred road. **MAPS:** Map 7 (page 267), Map 8 (page 268) and Map 9 (page 269); also Shell Tourist Map of Botswana. Map 7 gets you to Orapa Mine and Mopipi. Distances on Map 8 are counted from the petrol station on the north side of the road in Mopipi. The road is tarred as far as Rakops. **MAUN PROFILE:** page 98.

One needs to be cautioned about the abrupt and unsignposted right-hand bend just under 3 km west of Mopipi. A dirt track leads on but the tarmac swings right to cross a bridge. Twice I've missed this turning in the dark and ended up a very surprised and shaken driver! At 19.5 km from the filling station on the north side of the road is a well-used track, marked with a rusty and bent metal sign that sits low on the ground (and is therefore easy to miss!). This is a turn-off that will take you through cattle country and over seemingly endless kilometres (actually 27–33 km) of fine dust and bone-shaking calcrete until, eventually, one crosses into the most southerly reaches of **Makgadikgadi National Park** (see page 123). The rest of the journey to Rakops is signposted and straightforward.

It is perhaps as well to realise, as one drives through this country, that, for the whole way on your right (north or east) lies the **Boteti River**. It's not always easy to recognise it as a river but even in relatively recent times – early in the 20th century and certainly in the 19th – the river regularly flowed here and the southern end, between Xhumo and Mopipi, was a wetland full of birds and aquatic creatures. It's hard to believe that now!

It is more than ten years since the Boteti has reached Mopipi which, I am told, it has done only three times since 1963. In fact, the large, dry pan you see to the south of the village was modified so that water could be pumped in from the Boteti, turning it into a huge reservoir. From there, it was pumped the 50-odd kilometres to Orapa Mine. I saw water in Mopipi Reservoir in 1983, but not since.

The Boteti is an overflow from the Okavango Delta and draws its water from the Thamalakane, which flows past Maun. A low earthen embankment (bund) at the Boteti/Nchabe/Thamalakane junction was designed to divide the flow. The Okavango's flood does not reach Maun until July or August, and it takes many more months for the water to make its way down the Boteti. When the river is dry, however, as it is these days, it offers wonderful opportunities for exploration. There are beautiful acacia woodlands along its banks, cliffs of calcrete to investigate, birds in remarkable profusion, and, for the pho tographer, innumerable attractive rural scenes. Nearer to villages there's a maze of tracks leading everywhere; further out, you make your own. Be cautioned, though: the sand can make for slow, heavy driving. On his two journeys to Lake Ngami, the 19th-century missionary-explorer David Livingstone came this way with William Cotton Oswell. They found the sand so heavy and the trees so thick that they abandoned most of their wagons and went on only lightly equipped.

Three kilometres north of Rakops, on the west side, is the signposted turn-off leading 45 km to the Central Kalahari Game Reserve (CKGR) boundary and, beyond that, 8.8 km to Matswere Camp and permit office. The CKGR access road was in very poor condition in November 2000. It is possible that it will be abandoned and a new one cut, so keep your eyes open. You may rest assured, however, if a new road is cut, that the authorities will signpost it well.

If you were to take this track and drive 13 dusty and uncomfortable kilometres westwards, you will arrive at the top of an ancient sand ridge. This is either an ancient shoreline or an off-shore barrier beach of the old paleo-lake, **Gidikwe Ridge** marking its western margin at one time. Ascend to its summit and look back. If you do this in the afternoon, so that the sun is behind you, a stunning view unfolds. Even from this relatively low elevation the whole of the old lake-bed lies before you. The course of the Boteti is traced out with a dark green ribbon of riverine trees while, in the distance, the waters of the old lake still seem to shimmer and dance in the heat. It is incredible to think how changeable land-forms really are and how insignificant a human lifespan is against the immensity of geological time.

Aside from the fact that it is currently (November 2000) under construction, the road north presents few difficulties. Access to Tsoe is presently unsignposted, so you'll need to make enquiries once you get into the area (work on distances, and refer to Map 8, page 268). In the dry, you can cross the Boteti there and drive up the east side of the river, within the national park, to the game scouts camp at Xhumaga.

It is also at Xhumaga that you'll find **Leroo-La-Tau Safari Lodge**, a relatively new venture started by Sean Watson from Serowe. Located on the north bank of the river, at the bend, it offers both the advantages of a riverine environment – complete with perennial pools stocked with hippo and crocodile, giant trees, dense vegetation, superb birding – and, to the east, the rolling grasslands of Makgadikgadi.

At a point 35.8 km north of the microwave tower at Xhumaga, the Boteti River cuts its way through the Gidikwe sand ridge. There is interesting scenery to enjoy here. The ridge, as mentioned, is considered to be a barrier beach, related to paleo-lake Makgadikgadi and extending around this part

of its western shore for nearly 300 km. On the side of the road you will find one of Botswana's most enigmatic and unlikely road signs! I hope it won't be removed by the makers of the new road.

When the river is full, there are beautiful lagoons around Motopi. You can usually find your way up- or downstream on the north bank sufficiently far for reasonable privacy. The area is little known, but offers magical camping spots.

At Motopi, one can cross the Boteti, join the main tarmac road to Maun and be in town within an hour or less. If there is time, however, one can stay on the south side of the river, drive through the Makalamabedi veterinary fence and either cross the Boteti 10 km further west or go on to Samadupe Bridge (Map 9, page 269). The further upstream one travels, especially in these drier times, the more likely one is to encounter water in the river – and with it, all the attendant wildlife, including hippos and crocodiles. So beware! In addition, the river flows over long stretches of calcrete, especially in the Samadupe region, and among the rocks you will find hundreds of Early and Middle Stone Age tools. Please remember that these are state property and all the many sites in this area are protected by law. That should not, however, stop you from the fun of looking for, finding and admiring these artifacts, some of which may be more than 20 000 (Middle) or 300 000 (Early) years old.

The Makalamabedi fence is accessible either from this route or from the Nata–Maun road. Following it south is an interesting drive (Map 9, page 269): it leads you to 'Kuke Corner' (the infamous Kuke Fence, of Mark and Delia Owen fame) and thus to the boundary of the CKGR. Game scouts at Matswere Camp use the boundary cut-line and the Makalamabedi fence to get to Maun for their monthly shopping.

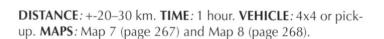

Route 7A

Part 2: Mopipi to Lake Xau

DISTANCE: +-20–30 km. **TIME**: 1 hour. **VEHICLE**: 4x4 or pick-up. **MAPS**: Map 7 (page 267) and Map 8 (page 268).

Find the track, off the road back to Orapa (see Map 8, page 268), that circles Mopipi Reservoir on its east and south side (the reservoir is that vast, circular grey, dry and dusty area before you, usually quite devoid of any water!). After about 9 km you will reach a junction where a road departs from the 'circular drive' and heads off to the southwest. Take this road.

In the next 30 km you will pass, on the right, **Lake Xau**, where once, when it had water, wildebeest used to herd in their tens of thousands, though now it stands as empty and as forlorn as its neighbour Mopipi. For additional interest, you can drive onwards to the **Kedia Hills**, past a smaller pan on your right.

Route 7A
Part 3: Orapa Pans

DISTANCES AND TIMES: Variable. **VEHICLE**: 4x4 essential. **RECOMMENDED MAPS**: Maps 7 (page 267), 28 (page 288) and 33 (page 293); also Republic of Botswana: 1:250 000 series, monochrome sheet SF.35.5 'Lake Xau', and sheet No 17 'Letlhakane'; 1:50 000 series, 2124B2, B4, 2125 A1 & A3 'Rysana', 2125 A2 'Guguaga', 2125 A2 & A3 'Nkokwane', 2125 B1 and B2, 'Ntsokotsa'. **ORAPA PANS PROFILE**: page 132.

It is not advisable to attempt these pans without the right vehicle together with, at least, the map in this book or preferably the two 1:250 000 series. There is, of course, no development or tourist infrastructure in the area and the nearest shops and fuel points are at Mopipi and Letlhakane.

Tracks link the major pans in this system, so one can get to any one of the bigger features. **Ntsokotsa**, in the east, is the most accessible from the village of Mmatshumo (see Map 15, page 275). Drive north along the road to Lekubung (Kubu) and, after about 9.5 km, when you reach the surface of a small pan, turn slightly north of east and cross the pan to its eastern side. Here you have to drive through the bush to reach GPS 21.02.52.3S/ 25.39.51.4E, which is a gap in a veterinary fence. Drive through and find your way carefully through the bush to the east. This will bring you to the shore of Ntsokotsa. If this doesn't work for you, another approach – again from the village of Mmatshumo – is to travel east on the gravel road to Mosu for 11 km from the telecommunications mast in Mmatshumo. Look for the cut-line running north at that point. Having turned, drive 10.6 km north to the sharp bend to the right. Beyond that the track continues for 1.9 km then turns north among the Mopane trees. Work your way first north, onto the grassy plain, then west around the prominent headland. After 4–5 km you will come to Ntsokotsa and find the obvious, spectacular campsite.

Rysana Pan is a little easier to reach. From the west gate of Orapa Mine, drive 24.5 km towards Mopipi. At that point you will find a track to the north at GPS 21.17.23.2S/25.04.58.2E. Opposite is a metal signpost bearing the name 'Kamkaxhono'. Turn north here for 6–8 km to reach the pan. A road at the north end of the pan will take you west to Tsokotsa Pan and beyond to the village of Mopipi (you re-join the main road near Mopipi at GPS 21.12.58.4S/24.54.12.6E). Or you can turn east and make your way to **Guguaga Gate** (see also Map 10, page 270). This route to Guguaga Gate is challenging and not easy unless you have the maps and a GPS. A better way is to return to the main road and turn east to the western side of Orapa Mine (see Route 7B, Orapa to Gweta, below) and follow the route north. Once at Guguaga Gate, turn east for just under 4 km. This track will take you straight down onto the grassy surface of the pan. Once on the pan surface, you can drive where you will.

We did find a way from Guguaga Pan to Nkokwane but it is complicated, necessitated quite a lot of bush driving and needs good maps, a GPS, great patience and a good navigator (that's Kerstin, my wife!). The easiest way is to return to the main road, get to the east side of Orapa Mine and drive 10 km east along the road to Francistown. At that point, about 50 m east of a substantial bridge, you will see a well-used sandy road going due north. Follow this for 20.6 km and you'll arrive at a large quarry where an ancient dune is being excavated for its sand. A few metres before this is a crossroads. A track west goes 4.8 km to Nkokwane Pan, while a turn east will take you 15.5 km to the village of Mmatshumo. Another way to Nkokwane Pan from the village of Mmatshumo is indicated on the map. Find the well and take the track that bears 319 deg. Mag. from it and starts at GPS point 'I' on that map.

ROUTE 7B
Part 1: Ntwetwe Pan: Orapa to Gweta

This area is divided into four route options, as follows: **NTWETWE PAN PROFILE**: page 126. **TOTAL DISTANCE**: 134 km. **TIME**: 4–5 hours. To get to Orapa see Route 9 (page 181). **VEHICLE**: A 4x4 or LDV is recommended. **PERMITS**: It's only possible to pass through the mine concession area of Orapa if a permit has been obtained by prior arrangement with Debswana, PO Box 329, Gaborone; tel 395-1131, fax 395-2941. Permits are not lightly granted. **MAPS**: Maps 7 (page 267), 10 (page 270) and 28 (page 288); also Republic of Botswana, 1:250 000 series, sheet SF.35.1 'Bushman Pits'.

On reaching the east gate, bypass the mine area by following the tar around to the south. A journey of 25 km will bring you, 1.8 km beyond (north of) a veterinary fence, to a T-junction. This in turn leads you to the original Mopipi road and the west gate. Distances are recorded from this point. Seek the mine boundary road that heads directly north from the west gate.

Drive directly north and continue in this direction. To begin with, the mine perimeter fence will be on your right. Soon, this turns abruptly to the east and the road diagonals to the northwest. After 5 km you will have a veterinary fence on your right hand. Follow it for a total distance of approximately 34 km from the start.

Having travelled through rather unattractive scrub lands, on roads of very indifferent quality, you will see the increasing occurrence of open grassy areas interspersed with woodland. When the sun is low, these grasslands, with the woodlands beyond, are quite breathtaking. Try to time your trip to take advantage of this.

After 34 km, you will come to the banks of the **Boteti River**, where it cuts through the base of the great tongue of land that juts into Ntwetwe from the south. North of this point are prairie-like grasslands of great beauty. They, and the reaches of the accompanying woodlands, extend along a further 36.2 km to the north, which will bring you to a veterinary fence and the edge of Ntwetwe Pan at Tchai Gate. This section takes about 1.45 hours from the start.

The next 20 km over the pan is very fast going, but care and common sense are required if the surface is wet. If you cannot, due to water, see the spoor of a vehicle in front of you, do not go on unless you are very sure of what you are doing. Please remember this; the track is heavily used by people commuting from Orapa to Gweta and if there is no spoor, you are either in the wrong place or the way is impassable.

Driving approximately 8.7 km north on the pan will bring you to the island of **Gabasadi**, which is difficult to recognise at first glance because it's nothing more than a low sandy prominence to your left (west). Actually, it's a stranded barchan (wind-formed) dune; if you climb up it you will at once see the typical horseshoe shape of such dunes; geography books brought to life! A further 12.6 km beyond Gabasadi brings you to the Gweta mainland. As you are racing across this exhilarating piece of pan towards the shore, look to the northeast and observe what a remarkable landmark **Chapman's Baobab** is! Driving north, you will see, 1.8 km from the edge of the pan, a turn-off to the east and you'll reach the tree after 5.4 km along this track. If you continue north past the turn-off for 11.1 km, you'll get to **Green's Tree** (also a baobab). It is 28 km from this tree to the village of Gweta.

Green's Tree can be difficult to find. You will notice, as you drive north, that the (appalling) track is very braided. Take the wrong 'braid' and you'll miss the tree, which is not large, and certainly no landmark; the trick is to keep your eyes open for a tall and obvious clump of vegetable ivory palm trees.These grow on the south side of Gutsha Pan and tower above every-thing. Green's Tree is approximately 300 m to the northeast of the palms. When you are that close, the baobab appears quite obvious.

If one is attempting the journey in the reverse direction – departing from Gweta – then seek the assistance of residents of that village to get onto the correct track. Ask for the Orapa road. A mistake can be enormously frustrating and, in the absence of signs, is easy to make.

Route 7B

Part 2: Ntwetwe Pan: the western islands

DISTANCES AND TIMES: Variable. **VEHICLE**: 4x4 essential. **MAPS:** Map 10 (page 270), Map 11 (page 271), Map 16 (page 276); Republic of Botswana, 1:250 000 series, sheet SF.35.1 'Bushman Pits'; 1:50 000 series, 2024 D2, D4, 2025 C1, C2, C3 and 2025 A4 (see below).

A safe route to Ntwetwe's Western Islands is to turn west at the point where the north–south track reaches the Gweta main-land. Careful observation may show you the spoor of previous travellers in this area but, from this point on, it is best to rely on a map. A general, but not very helpful, picture of the region can be obtained from the 1:250 000 'Bushman Pits' mono-chrome map. However, for navigating through the islands and the areas referred to in this text, you should have the maps specified above.

Some of these are full colour, costing P20 each; others are black-and-white photographic mosaics (P10 each). They can be obtained from the Department of Surveys and Mapping, P/Bag 0037, Gaborone; tel 395-3251. They are what I consider to be the minimum in order to navigate successfully. Your own experiences and individual requirements will determine whether you need a wider spread. Any competent geographer will be able to help you plot these maps out onto the 1:250 000 so that you can see those areas covered in detail.

Route 7B
Part 3: Ntwetwe Pan: Nata–Maun road to Gabasadi Island

TOTAL DISTANCE: Approximately 75 km. **TIME:** 2–3 hours. **VEHICLE:** 4x4. **MAPS**: Map 10 (page 270), Map 16 (page 276); 10 mm,1:50 000 series, 2024 D2, D4, 2025 C1, C2, C3 and 2025 A4. Also Republic of Botswana, 1:250 000 series, sheet SF.35.1 'Bushman Pits'.

A different and interesting route into the Ntwetwe area is from the Nata–Maun road. At a point of 51 km from Nata, the north-east 'finger' of Ntwetwe crosses that main road and it is easy to get down onto the pan surface. It is not so easy to drive south-west, or 'down' the finger. The exercise is fun but requires some directional skill, a lot of common sense and some luck too, for you have to work your way round, between or over areas of tussocked grassland. More than once I have seen heavily laden vehicles sink through the surface – but then escape with relative ease. But driving with care can avoid these annoyances.

Large areas of grass make it difficult to find a clear 'open pan' surface, especially in the northern reaches. Eventually, however, patience is rewarded and you'll find an excellent route *if you stay close to the western shore* of the 'finger'. This is important in the early stretches of open pan – even if you feel you are going too far in that direction. Several times I have ignored this advice, only to find myself finally reaching the open pan surface at the end of a long reach of grass only to face frighteningly vast bays to the east and west – bays so wide

I couldn't see land in either direction. In such a situation I either had to drive across to reach the 'shore' or retrace my steps. I can assure you, driving across knowing what can go wrong is serious, nail-biting stuff! Stay west! Once you've found the shore, you can follow it round to the south and then west to meet up with the north–south Orapa–Gweta track that passes Gabasadi Island.

On the journey along the 'finger', you will encounter a track coming out of the open pan and running from southeast to northwest (see Map 11, page 271). You can either turn northwest along this route to Gweta, southeast to Kubu Island, or continue southwest along the present shoreline. The latter option will, after 5–8 km, bring you to a concealed bay. Its narrow entrance is inviting and usually marked by a number of prominent aloes and you'll see many cattle. Follow the snaking bay, and within a kilometre or two you will come to a natural spring. Here there's a hunting blind on the north side of the pool, together with many **Stone Age artifacts** strewn about and large numbers of birds (and – if the cattle are there – flies!). This approach is a scenic and exciting route into the area.

Route 7B
Part 4: Ntwetwe Pan: Kubu Island to Gweta

TOTAL DISTANCE: About 95 km. **TIME**: 3–4 hours. **VEHICLE**: Pick-up or 4x4. **MAPS:** Map 11 (page 271), Map 14 (page 274) and Map 16 (page 276). Route 7B (4): Kubu Island to Gweta.

Travel north from the Kubu turn-off on the north–south track from Mmatshumo to Zoroga and Nata, travel north. After 8,4 km you may notice a small borrow pit (formed by the extraction of road-building material) on the right. Then after 12,4 km from the turn-off you will reach the pan edge where the bush begins again. There is a turning to the west 1,5 km beyond this with two or three huts in evidence; ignore it. A further 2,3 km north brings you to a crossroads which includes another turning to the west. This crossroads is the start of the track to Gweta. Set your odometer to zero here. Your are 16,2 km from the Kubu turn-off, roughly due south of you.

To ensure that you have the correct turn-off, verify that there is a single baobab in sight on the west side of the road and that a track passes between it and a group of huts on the right with an acacia tree growing inside a wooden palisade surrounding the huts.

From this starting point, drive north for 4.6 km to the veterinary fence gate. After going through the gate, turn west on its north side for 4.1 km. At this point turn right (north) onto the main track that continues to the northwest.

At about 18 km from the starting point at the crossroads, open grasslands are reached on the north side. Some 4 or 5 km further, the grasslands open out on both sides of the track. On the southern margin of this great plain, three large and beautiful *Acacia tortilis* once stood. If you knew them, I regret to report that all are now dead.

The grassland that begins here and stretches to the north is almost too beautiful for words – especially in March when the stands are high and full. Once, when passing through, Alec Campbell and I climbed onto the canopies of our respective vehicles and looked down in wonder at successive waves of wind as they bullied and buffeted the grass, which bobbed and bowed before their passage. We shot off countless pictures and shouted like children with the sheer joy and the beauty of it all (I now have a large collection of rather uninteresting pictures of blurry grass. Still cameras simply don't capture the thrill of such moments!)

When you reach 25 km from the starting point, you will be on the edge of the first Ntwetwe Pan crossing. Before setting off, take a few minutes to look around. In the exposed sides of the sand features all about you, you will find fossil reeds and mollusc shells, reminders that the place where you stand was once, not all that long ago, swamp-like in nature. When you continue on, you will be moving on across the surface of Ntwetwe Pan but, after 12.5 km of a high-speed, thrilling drive (it's all relative really; one is just not used to driving at 60 km/h!) the road returns to the mainland again along a 12.8-km stretch before, at approximately 49 km from the start, reaching the 'finger' of Ntwetwe. This second venture out on to the surface of Ntwetwe is 9.7 km and then there remains 31.4 km to the village of Gweta.

When you start from the Gweta end, the track will be extremely difficult to find. You are best advised to ask for directions and, when enquiring, use such names as Kubu, Lekhubung, Thabatshukudu, Tshwagong, Thitaba or Mmatshumo (all of which villages are accessed from this route).

ROUTE 8, Option 1A

East Sowa Pan (land route)

MAPS: Maps 12 (page 272) and 13 (page 273). There are several options here. The following sections profile five of them. **SOWA PAN PROFILE:** page 135. **DISTANCE AND TIMES**: 100 km, 3–4 hours. **VEHICLE**: A 4x4 is not essential for this route in winter, but I think it most advisable. In the wet, you'll certainly need one: there is block-cotton soil and two rivers to cross. **MAPS**: Maps 12 (page 272) and 13 (page 273); also Republic of Botswana, 1:50 000 series, 2026, C2, C3, 2126 A2; 1:250 000 series, sheet No 12 'Nata'.

A little-known track, maintained by Botswana's Veterinary Department, runs near the east side of Sowa Pan and gives excellent access to the area.

The southern end of this track begins on the Francistown –Orapa road at the Tlalamabele veterinary fence (about 144 km from Francistown). The fence forms a barrier across the main road, which is manned 24 hours a day. Approaching from Francistown, the track you seek begins on your right-hand side, immediately *before* going through the barrier.

Once on the track, which, at the moment, lies in the middle of the double fence, in a northerly direction, the going, although a little rocky in places, is on a firm, smooth surface. As you drop down, off the escarpment, you will occasionally be driving on the edge of the pan. This can be slippery when wet. After 20 km and about 45 minutes you'll reach Tlhapane Gate. This point is a crossroads; east takes you about 3 km to Tlhapane Hill and the **Zimbabwe** *site* (ruins; see page 139) on its summit; beyond that there are various cattle posts.

If you travel west for 35 km you will reach the village of Mosu. The Mosu track allows access to the whole fascinating escarpment area of southern Sowa Pan and some rather dramatic camping spots. Feel free to explore this area. There have been a large number of new and very exciting (as well as important) archaeological discoveries in this region but you would have to do a lot of climbing and walking to find them (if you are really interested, contact me for details; see page 15).

Another 28.6 km north from Tlhapane brings you to a second veterinary fence and a pair of gates. On the way, you pass through two rather beautiful stretches of mature mopane woodland. I've always thought this would be a nice place to camp but, unfortunately, the track at this point passes between the two fences – at present (November 2000) it is impossible to get off the road here (although circumstances frequently change).

Just before the gate, to the west, you will notice a rather large and very striking baobab on which you'll see, among others, the name 'Ker' and a date (see also page 115). This tree was clearly on the 'Western Old Lake' route used from 1880 to the early 1900s by those travelling north to Mpandamatenga, the Zambezi and Barotseland. I have no idea at the moment who Ker was, but I am very glad to have found this trace of an original route in which I have been interested for some time.

The gate you arrive at is Kwadiba. If you turn west immediately on passing through, you will see a well-worn track leading to Kokonje Island. This island has become something of a popular destination but you can avoid the crowd and 'churchmouse' your way around the pan's edge until you get to a point due north of it. You will see a low ridge there, and will need to pick your way through the bush and camp on top of it. The site is fantastic: the sun sets on your right as you look south and the view from this slightly elevated position is quite amazing.

Between the Kwadiba and Tlhapane gates on the veterinary fence there is a turning to the southeast (7.2 from Tlhapane Gate and 21.4 km south of Kwadiba), at a point where there's another gate (the Mea). From here, a track leads to the very beautiful **Mea Pan**, a favourite haunt of local 'twitchers', (bird- watchers) and beyond to the village of Mokubilo. This village is also just a few kilometres from the large and striking Mokubilo Pan. Both pans are good places to camp. (See Map 28, Francistown to Orapa, page 288.)

To complete the journey to Dukwe from Kokonje, return to Kwadiba Gate. From this point it is just under 50 km, on a reasonable track, to the tarred Francistown–Nata road. You emerge at the Dukwe veterinary gate, approximately 133 km from Francistown. Note that there are two rather steep stream crossings on this section. If there's rain about, they may prove difficult or impossible to ford (see Map 13, page 273).

At 9.5 km on the route towards Nata from the Dukwe Gate, you'll find a signposted turning to the left labelled 'SUA'. This will take you to what is known as the Sowa Spit – a long tongue of land that juts far out into Sowa Pan. It is approximately 40 km to the base of the spit, to Sowa town and the site of Botswana's Soda Ash project. The road is tarred. An additional 18 km of sand track will take you along the spit to its western extremity.

You used to be able to find a track going northeast from the base of the spit, more or less along the shoreline, but I'm informed that there is a veterinary fence there now and that one can no longer get through. I haven't been there for many years.

Returning to the main Nata road, a drive 27.2 km towards Nata will bring you to yet another veterinary fence and, 3 km beyond, to Nata Sanctuary (see page 220). The prominent baobab tree to the west of the road, which used to mark this spot, was blown over (yes, blown over – so what hope your tents!) some years ago. But life is resilient and persistent. The tree still grows and I watch its progress carefully. I am amused by the single finger-like branch that still points defiantly to the sky, barely visible above the tree-line!

Route 8, Option 1B

East Sowa Pan (pan surface route)

DISTANCES AND TIMES: Variable; between 150 and 200 km. **VEHICLE**: 4x4 absolutely essential. **MAPS**: Map 12 (page 272), Map 13 (page 273), Map 28 (page 288) and Map 31 (page 291); also Government of Botswana, 1:50000 series, 2126 A1 and A2, 2026 C1 and C31:250 000 series, sheet No 12 'Nata'.

Since first writing these directions I have continued to explore and open up new areas. Without doubt, one of the most beautiful and exciting journeys is that along the east side of Sowa Pan – on the pan surface – from south to north. The journey is not without certain risks (I would hesitate to do it alone; someone always gets stuck) but it is great fun and hugely rewarding.

There is no formal starting point so, for convenience, I'll talk about the southeast corner, because that is where I usually start from. The first step is to get onto the pan surface, and you can do this easily from the Tlhapane or Kwadiba gates (see Route 8, Option 1A: East Sowa Pan, land route, page 173). Turn west at either of these gates and follow your nose. In both cases there are tracks that take you onto or near the pan. I drive on the pan surface, never stray too far away from the shore and simply work my way north.

Beyond this, the directions are simple: follow the shore-line. But I have other vital pieces of advice: stay in four-wheel-drive, keep your speed up, no sudden braking, no sudden swerves, never try the trip when the pan is wet, *drop your tyre pressures to 1 bar* (this makes the most amazing difference to your traction and it really does make driving much safer). Study the guidelines suggested in 'Driving on pans' on page 86. Enjoy the pan-driving experience. Another suggestion: it is wiser always to take a longer journey around a bay than to rush across it – the pan surface is utterly unpredictable and a 'sticking' will delay you an hour or two. Be wary, too, of places where rivers join the pan. Although there may be no surface water, the sub-surface may be wet and, therefore, the surface even more than usually undependable.

Map 31 (page 291) indicates the Shuane-Mosetse river valley and the route from the pan to Toranju and Tshwaane, together with their GPS co-ordinates. From these sites one can either travel directly north to the tarmac road at Sowa town and the main Francistown–Nata road, or return to the pan, continue north along the shore for a short distance, find the vet fence and follow it northwards for 12 km to the same road.

The map also shows a track leading down from Sowa Spit to Kwadiba Gate. This track is shown on other maps inaccurately. While in some places – along most of its length – the track is exceptionally good and lovely to drive on, it goes only as far as two very large cattle posts in the south – known as Kwadiba. From this point on, the southern extension is difficult to find and dramatically different in nature. It winds through thick vegetation and in and out of many small sandy stream beds. It isn't easy to get lost here, but it is easy to *think* that you have it wrong. Eventually the track brings you out on the west side of the veterinary fence, which you can follow for a few kilometres south to the Kwadiba Gate.

My suspicion is that this track is the remains of the old 19th-century wagon route, and I am delighted to find a surviving fragment. While I have twice used the route from north to south, I have not yet tried it in the opposite direction and suspect it would be difficult to find from the south end. I last used it in 1999, and at that time noticed that another vehicle had recently been down before me. It may be that my first trip reopened the route, and that others have followed. If so, it may become easier to find and to use.

Route 8, Option 2A
West Sowa Pan: Nata to Kubu

DISTANCE: North to south 120–130 km. **TIME**: 4 hours. **VEHICLE**: This section can be travelled in a pick-up vehicle but a 4x4 is strongly recommended. **MAPS**: Map 13 (page 273) and Map 14 (page 274); also Republic of Botswana, 1:250 000 series, sheet No 12 'Nata'; 1:50 000 series, 2125 B1, B2 and 2025 B4, D2, D4.

Nata is the starting point for this section (for directions to Nata, see Route 9, Francistown–Maun, page 181, and Map 13, page 273). There are three main routes on the west side of Sowa Pan, and all three pass through a single gate in the veterinary fence 9.7 km south of Thabatshukudu.

One route follows a series of tracks down the dry (and very dusty) mainland between the two pans; another is on the pan surface itself; the third is along the western shore of the pan – the most beautiful and interesting of the drives. The start of all these routes is one of the turn-offs at various points along the first 20 km of the Nata–Maun road.

The most exciting and exhilarating approach is to drive south on the pan surface but, be warned, *this is a highly risky route*. It's fun, but one can get badly stuck and there will be no help. Do not take this route lightly. To begin, drive west from Nata on the tar and look to your left, towards the old road where, at about 10.6 km along the latter, you'll see, opposite a distinctive grass-covered mound on the north side, a track to the south. At that point, turn and meander south through the grasslands for 9.7 km. Whenever there is a fork in the road, always choose the southerly alternative. There is one particularly difficult junction on a sharp bend. Close to the pan's edge you may pass a few borehole liners which have been lying there, rusting, for over 20 years.

If you've been lucky and found the right tracks, you will find yourself on the pan surface at some spoil dumps I call the 'Pyramids' – a name suggested by the shape of the spoil dumped when the trench was dug. The trench is part of an exploration exercise for what is now the Sowa Pan Soda Ash project, which extracts salt and soda ash from the sub-surface saline brine. Do

stop. Note how high the water-table is and how saline the water. Swim in it and notice the unusual buoyancy. Carefully examine the strange aquatic life, which assumes grotesque and repulsive forms. But treat it with great respect for it is a scientific wonder: it includes stromatolites, an algal growth mat and one of the most ancient forms of life on earth!

The next section is not for the faint-hearted and *under no circumstances attempt it when the pan is wet or in the rainy season.* From the Pyramids on, you have to rely on your sense of direction and common sense. The island of Kubu lies 81 km to the south, across the open pan. Stay close to the shore, and good luck. It's an exhilarating drive! Regretfully, one cannot now go all the way to the island: a new veterinary fence extends into the pan about 60 km to the south and reaches too far east into the pan for vehicles safely to drive round it. When you reach the fence, turn west along it until you get to the gate. Thereafter follow the route as shown in Map 14 (page 274).

For the nicest and safest route, continue westward *on the main tarred road to Maun* for 17.5 km from Nata. There you will see a standard road sign indicating 'Lekubu 72 km'. Follow this track, which will lead you to the route down the mainland between the two pans. You turn south and pass a small quarry, half a kilometre to the west of which is a good and well-used track and a T-junction. One branch heads north, back towards the main road, but ends in a small collection of huts before getting there. Turn southwest at that junction, for it is the track you seek. On this section, the object is to maintain a southerly course, but deviate to the east whenever forks or junctions give you a choice. You'll always recognise Sowa Pan when you see it! Keep it close on your left.

Gradually, the track turns south and you will soon find yourself in an elevated position on top of one of the long, low shorelines, immediately overlooking the pan, that mark the west side of Sowa. On a clear day you can see across the pan to the soda ash factory and, if the sun is in the west, the wash of colour over the pan and the scenery before you are quite superb. This elevated position is important; the views through the acacia trees characteristic of the route. If you don't see all this, then you're not on the right track! Work your way further east.

A key point, especially for those using this route from the south, is the blue-green-painted, minuscule 'small general dealer' store at Thabatshukudu. It is important to locate this and to take the correct route – otherwise Zoroga can end up as your final and unexpected destination (see Map 14, page 274).

Just under 10 km to the south of the store is the veterinary fence. To continue south will deliver you to Mmatshumo and, ultimately, the Francistown–Orapa road (74 km). To reach Kubu, bear left after 2 km. A further 3.2 km will take you to Kebetseng's cattle post from which, turning left again, it is 14.4 km to Kubu (Map 14 or 15, pages 274 or 275).

The third route south is really not very attractive. It threads its way between the two pans and is out of sight of both. Usually, one gets on to it in error – by straying too far west. It is a useful route, however, for people coming from the Maun direction. They turn south through the village of Zoroga on the main road. The track is firm, but in places exceptionally dusty, and impossible in the wet. In the dry, it bears a fine, black dust which once formed the old lake-bed on which you are travelling. The road is excessively braided and, in the absence of any landmarks, it's difficult to know quite where you are. Use the sun to help you keep heading south, and have the confidence to realise that nothing much can go wrong: you'll either hit a pan on the left, a pan on the right or the veterinary fence in front of you!

The village of Thabatshukudu is not signposted, nor has it any facilities (it is little more than a large cattle post) but is distinctive in its position – it's perched on a very low ridge. If you've come down the central route from Zoroga or thereabouts, it will be from this vicinity that you'll have your first clear view of Sowa Pan to the east.

Route 8, Option 2B
West Sowa Pan: Letlhakane to Kubu

DISTANCE: South to north, 83 km. **TIME:** 1.5 hours. **VEHICLE:** This section can be travelled in a pick-up vehicle but a 4x4 is strongly recommended. **MAPS:** Map 7 (page 267), Map 15 (page 275) and Map 28 (page 288); also Republic of Botswana 1:50 000 series, 2125 B1, B2 and 2025 D4; 1:250 000 series, sheet No 12 'Nata'; 1:250 000 series, sheet No 17 'Letlhakane'.

The starting point is at Letlhakane (for directions to Letlhakane see Route 7, page 160, and Map 7, page 267). From Letlhakane, take the gravel road for 12 km northeast, to the point where it crosses the Francistown–Orapa main tar road. Directly opposite is another gravel road that leads 22.7 km to Mmatshumo, which has a small general dealer and a bottle (liquor) store.

Just over 5 km north of this village the road abruptly becomes very stony and drops steeply. This is the highest and oldest of the great, ancient lake's shorelines. If you examine the stones under-foot you will see that they are all smooth and rounded – the remains of a former pebble beach! As you descend further towards the pans (especially at lower levels, and if you stop and look back) you'll notice a succession of shelf-like shorelines which mark progressive reductions in lake levels.

The road surface, before you reach the pan, leaves something to be desired. Lake-bed deposits are particularly fine and deep ruts have been worn in the track. Many alternative tracks have been created, and it is wise to make use of these to avoid the worst places. If you're in an ordinary vehicle, it is here that you will have the most trouble. In fact, when this section is wet, you can expect to have difficulty in any vehicle. At 15.3 km from Mmatshumo, you reach the edge of the pan, an obvious feature, easy to spot. A veterinary fence is in place 6 km on.

Once through the fence there is a further 7.4 km to the Kubu turn-off. I have not been here for some time but I suspect that this point is now marked in some distinctive way. Stone cairns come and go. The most reliable clue is to watch carefully for vehicle tracks heading out through the patches of grass, into the pan beyond. You have 19.5 km to go to Kubu Island, one of the most amazing camping places in the world (see below)!

Route 8, Option 3
Southern Sowa Pan

DISTANCES AND TIMES: Variable. **VEHICLE**: 4x4 highly recommended. **MAPS**: Map 7 (page 267), Map 15 (page 275) and Map 28 (page 288); also Republic of Botswana 1:50 000 series, 2125 B2, 2126 A1, A2; and 1:250 000 series, sheet No 17 'Letlhakane'.

An interesting route is that east from Mmatshumo for 34 km on a passable dirt road to the village of Mosu.

Mmatshumo, the starting point, is 22.7 km from the main Orapa–Francistown road. The junction is directly opposite the point where a gravel road leads 12 km south to join the Orapa–Serowe road at Letlhakane village (see Route 7, page 160, Map 7, page 267, and Map 15, page 275). The intersection is a major one and difficult to miss. It is 14.5 km west to Orapa's east gate and 216 km from Francistown, all of which is tarred. From Mosu it's a further 27 km on a similar road to the veterinary fence back on the main Francistown–Orapa road at Tlalamabele.

About 3 km to the west of Mosu, on top of a low hill overlooking Sowa Pan, is the small but beautiful and well-preserved Khami ruin known locally as **Mmakhama's**. Ask for directions; it's well worth visiting. From Mosu one can gain easy access to the southern end of Sowa Pan. On rough tracks it is possible to travel either east or west, meeting up with Maps 12 (page 272) and 15 (page 275) respectively. This is really out-of-the-way country. You are not likely to meet anyone, and you'll find yourself at liberty to wander where you will in perfect freedom.

ROUTE 9
Francistown to Maun

TOTAL DISTANCE: 497 km. **TIME**: 5 hours. **VEHICLE**: The road is tarred all the way. **MAPS**: Map 13 (page 273) and Map 16 (page 276); also Shell Tourist Map of Botswana.

Starting at Francistown, travel northwest along the main tarred road towards Kazungula. There are two veterinary fences to pass through before reaching Nata (190 km from Francistown). The first of these, the Dukwe fence, will be found at 132.6 km; the second (a new fence) is at 169.3 km. Nothing is required of you at these fences, except that they do provide you with information on where you've come from and where you're going to. Your vehicle registration number will be recorded. If you have a dog with you, you must produce a veterinary permit authorising its movement about the country (see page 181). The turn-off to Botswana's Sowa Pan Soda Ash project, to the west, is signposted at 142 km from Francistown.

Just after the second veterinary fence is **Nata Sanctuary** (see Route 8, Option 3: Southern Sowa Pan, and page 181). At 11.3 km beyond the fence is **Nata Lodge**, a haven for long-distance travellers (181 km from Francistown or 9 km out of Nata). Apart from a welcome pool, a bar and excellent meals, there is also good accommodation in chalets and for campers.

It is at Nata that one turns left and begins the 307 km journey to Maun. This is the last petrol station before Gweta, 100 km further to the west. Nata is also a good place to fill up with water.

The tarmac road to Maun is a delight to drive on (but, at night, do be aware of vehicles parked without lights on the verges, and of cattle on the road – especially in winter when the road's radiated warmth attracts them). If you are planning to drive southwest along the 'Ntwetwe Finger' to Gabasadi (Map 10, page 270), your turn-off onto the pan is at 51 km from Nata. A place I've never explored (but, like so many other things, 'always mean to') is to turn north here. It was at the northern extremity of this pan that two young pilots landed their aircraft when it ran out of fuel. They were on a training flight from Bulawayo during World War II, and apparently surprised some Bushmen, who might have been illegally hunting giraffe, and were murdered by them. A number of San were arrested and tried but the evidence was too circumstantial and they were released. Later the plane was recovered, refuelled and flown back to Bulawayo.

At the 99-km mark is a signposted left turn to Gweta, where there is water, petrol, a general dealer, a safari camp and a bottle (liquor) store. It is also an access point for the Makgadikgadi Pans and grasslands (see Map 10, page 270).

An interesting point is that at 199 km from Nata (Map 16, page 276). Here, the road cuts through the **Gidikwe Sand Ridge**, and road engineers have built a short off-ramp that takes you to the crest, which offers a magnificent view. Do drive to the top and have a look. Apart from the view, one gains a sense of the size of the old lake, for everything to the east of you once lay under water. Climb onto the roof of your vehicle, if you can, and look both north and south. You can see the ridge of sand – an off-shore barrier beach – stretching away in either direction.

At 59 km from Maun you will be stopped at the Makalamabedi veterinary fence (the gate is manned 24 hours a day). All facilities are available in **Maun** – good shops, fresh meat and vegetables, fuel, health services, international communications, hotels and camp grounds (see page 221).

ROUTE 10
Makgadikgadi to Nxai Pan National Park, from the Nata–Maun road

(Makgadikgadi grasslands)
DISTANCE AND TIME: Variable. **VEHICLE**: 4x4 essential in places. **MAPS**: Map 16 (page 276) and Map 17 (page 277). **MAKGADIKGADI/NXAI PROFILE**: page 123.

There are three entrances to this section of the now-combined national park (see Map 17, page 277), which consists of the former Makgadikgadi Pans Game Reserve and Nxai Pan National Park. There are two manned entrances, at Xhumaga in the west and at Makolwane in the north, just to the south of the Nata–Maun road, and a third entrance from the south. The latter isn't official but is likely to be manned in years to come and, for many travellers, it's convenient, so for the time being persons using this southern entrance will be required, on exiting, to obtain the appropriate permit at one of the other gates.

The most commonly used gate is Makolwane. The turn-off to it is 140.7 km from Nata and 165 km from Maun. The permit office itself is 8 km south of the main road. At both entrances there's a painted map board, and I advise visitors to note down the details shown thereon (we in Botswana are still some way from being able to guarantee a reliable supply of maps for visitors, but you should receive copies of maps with your confirmation slip). Remember that *campsites have to be booked and paid for in advance* (see page 207).

To explore the park, begin at Makolwane game scouts' camp (where you will enter; a turn-off after a few hundred metres goes a short distance to an artificial waterhole – well worth spending a few hours at).

Travel 14 km southwest, at which point there is a T-junction (unsignposted) to your left. The route straight on will take you to Xhumaga, the Boteti River (check at the entrance gate to establish if the river has water in it) and its riverine forest. Turn left, and after a further 6.2 km (during which you may have noticed the **Njuga Hills** looming above the scrub to the southeast) you will reach a second T-junction. If you turn left here it is but a short distance to Njuga Hills and the astonishing views that unfold from them. The dominant tree on this massive ancient dune is *Albizia anthelmintica*, a species rarely occurring in South Africa but common on the watershed in Zimbabwe. Its bark is known from Namibia to Somalia and Ethiopia as an anthelmintic (cure for worms).

If you wish to return to the main road from Njuga via a different route, drive east from the hills for 11 km. This will bring you to a distinct group of palm trees, known as Makolwane a ga Wateka, and to what appears to be a T-junction with one track continuing to the east (it goes 40–50 km to Gweta but it is not a very good track) and another turning north. Take the latter which, after 12 km, will deliver you to the old main road. Turn left (west) and, after 3.2 km, you will be back at the Makolwane game scouts' camp. As a matter of interest, there used to be a cut-line leading south from these palm trees into the northwest corner of the area I call 'The Land of a Thousand Islands' (see Ntwetwe Pan, page 126). I've not been able to see it easily from the ground but I flew over the trees in August 1995 and the track to the south was still plain. You might like to look for it, and to explore this incredible area (but make sure you have your maps with you).

If you do not wish to visit Njuga, turn right at the T-junction mentioned and travel southwest and south for about 16 km. This will bring you to a third turn-off to the left (south). Take this turn-off and drive due south along the cut-line for 43 km.

On the way you'll pass Nomad Pan, named after a vehicle once abandoned there, many years ago. At the end of the 43 km will be another turn to the left. Take this and you will shortly be out of the park and into cattle country. After some 27 to 33 somewhat trying kilometres (distance depends on which of the many tracks you follow southward) you'll reach the tarmac between Mopipi and Rakops, at a point 19.5 km from Mopipi (see Map 8, page 268). Turn left for Mopipi.

Approaching this route from Mopipi and the south, one needs to be aware of several sharp right-angle bends (which confound, especially, the night-time motorist) encountered when travelling west, soon after you leave the petrol station at Mopipi behind. At 19,5 km you will discern a track to the right (north), which is not signposted. A low, rusty sign is on the left-hand side of the turning. It has nothing written or marked on it, and you need to be watching carefully to locate it.

ROUTE 11

Nxai Pan from Nata–Maun road and Baines' Baobabs

DISTANCE: Variable. **TIME**: From main road to entrance, 1.5 hours. **VEHICLE**: 4x4 essential. **MAPS**: Map 16 (page 276) and Map 17 (page 277). **NXAI PAN PROFILE**: page 124.

The turn-off to Nxai Pan National Park is from the main Nata–Maun road, about 165 km from Nata and 140 km from Maun. The sandy track that leads 37 km to the park gate is in an execrable state; it always has been bad but it is now (November 2000) worse than I have ever known it. It takes an hour and twenty minutes or more to the gate – and it is only that quick because the last 12.5 km are on broken calcrete, where speeds of up to 50 or 60 km/h are possible. For the rest, it is mostly low-ratio, first-gear work. Be warned! In fact I am told that there are plans to build a new access road, but I've heard no date so don't hold your breath!

Starting north up the track, you will reach a crossroads at 18.9 km (as a matter of interest, this is one of the original Nata–Maun routes, known then as the 'Wenela Road'; I think there have been three others since). Going north, the track continues for another, slightly less agonising 18.4 km to the Nxai Pan gate. Remember, you need to *book and pay in advance* for a campsite in this national park. The staff will direct you to your campsite. Remember to examine, and make notes on, the map of the park which is on the wall in the entrance hut.

There is a better way to the park gate, and a much quicker one for those approaching from the east. This route is longer for those coming from the west but is kinder on the vehicle and takes about the same time. For details of this route see the approach to Baines' Baobabs below.

Access to **Baines' Baobabs** (Map 17; page 277). The vicinity of Baines' Baobabs has become increasingly popular, but note that it is now no longer possible to camp at the trees (although camping near them is allowed). The crossroads described above, 18.9 km north along the Nxai Pan track, is the official access route for Baines' Baobabs. As is illustrated in Map 17, turn east here and drive for 0.9 km to a fork in the road. You can go either left or right at this fork but the latter is recommended. The road leads 11 km directly to the baobabs on a fair surface.

The alternative route is longer (17 km, and requires that you know where to make a right turn after 13.3 km), and less comfortable, but vital for the wet season when the shorter route may be flooded or too wet for safe travel.

The disadvantage of this route is its notorious first 18.9 km. There is, however, another much better route that is also, for those approaching from the east and south, much shorter (see Map 17, page 277). Turn north for 19 km along the western boundary of Odiakwe Ranch (132.3 km from Nata); then turn left (west) onto the old Nata–Maun road for 16.3 km. At that point you will see a well-used track turning to the south and to Baines' Baobabs, 3.7 km away.

This route saves 'easterners' a total of 24 km and about an hour in time. Motorists approaching from the west will have to travel an extra 40 km, of which 32 km are on tar. However, I suspect they may agree that the longer approach is the better choice.

As mentioned above, this is, of course, also a way of getting to Nxai Pan itself, and one that will avoid the worst of the present access road.

ROUTE 12
Ghanzi to Maun

TOTAL DISTANCE: About 280 km. **TIME**: 3 hours. **VEHICLE**: ordinary saloon. **MAP**: Shell Tourist Map of Botswana.

This road is being tarred and should be completed by mid-2001. At the time of writing (November 2000), the tar from Ghanzi has reached the gate at the Kuke vet fence. It is from Ghanzi that one can visit the famous **Bushman Centre** at D'Kar, 38 km north on the Maun road, or 245 km south of Maun (see page 98). On the same road, 25 km north of Ghanzi, is **Dqãe Qare Game Farm** (page 115), owned and staffed by San.

Until Kuke, one is passing through the Ghanzi freehold farms. Kuke Gate is manned 24 hours a day; only basic information is required by the attendant, and you'll need a permit if you have a dog with you. At this point one is diverted onto the old gravel road to Toteng (which is being maintained in good condition) where you rejoin the existing tarmac road.

In the meantime, from Kuke, the new tarred route turns a little to the north and goes direct to Sehithwa on the north side of Lake Ngami, where it joins the existing main road. From Sehithwa, turn northeast for 99 km to Maun or northwest to the western side of the Okavango Delta.

ROUTE 13, Part 1
Okwa River East

This route is described in two parts, as follows:
DISTANCE: Plus-minus 150 km. **TIME**: 2–3 days. **VEHICLE**: 4x4 essential. **MAPS**: Map 5 (page 265) and Map 24 (page 284); also Republic of Botswana, 1:250 000 series, sheet SF 34-11 'Hanahai', sheet 21 'Okwa'.

No formal road or track exists down any part of the Okwa – this is a wilderness route. One can enter it at any point along its length and travel, with varying degrees of comfort and convenience, to any other. The following is suggested as a

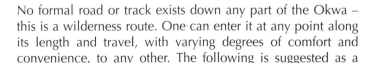

sample of what can be done; once you have the experience and the idea, try a section of your own choice. In my experience, there is no substantial part of the river that cannot be traversed. This route goes from the Kang–Ghanzi road to the boundary of the **Central Kalahari Game Reserve** (CKGR).

Turn off the main road at a point 183 km north of Kang at GPS 22.24.09S/22.43.41E (Clarke 1880). Travel 12.3 km down this gravel road to its intersection with the old main road. Directly opposite you, a narrow track leads onwards to the east. Take it. Distances are measured from this junction. There will be a large quarry on your right and the track goes directly and shortly to a fenced cattle post. You will find a track passing round the enclosed area to its south. It's rough, but follow it, and after passing the farm you will find yourself on an excellent sand track. This continues down the Okwa for 50 km and is the most magnificent of drives.

At 6.5 km you will find an excellent campsite and some rather interesting petroglyphs. At this point, on the north bank, just below the highest part of the bank, there is a wide sheet of basalt in which some 44 grooves have been cut. The position of the point is GPS 22.24.37 S/21.53.33 E (Clarke 1880 datum)

A faint north–south cut-line bisects the track at 30.3 km (GPS 22.24.14S/22.04.58E; I have not explored this feature) and at about 44 km a large tributary appears to join the main river from the south. At approximately 50 km, the track turns somewhat abruptly out of the river and climbs the south bank towards a ridge. Before reaching the crest, it turns back on itself and plunges into the riverbed once more. From this point on the track markedly deteriorates, becoming very sandy and overgrown. At 59 km, still in the riverbed, it all but vanishes at an unused borehole marked 3359 at GPS 22.25.01S/ 22.18.40E. From this point on you have to find your own way down the river, through the bush. There is no track to speak of.

At 125 km, you reach the boundary of the Central Kalahari Game Reserve (GPS 22.22.33S/22.47.52E). In the same valley to the south, and within 2 km, are two boreholes with pumps. These supply water via a pipeline to the new Xade settlement further north. There is a tap on the boundary track near the boreholes and (if all is in working order) you may be able to obtain water here. In April 1998 this water was potable.

It is illegal to enter the CKGR at this point and thus you need to turn north on the track along the boundary until you get to the main Ghanzi–Xade road after an estimated 10–15 km (I have not actually driven the stretch). From this point you can either continue into the CKGR and exit via Deception Valley or Khutse, or return to Ghanzi.

Route 13, Part 2
Okwa River West

DISTANCE: About 200 km. **TIME**: 2–3 days. **VEHICLE**: 4x4 essential. **MAPS**: Map 5 (page 265) and Map 25, (page 285); also Republic of Botswana, 1:500 000 series, sheet 6, 'Kang'; 1:250 000 series, sheet SF 34-11 'Hanahai', sheet SF 34.10/14 'Mamumo'. The following maps are very useful even though they cover only the western half of the route: Republic of Botswana, 1:100 000 series, sheets 2220A and 2220B 'Xanagas Farms A and B'. A GPS and maps are highly recommended.

Turn west off the main road at a point 183 km north of Kang at GPS 22.24.18.8S/22.43.46.2E (Clarke 1880). The aim is to use existing tracks to follow the valley floor. We found that the local farmers who use this route are usually more interested in getting from one place to another directly rather than exploring the river. For this reason, the track will often climb suddenly out of the valley, only to drop back into it again later after 'cutting off' a loop or bend. This is confusing at first but one soon gets a feel for it. Use your common sense, plus maps and a GPS, and you won't get lost. About 17 km from the start, there is a very clear crossing of the Okwa at GPS 22.20.24S/21.37.37E, .

An important point is reached near GPS 22.26.38S/ 21.19.54.01E. Here a major tributary comes in from the north and the track splits. I suspect the well-used northwestern track will go, eventually, to the Mamuno main road but I have not yet checked it out. Continue southwest, following the Okwa. There is a rather nice campsite, at GPS 22.20.16S/21.05.04E, in a small clump of trees. Firewood is not plentiful around this place so you need to have been collecting it along the final 0–15 km.

There is a large and very interesting cattle post about 3 km to the west of this clump of trees, at GPS 22.20.55S/21.03.34E, and a good supply of very pleasant-tasting water. The route to follow lies along the valley but you'll encounter a fence right across the river at GPS 22.24.19.5S/20.42.23.6E. At first sight this is something of a blow – until one discovers that a 50–m section of the fence has been removed (many years ago) 200 m from the river on the south bank (GPS 22.24.38.1S/ 20.43.26E). Drive through here and resume your journey through the valley.

In the unlikely event that this fence has been or ever will be repaired (it has stood like this for some 15 years, we were told), then all is not lost. Go back, east along the Okwa, for about 6 km to the last big cattle post (either Makgabalo or Nxogodimo) and ask for the road to Tsawe village. We later passed a sign at Tsawe that told us it was a good sand road and that it was 13 km to these cattle posts. As we continued west along the Okwa, to our absolute surprise, we came across a large village, complete with police station and school, perched high on the south bank. It appeared on no maps but proved to be a new San settlement called Tsawe (GPS 22.25.26S/20.39.18E).

The main road west leads out of this village, crosses a major tributary coming into the Okwa from the south, and climbs the steep bank on the opposite side, passing through a gate in a fence as it does so. We believe this good road continues west to Makunda and can be used to get there if you're in a hurry. We chose to turn right, immediately on passing through the fence, followed it a few metres, and then turned left once more to travel along the Okwa.

From this point on there was little difficulty in following the river until we reached a cattle post at GPS 22.23.27.5S/ 20.17.57.6E. Here, as the map indicated, we could find no way through along the river and so took the main (at that point) north–south sand road to the north. We arrived at Makunda after taking care to follow every reasonable left-turning intersection. From this village, seek out the wrecked white truck body on the south bank of the river, on the west side of the village beyond the houses, and locate the faint track that heads west from there. Follow this west to the border. There is a very nice camp in the bed of the Okwa, 2 km north of where you strike the Botswana/Namibia border at GPS 22.25.20.4S/19.59.58.7E.

It is a short (about 15 km) drive north to the Mamuno border post. Follow the track when it curves away to the east at the border. It will eventually lead you to the back gate of the Customs and Immigration residential quarters. The gate is not locked. Go through it to the main road. An Engen filling station, where you can also get ice-cold drinks, lies just 6 km to the east.

Those attempting the journey the other way will find the government quarters immediately west of the fence that crosses the main road, some 700 m from the border post. Enter the grounds and drive to the back (at the east end), where you will find the gate.

ROUTE 14

Maun to Lake Ngami

TOTAL DISTANCE: About 120 km. **TIME**: 1.5 hours. **VEHICLE**: 4x4 essential if you intend going off-road. **MAPS**: Map 18 (page 278); also Shell Tourist Map of Botswana. **LAKE NGAMI PROFILE**: page 121.

If you are going to explore the Lake Ngami area and embark on a lot of off-road travel, the heavy sand in the west and east (and elsewhere) make it essential that you have four-wheel-drive. Remember that the lake is presently dry and has been so for many years now. There does not seem to be any immediate prospect of this situation changing, although a trickle of water reached it in 2000.

There are two approaches to the lake, one from the east and the other from the west. Both involve travelling from Maun to Toteng, a distance of 65 km, now fully tarred. At the latter village there is a road to the left, which crosses the Lake River and turns southwest towards Ghanzi (Route 12, page 187). You can try and make your way along the banks of the Lake River from this point. The best way, however, is to ignore the Toteng turning and continue on another 30-odd kilometres to the village of Sehithwa.

From Sehithwa, according to Geoff Tucker, the best way down onto the lake is via a track from the 'Three-way Trading Store' at the old crossroads in the village. The track starts to the left and behind the store and runs in an easterly direction, right across the lake and out the other side, over some very sandy dunes. It eventually links up with the gravelled Ghanzi road on the east side of the old lake, and will lead you back to Toteng and Maun or, in the opposite direction, to Kuke Gate and Ghanzi. It's an interesting and enjoyable drive across the lake. There is much to see in this area, so feel free to explore where you will.

The **Dautsa Ridge**, at the west end of the Lake Ngami basin, is another offshore barrier beach associated with the paleo-lake Makgadikgadi and to the west of the ridge are the Dautsa Flats, equally fascinating.

ROUTE 15
Maun to Drotsky's Cave

TOTAL DISTANCE: 273 km. **TIME**: 6.5–7.5 hours. **VEHICLE**: 4x4 essential. **MAPS**: Map 18 (page 278) and Map 19 (page 279); also Republic of Botswana, 1:250000 series, sheet 5 'Nokaneng'; 1:250000 series, sheet No SF-34-3 'Tsau'; Shell Tourist Map of Botswana. **DROTSKY'S CAVE PROFILE**: page 110.

The easiest route by which to reach these caves is from Maun, via Sehithwa and Tsao. The whole of the western side of the Delta is tarred to Mohembo and so getting to Tsao, the turning-off point for Drotsky's, is much faster than before (see Map 18, page 278). If one is starting from Gaborone it is actually shorter to travel via Ghanzi and Sehithwa, the road being now all tarred.

At 10.4 km past the turning (northeast) to the village of Tsao, and the microwave tower, you will see a turn-off to the left (Map 19, page 279). It is not marked with any sign. From the turning, the track is sand for 133.5 km to the lower cave entrance. A four-wheel-drive vehicle is essential. Fold your wing mirrors back at this point!

The first third of the journey passes through wooded, undulating, sand country, without any distinct pattern in the low dunes. This area was once flooded and part of the Okavango. Later you will come upon more distinct and larger fossil dunes in a regular pattern. They mark the furthest reaches of the once far more extensive Delta (Map 19, page 279). From here the sand can be heavy and the undulating going somewhat slow.

The journey from Tsao will take you 5–6 hours. An important junction not to miss is the signposted turning, which reads 'Xhaba Borehole', at 91 km from Tsau or 81 km from the start of the track. This is a short-cut to the caves that saves 35 km and an hour-and-a-half in time. Turn left here. This route will take you past the borehole, an equal distance beyond it to the Gcwihaba River and the caves beside it.

The longer route is more arduous but worth doing, even if one is not going to Caecae. At 152 km, after crossing a particularly sandy dune, look out for a magnificent view over to the west. About 30 km away to the northwest you will see the Aha Hills. On the downhill slope there is a bush track that follows the river valley for 27 km to Drotsky's Cave. Continue straight on at this point for 9,6 km to Caecae.

It is interesting to note that as Botswana's elephant population continues to multiply that these animals are becoming more and more commonly seen. I was in the caves in early 2001 and saw spoor at the entrance and some of the animals themselves whilst travelling to and from them. At that time, also, the resident leopard at Gcwihaba was also, definitely, in residence!

ROUTE 16
Drotsky's Cave to Aha Hills

TOTAL DISTANCE: 47 km. **TIME**: 2 hours. **VEHICLE**: 4x4 essential. **MAPS**: Map 18 (page 278) and Map 19 (page 279); also Republic of Botswana, 1:250000 series, sheet 5 'Nokaneng'; 1:250000 series, sheet No SF-34-3 'Tsau'; Shell Tourist Map of Botswana. **AHA HILLS PROFILE**: page 103.

The Aha Hills can be reached from the main Maun–Shakawe road. The easiest route is to turn off at the Drotsky's Cave turning, just north of the village of Tsao. (For details of the first section, see Route 15: Maun–Drotsky's Cave, Maps 18 and 19.)

Continue on that track for 153 km to the turn-off to Drotsky's Cave, beyond which the village of Caecae is about 9,6 km. At this village the road turns north to the Hills 10 km away.

You can also get into the Hills from further west by driving 9,2 km west of Caecae and turning north along the border fence on a perfectly adequate and frequently used track. Regardless of which route you take into the Hills, it is possible to return via Quangwa and Dobe in the north. To do this, on either road, drive north for about 50 km. After that distance, the border track turns due east for 20 km past and takes you to Dobe and beyond it to Quangwa. On the more easterly track, the one that led directly from Caecae, you will come to a T-junction. Turn west to Dobe or east for Quangwa and a direct track to Nokaneng. The 160-odd kilometres to Nokaneng is now gravelled but is not a particularly comfortable drive. A four-wheel-drive vehicle is not a necessity, however.

ROUTE 17
Maun to Tsodilo

DISTANCES AND TIMES: Via Sepopa: 365 km, time: 5–6 hours; via Ncamaseri: 385 km, time: 6–7 hours; Shakawe to Tsodilo: 68 km, time: 3 hours. **VEHICLE**: 4x4 essential. **MAPS**: Map 18 (page 278); also Republic of Botswana, 1:250000, sheet 1 'Tsodilo'; 1:100000 series, sheet 1821D; Shell Tourist Map of Botswana. **TSODILO HILLS PROFILE**: page 141.

There are now three tracks to Tsodilo, two from the south, and one from the north. All lead from the fully tarred Maun–Shakawe road on the west of the Delta (see Map 18, page 278). A four-wheel-drive vehicle is essential for Tsodilo access from this road, however.

From Maun to the nearest turn-off at Sepopa is 320 km; the last petrol is at Etsha-6. The turn-off is signposted with the National Museum's zebra logo and is 0.6 km *before* Sepopa. It is 57 km to the Hills. The first part of the journey, 32.4 km, is on a firm bush track. It is advisable to remove, or fold in, your wing mirrors. Just after halfway you will encounter dune country – the valley floors are hard and driving is easy, but the route lies diagonally across the trend of dunes and a number of them must be crossed. The sand on the dunes can be very thick and loose. The last 24.6 km is exceptionally sandy and slow. Total time from Sepopa turn-off to the Hills can be anything from two to three hours.

A route generally considered much better is that 25.5 km north of Sepopa: you'll find it exactly 2.2 km *before* the Ncamaseri turn-off and some 300 m before a sign on the left side of the road indicating 'Shakawe 32 km'. For a GPS reference of this important junction, see Map 18 (page 278).

If you turn and face the track you will notice a lone tree to its left, the palisade of a village to the right and a rough track behind you; there is no sign. It is 39 km to the Hills from here. This route is slightly longer but the additional mileage is on tar, the route itself is shorter (39 km) and my experience suggests it is the better surface (though still not great). This is now the recommended route.

Those approaching from the north should note that the old Shakawe route (turn-off some 8 km south of the village) is no more, and has been replaced by an appalling alternative. Barry Pryce from Shakawe now drives down to the Ncamaseri track, which he finds faster although longer.

If you want to try the Shakawe alternative as you are coming from the north, do not take the track opposite Shakawe Fishing Camp (the old starting point). Instead, drive 5.5 km south on the tar until you hit the Samochima fence. This was a new veterinary fence erected as an emergency measure to stop the spread of cattle lung disease in Botswana's national herd. Infection broke out in the area north of the fence and the idea was to contain the disease at this front line. The Thamacha fence, through which one passes between Etsha-13 and Sepopa, marks the perimeter of a still larger 'containment area'. The disease has now passed. In the end the government oversaw the slaughter of all the cattle in Ngamiland – over 250 000 animals. But cattle numbers are building up again.

Pass through the Samochima fence, turn west and follow it until you pick up the old road again on your left. But the route is not recommended – not only is it longer (about 54 km of sand) but it is also extremely tough driving. You will have a foretaste of what lies in wait by looking at the sand facing you as you turn off the tar road onto the south side of Samochima.

Note that Shakawe village has a clinic, several stores and small supermarkets as well as good telephone contact with the rest of Botswana. There is no petrol in the village. Customs and Immigration now operate in Mohembo, at the border itelf.

ROUTE 18
Maun–Moremi–Savute

DISTANCES AND TIMES: By-passing Moremi: 183 km, time: 3–5 hours; via Moremi: 229 km, time: 5–8 hours (including grand tour of Moremi); total distance plus-minus 350 km. **VEHICLE**: 4x4 recommended. **MAPS**: Map 23 (Maun– Moremi–Savute–Kasane, page 283); also Republic of Botswana, Chobe, 1:350 000 and Okavango Delta, 1:350 000; Shell Maps of Moremi and Chobe by Veronica Roodt; Shell Tourist Map of Botswana. **MOREMI PROFILE**: page 125. **MAUN PROFILE**: page 98. **MOREMI GAME RESERVE PROFILE**: page 125. **CHOBE PROFILE**: page 109. **SAVUTE PROFILE**: page 133.

Some people manage this route in an ordinary vehicle but this is not recommended. There are no facilities for the general public, and no fuel, but water is obtainable.

For directions to Maun, see Route 9, Francistown to Maun (page 181) and Maps 13 (page 273) and 16 (page 276). It is not in the scope of this book to provide detailed maps of national parks as these are usually available from the Department of Wildlife. For this reason, only a large map of this section is included. For more detail, consult the *Shell maps* of Moremi and Chobe by Veronica Roodt, available in Botswana and South Africa. I am grateful to these maps and to Ms Roodt for verifying certain information. There is little I can add to them except the GPS references on Map 23 (page 283).

Remember, no campsites are available in Moremi or Chobe unless *booked and paid for in advance*.

All the roads in this section are sand except for a tarred stretch between Maun and Shorobe. After this point the surface is mostly sand or clay which, in places, can be very slippery when wet. Crossing the Mababe Depression, when the 'black-cotton' soil there is wet, is extremely difficult.

The most direct route to Savute (but one which avoids all the fun) is to head northeast out of Maun on the tarred road to Shorobe (28 km; distances are calculated from the last traffic circle in Maun, near Crocodile Camp). At Shorobe it is possible to purchase high-quality locally woven baskets.

Beyond Shorobe, and 9 km from it, is a fork to the left. This leads past San-ta-wani to the Moremi South Gate, but the road is exceptionally sandy, the going slow and it is not recommended. Continue beyond Shorobe to where the tar ends 2 km further on (30 km from Maun) and you will arrive, after an additional 19.4 km and 49.4 km from Maun, at the Buffalo fence.

There is a critical junction 1.8 km beyond the fence. To the left is the main route to Moremi South Gate (34 km) and the **Moremi Wildlife Reserve**. For Savute, however, continue north to Zankuyo village (24 km), 1 km beyond which the road splits. Either choice will get you to Mababe Gate and Savute but the right fork is recommended as this will lead to Mababe village (30 km) and avoid the difficulties of Magwikhwe Sand Ridge.

You will have to turn west out of the village and, after crossing the cut-line of Chobe National Park, turn north again. From Mababe village to Savute is 77 km. At 10 km north of Mababe Gate in the Chobe National Park, the road splits. Both roads go to Savute; the right-hand route is about 8 km longer and passes the margin of what used to be Savute Marsh.

The public campsite at Savute is undergoing reconstruction. Check with the Department of Wildlife in Maun (tel 686-1265, fax 686-1264) before laying elaborate plans that include staying there. If you choose to pass through Moremi you will arrive at the manned South Gate, where there is a public campsite.

From South Gate, there are two routes. The first (and more leisurely) is a drive around the Moremi peninsula to North Gate. Mboma (plus-minus 50 km) is the western extremity. Continuing the circular drive you will come to Third Bridge and Xakanaxa before arriving at North Gate (Khwai), having covered a total distance of about 120 km.

The shorter, more direct route is from South Gate directly to North Gate (30 km), crossing a wooden bridge over the River Khwai just before the exit. From North Gate the road turns east for 40 km and joins up with the main road from Maun to Savute. About 34 km from North Gate you will come to the **Magwikhwe Sand Ridge**. This fascinating feature (best seen in the vicinity of Savute) is a relic barrier beach from the time of

Botswana's super-lake (see page 133). Its summit stands at the highest level ever reached by the lake: 945 m above sea level. But the immediate problem is to cross it and a 4x4 is needed: the sand is especially deep and soft as you negotiates the ridge. Beyond it the road descends to the hard surface of Mababe Depression and you should have no further problems. It is some 12 km from the eastern foot of the ridge to the park boundary.

The South Gate of Chobe National Park (also manned from dawn to dusk) is 58 km from Savute. As at Moremi, there is an entrance fee. The only official camping place is the public campsite on the banks of the Savute Channel.

ROUTE 19
Savute to Kasane

DISTANCES AND TIMES*: Via Nogatsha: 195 km, time: 6-8 hours; via Kachebabwe: 164 km, time: 6–8 hours. **VEHICLE***: 4x4 essential. **MAPS***: Map 23 (Maun–Moremi–Savute–Kasane, page 283); also Republic of Botswana, 1:350 000 'Chobe'; Shell Map of Chobe by Veronica Roodt; Shell Tourist Map of Botswana. **KASANE PROFILE***: page 102.

It is not in the scope of this guidebook to provide detailed maps of national parks since these are usually available from the Department of Wildlife. For this reason, only a large-scale map of this section is included here (page 198). For more detail I recommend the *Shell Map of Chobe* by Veronica Roodt, which is widely available in Botswana and in South Africa. I am grateful to that map and to Ms Roodt for verifying certain information.

Two routes lead from Savute and the Mababe Depression northwards towards Kasane. Most take the more northerly one, which, although it is the shorter, is far more difficult because of its long stretches of deep sand. It does not appear to save time.

The longer but generally easier route from Savute is eastward via Ngwezumba Dam. Not only do you see more of the park and, at certain times of the year, very much more game, but the sand road is often good, particularly after rain, and invariably better than the deep, loose sand of the western route. But *be warned*: the nature of roads in this part of the world is exceedingly variable; always expect the worst. To follow this route, start at the crossing of the Savute Channel itself and take the main road north, past the signposted turning to Linyanti. Shortly – just after crossing an old and faintly discernible river channel – turn right to what is known as Harvey's, or Khearoga, Pan (going north here is the 'direct' route that passes through Kachekabwe and Ngoma Bridge on the way to Kasane). Continue east, passing Quarry Hill – which you can see clearly from the pan – on your left.

At the 35-km point from where you turned off to Harvey's Pan, another track joins yours from the right, and you now begin to swing increasingly northeast. Within 20 km, you start to follow the dry bed of the Ngwezumba River. After 114 km from the start you reach a signposted junction. If you turn right here, you enter the complex of roads around Ngwezumba Dam, and will have access to Tchinga and Nogatsha campsites.

To get to Kasane by the most direct route, do not turn right but continue straight on. After 22 km you will come to a second intersection, where a right turn will also give access to Nogatsha and Tchinga. Continue straight for 36 km until you arrive at Nantanga Pans, 1 km beyond which is the main road from Kasane to Ngoma Bridge. Turn right for Kasane (22 km) or continue straight on to reach Chobe River (10 km).

ROUTE 20
The Hunter's Road (another adventure!)

This route is profiled in two parts. **DISTANCES AND TIMES**: See individual sections. **VEHICLE**: Note that a 4x4 is essential, although not at all times and in all places. **WARNING**: Under no circumstances, unless you are a complete nut, attempt this road at the height of the rainy season. If there is standing water on flat ground, the route will be impassable. The timing of your visit is also critical to success: if it's too wet, you can't get through, if it's too late in the year, the pans will be dry and there will be no game. April/May through to July is probably the best time. **MAPS**: Map 20 (page 280), Map 21 (page 281) and Map 22 (page 282). Also refer to other maps as recommended in the separate parts. **HUNTER'S ROAD PROFILE**: page 114.

Route 20, Part 1
Hunter's Road: Nata to Mpandamatenga

DISTANCE: 239.2 km. **TIME**: Minimum 1 day (if you're lucky); recommended time 2–3 days. **MAPS**: Map 20 (page 280) and Map 21 (page 281); also Republic of Botswana, 1:250 000 series, sheet 12 'Nata', sheet 8 'Basutos', sheet 4 'Kasane' (not absolutely necessary, but fun if you are into maps); 1:50 000 series, 1926 C1, 1926 A3, 1925 B2, 1825 D4 and 1825 D1.

Begin at the high-level bridge in Nata and take the tarmac road to Kazungula. You cross a remarkable grassed pan at 30 km and reach a veterinary fence at 60.2 km. Four kilometres after this, a sign indicates 'Ngwasha Veterinary Camp' to the right (names and spellings are always a problem in Botswana; the place is referred to as both Ngwasha and Ngwahla). Turn right and, at about 14.5 km, take the right fork which will lead you to a T-junction, on the border track, about 23 km from the tar. At this point the border is fenced – it is just over a metre high and includes two steel cable strands. I don't know why, as it extends only for about a kilometre north, but that's Africa for you.

Turning north, the first part of this route is sand but the last third is 'black-cotton' soil into which, when it's wet, your vehicle will sink like a stone into quicksand. The soil needs at least five or six days of hot sun to dry out. Average speed on the sandy track (which was damp on both my visits) was about 10 km/h for the first 40 km. At 41 km from Ngwahla (or Ngwasha) a firm track from the southeast joins the border road on which you are travelling. I have not investigated this joining road, but from here on the border track improved greatly and speeds of 20–25 km/h were possible all the way to Mpandamatenga. I engaged four-wheel-drive only twice and then only for a few minutes. The vegetation is varied, but look out for the Baikiaea woodlands, notably those at 5 km and 12 km from Ngwahla.

There are beautiful pans to be seen all the way. You reach Tamafupa after 27 km; at just over 34 km from the start is the group known collectively as Domtshetshu Pan. A little more than 200 m north of the 41-km junction with the road from the southwest, on the east side, is a feature rather unromantically called 'Cement Pan'. I do not know how it won this unfitting name for, when it has water in it, it is indeed a beautiful sight.

Then follow, in succession, Kidney Pan (the name reflects its shape), Stoffel's Pan (200 m into Zimbabwe; I didn't visit it), Leadwood Pan (five leadwood trees, including one to the north, four to the east), Hendrick's Vlei (three leadwoods to the north, one to the south), Tibukai Pan (a small, circular mud-hole), and Jolley's Pan (there's a pair of tall mopane trees to the southwest).

North of Jolley's Pan, you leave the sandveld country behind. Dune crests are replaced by a rocky substrate (decomposing basalt) that offers firm, fast and easy driving; the valleys that now start to appear are filled with black-cotton soil – *lethal* when wet! As you rise north out of Jolley's, you'll find a large tree on the left, which provides a nice spot for lunch and gives you time to regroup before tackling the first vlei. After this comes Cream of Tartar Pan (six mopane trees on the west side). **Note:** at a point 6 km north of Cream of Tartar Pan is an *important junction.* If you turn southwest here you can reach the main tarred road at a point 161 km from Nata (and 137 km from Kazungula) after a drive of 23.2 km. From the main road, the microwave tower is a good indicator of the turn-off.

From this junction on the Hunter's Road onwards – the remaining 40-odd kilometres to Mpandamatenga – the route is alternately hard basalt and soft black soil. Watch out for Border Beacon BB620 and the magnificent view from its ridge crest as you reach the watershed of Deka River. Dawdle along the rest of this route, for it is beautiful scenery. Before reaching Mpandamatenga, find the place where George and his wife 'must' have bathed on their journey home (George Westbeech pioneered this route to the Zambezi and Barotseland beyond in the1870s); view the stand of acacia (*Acacia polyacantha*) just before reaching Mpandamatenga. Notice the track to the west just before you get to the border post, and turn there onto the road.

Route 20, Part 2

Hunter's Road: Mpandamatenga to Kazungula

DISTANCE: 102 km. **TIME:** Minimum 2.5 hours; recommended 1 day. **MAPS:** Maps 20 (page 280) and 22 (page 282); also Republic of Botswana, 1:250 000 series, sheet 4 'Kasane'.

This is a much easier and much more forgiving trip than that described in Part 1 (see page 201). It is shorter and the roads are better although, in the wet, you can cross Kazuma Pan only by using a kilometre or two of the Zimbabwe side (the two tracks are just 20-odd metres apart).

Seek the assistance of the Customs officials at Mpandamatenga, who will show you how to get onto the border road – although you ought to be able to see where it curves off to the left a metre or two before the boom on the Botswana side. You don't need to clear Customs or Immigration.

You reach the edge of Kazuma Pan after 25.8 km. Here there's usually game to be seen at the waterhole on the Botswana side, and the pan stretches 15 km before you. The rest of the journey is straightforward and the accompanying map (Map 22, page 282) should help you get through without difficulty. North of Kazuma the track is hard sand and excellent. Observe the Leshoma River in the east about 88 km from Mpandamatenga, and enjoy the open acacia woodland in the river's wide valley. These last 15 km are a wonderful (and free) game drive. The track north divides just before you get to the Botswana and Zimbabwe border posts. Turn to the left (west) to join the tarmac road that leads 2.6 km to the Kazungula junction.

ROUTE 21
Cattle Trek Route

DISTANCE: 195 km. **TIME**: Minimum of 1.5 days, preferably 2. **VEHICLE**: 4x4 essential. **MAPS**: Map 20 (page 280), Map 29 (page 289) and Map 30 (page 290); also Republic of Botswana: 1:100 000 series, 1924 B, D and 1925A' ;1:50 000 series, 1825 C3, C4. **CATTLE TREK ROUTE PROFILE**: page 105.

This is a really interesting journey, but it most definitely is *not* for the faint-hearted, the ill-equipped or the inexperienced (or those with highly treasured paint surfaces!). The road is unmarked, unserviced and infrequently used (it passes through one or two concession areas, but that does not mean anyone will be using the road when you need them).

Some thoughtless and irresponsible individuals apparently once tried it in a saloon car. They got stuck, the vehicle broke down and half of Botswana searched for them for some days. Fortunately no one died, but it is extremely silly to attempt this trip without being properly prepared.

For convenience, I start the route description from the south, from the entrance to Nxai Pan National Park (see page 124). It's a pity to have to do this. Originally the route went almost directly from the Mpandamatenga road to the Maun–Nata road. I drove down it in 1997 from the north, ignored the Nxai Pan exit and continued on to the south. I did get through, but it was difficult. Thorn trees have grown across and, in the road south of the turning into the park, the track is very faint and little used, almost impossible to follow in some places. The journey did not do my vehicle much good. It's more sensible to cut through Nxai Pan. I have heard of a track that goes somewhere up the east side of the park, but have yet to find it. (It may not serve the purpose I want and, in any case, it'll have to wait for another edition.)

Use the Nata–Maun road and the directions in Route 11 (page 185) to get to the entrance of Nxai Pan National Park at (GPS 19.56.00S/24.45.46E). You may be able to persuade the game scouts there that your intention is to pass immediately through the park, or you may have to pay the entrance fee.

Once through the gate, turn left and follow the road round to the west. It tracks the pan margin, swings gently north and reaches a T-junction after 9.4 km. Here you turn left (west) for 5.2 km, and this brings you to what I have chosen to call the start of the Cattle Trek Route that, at this point, forms the western boundary of Nxai Pan National Park at GPS 19.50.45S/24.41.48E. Turn northeast. The next section is easy driving through several stretches of beautiful mopane woodland.

After 6.5 km from the park exit, one passes a disused borehole at GPS 19.47.52S/24.43.45E. A further 18.7 km leads to another broken borehole, together with a collapsed windmill. I do not know where the track that leads west from this point goes to.

An additional 14.5 km from the windmill brings one to a critically important *Y-junction* (39.9 km from the park exit and at GPS 19.32.05S/24.51.50E). The track to the left (northwest) leads to one of the concession areas; the straight-on (northeast) one is a continuation of the Trek Route.

Some 37 km northeast of the 'Y' one reaches the first in a series of mongongo-tree forests (*Phytodendron rautaneii,* known as manketti trees in South Africa). The monongos appear to favour their own company and will suddenly appear, giants among others in the veld, dominating everything. I have done this trip twice in the wet season, around December and January. Not only was the area alive with elephant but some of the flowers were remarkable. I particularly remember the displays of flame lilies. At GPS 19.13.25S/ 25.02.31E you pass beacon BPS 572 (40.3 km from the 'Y'). Ignore the east–northeast trending track that splits away at GPS 19.09.31S/ 25.04.34E (48.6 km from the 'Y') and continue in your original direction. Notice the small pan after a 'thorn tree-island' at GPS 19.03.12S/25.08.31E (62.5 km from the 'Y'); find beacon BPS 432 at GPS 19.00.47S/ 25.09.48E (67.7 km) and beacon BPS 431 at 18.53.19S/ 25.14.16E (84.1 km from the 'Y').

There is a very distinct right-angle bend to the east at GPS 18.48.47S/25.17.45E (93 km from the 'Y') and an equally abrupt turn to the north at GPS 18.48.17S/25.23.06E at 105.4 km, 12.4 km later. Your map will indicate a track going east from this point, but I couldn't find it; only a strong elephant trail went off in that direction.

One and a half kilometres north of this last turn, you will encounter a wrecked vehicle whose age we tried to estimate. The presence of a cable-tie in the canopy suggested it was much more modern than we first thought (it's at GPS 18.47.26S /25.23.32E). Once again, in this last 10 km, one is driving through beautiful woodland with big, high trees widely separated, giving the appearance of a parkland. The modern end of the Trek Route is at GPS 18.42.52S/25.25.53E, at the point where it intersects with an east–west track coming from the Nata–Mpandamatenga road. This intersection is 117 km from the Y-junction, 156.9 km from where you exited the Nxai Pan National Park or a total of 172 from the south gate of Nxai Pan. From here it is 22.8 km east to the tarmac road between Nata and Mpandamatenga, making a total distance of 195 km for the whole journey.

The northern end of the Cattle Trek Route is extremely difficult to locate. There is nothing of any particular note near the starting point that makes it distinctive; there is no obvious junction of two tracks. I noted that, approximately 1 km to the west, there is a road junction (not signposted). In the immediate vicinity there's a very tall tree, with a straight trunk and the first fork at least 7 m long (previous fork, on the eastern side of the tree, had been broken off some time in the past, and the base had been damaged by fire). I don't know what species it belongs to. The tree is about 40 m to the southwest of the junction, and very distinctive – there was no other tree like it in the immediate vicinity.

The start of the Cattle Trek Route, as I say, is extremely indistinct and only becomes clearer between 200 and 300 m from the main track. You'll have to search for it carefully, on foot. Note from Map 29 (page 289) the unusual angle at which the Trek Route strikes the main track. One is inclined to expect it to be at right angles, whereas it is really at about 50 degrees. I have a note that there is a 'Fire Warning' sign ('Se Tshube Naga' in Setswana) within 280 and 300 m but forget in which direction it lay.

ROUTE 22

Tswapong Hills

DISTANCE AND TIME: Variable. **VEHICLE**: 4x4 highly recommended. **MAPS**: Republic of Botswana: 1:250 000 series, No 24, Palapye and the Shell road maps. **TSWAPONG HILLS PROFILE:** page 143.

There are no maps in this guidebook to assist you in exploring these Hills. Basically, they are some 60 km from east to west and about 20 km from north to south. They can be approached on tarmac road from any direction. Key approaches are Martin's Drift on the South African border and Palapye on the main Gaborone to Francistown road.

The roughly rectangular massif is completely surrounded by roads and tracks. The deep gorges – which are so much of the attraction of these Hills – can be seen from a great distance and will be found near the villages of Go-Sekweng and Go-Tau, Lerala and Lecheng in the south and, most notably, Moremi in the north. All of these villages are marked on standard road maps of Botswana.

WHERE TO STAY IN BOTSWANA

With the growth of the tourist industry and the general development of the country there is an increasing range of places to stay in Botswana. But there are still some notable gaps, for example, no youth hostel facilities exist anywhere, and most towns are short of camping facilities.

This section is divided into five categories – National Parks and Reserves, Smaller and Private Reserves, Private Camping Grounds, Hotels in the Major Centres, and Lodges and Country Hotels. Hotels in the main centres of Gaborone, Francistown, Lobatse and Selebi-Phikwe are used mainly by business people and government officials. Although this is changing, tourism is at present largely focused on the wildlife areas to the north, where visitor accommodation is mostly at campsites and in lodges; I have tried to capture the unique character of these lodges.

National parks and reserves

Botswana is doing much to upgrade its national parks and reserves and to manage these protected areas in an ecologically sound manner. In an attempt to prevent overcrowding, a booking system was introduced in 1995 and new facilities are constantly being added.

Overview

National parks and game reserves in Botswana are open throughout the year. Altogether some 17 per cent of Botswana is devoted exclusively to wildlife sanctuaries, apportioned as follows:

Three national parks: Chobe National Park, Nxai Pan and Makgadikgadi National Park and the Kgalagadi Transfrontier Park (which also incorporates the old Mabuasehube Game Reserve).

Seven game reserves: Central Kalahari Game Reserve, Gaborone Game Reserve, Khutse Game Reserve, Mannyelanong Game Reserve, Maun Game Reserve and Moremi Game Reserve.

Gate times at parks and reserves, except for the Kgalagadi Transfrontier Park (see page 211), are 6 am–6 pm from March to September, and 5 am to 7.30 pm from October to February.

Camping sites: At present, campers need to make advance reservations for the campsites in all the parks and in the Khutse, Central Kalahari and Moremi reserves.

Public camping grounds in the parks are divided into individual camping sites, each of which is designed to accommodate a maximum of six people. Groups of more than six people are required to book additional sites. Most public camping grounds are serviced by ablution blocks with flush toilets, showers and hand basins; many individual sites have concrete table/bench units and braai (barbecue) stands. Water standpipes and litter-bins are provided within most camping grounds, but not all.

At the same time, although shower and toilet facilities do exist in many parks, water is frequently a problem. (In the Kgalagadi Transfrontier Park some of the campsites have showers but you bring the water!) Supplies may be temporarily suspended for one of many reasons, including drought and the activities of game, especially elephant.

To repeat: it is essential to make advance reservations, as any camper arriving without a prior reservation may find that the camping grounds are full and will thus only be allowed access into the park for the day.

Making your reservation

Booking applications and enquiries should be directed either to:

Gaborone: Parks and Reserves Reservations Office, PO Box 131, Gaborone; tel 318-0774, fax 318-0775, email DWNPBOTS@global.bw. The Gaborone office is located on the ground floor of the Department of Wildlife and National Parks offices on Khama Crescent, near the north end of the main Mall.

Maun: Parks and Reserves Reservation Office, PO Box 20364, Boseja, Maun; tel 686-1265, fax 686-1264. The reservation office is located near the Police Station and is clearly signposted. It is open every day of the week throughout the year, including public holidays, from 7.30 am to 4.30 pm.

Reservations are accepted up to 12 months in advance and may be made personally or by telephone, fax, telegram or letter (not email yet). The information required when making a booking includes the name of the park or reserve, the name of the public camping ground, the dates of arrival and departure, the total number of intending campers and whether they are Botswana citizens, residents or non-residents.

After making a reservation, a provisional booking form will be sent to you by the reservations office. Full camping fees are payable in advance, the amount of which will appear on the form. The date by which payment is to be received will also be indicated. This payment date will usually be due within two to four weeks, depending on the location of those making the booking and provided the date of visit allows this. Entry fees are payable at the gate of the park or reserve.

All payments must be in Botswana pula (see Money, page 55). Payments made to the Reservations Office may be submitted in one of the following ways:
• Bank certified personal cheques;
• Postal orders or money orders, crossed a/c payee only;
• Bank drafts;
• Cash, but only when the payment is made personally at the Reservations Office (see page 207).

Payments made at park or reserve entrance gates must be in cash. When pre-payment for a reservation is received, an official receipt and confirmation form will be issued. It is essential to safeguard this form as you will not be allowed to occupy the campsite without presenting it at the park or reserve entrance gate. A second copy of the confirmation form, marked 'station copy', will also be issued. This must also be presented at the entrance gate and will be retained by the gate attendant. Campsite reservations not taken up by 5.30 pm will be subject to re-letting at the park, and pre-payments will be forfeited.

The reference number that appears in the top right-hand corner of the provisional booking/confirmation form must be quoted in any further business connected with that reservation.

Requests for alterations to your original booking should be made in writing or by visiting the Reservations Office personally. The alteration must be initialled to avoid any dispute at a later stage. Should there be an increase in the number of persons or length of stay, the difference can be paid on arrival at the park or reserve.

Refunds of pre-payments will only be made if notice of the cancellation is received in writing more than 30 days prior to the effective date of the reservation. Any applications for refund should be accompanied by the original receipt. If you wish to transfer your booking, then you must cancel your original booking and re-book, and the pre-payment will then be transferred to the new booking. Only one such transfer of pre-payment is permitted.

The schedule of fees that follows on pages 247–249 is that introduced for 2000. However, fees are subject to alteration without notice. The booking system in Botswana is relatively new and no-one will deny that it has had its share of teething problems in the recent past. DWNP are well aware of this and have worked hard to improve it.

FEE STRUCTURE: NATIONAL PARKS AND RESERVES

Note: A separate schedule of fees and opening times apply to the Kgalagadi Transfrontier Park; see page 211.

I. FEES FOR PARKS/RESERVES, CAMPING AND OTHER ACTIVITIES (1)

Description	Citizen	Resident	Non-Resident
A. PARK/RESERVE FEES – Pula per day			
1. Private visitors, per person per day *	10.00	30.00	120.00
2. Clients of Botswana tour operators, per person per day (2) *	10	30	70
3. Professional guides and staff of Botswana tour operators, per person per year (3)	0	1000	N/A (8)
B. CAMPING FEES			
4. Camping fee per person per night (4),	5	20	30
C. SPECIAL ACTIVITIES			
5. Camping at wilderness campsite per person, per night (4)	50	100	200
6. Overnight stay at observation hide per person, per night (4)	50	100	200
7. Participation in walking safaris in designated area, per person per day	50	100	200
8. Use of wilderness trail, per person per day	50	100	200
9. Participation in animal-back safaris	50	100	200
10. Participation in night game-viewing drives	5	20	30
D. RESEARCH/FILMING ACTIVITIES			
11. Research, per person, per month or part thereof (composite fees) (5)	250	500	1000
12. Filming: commercial still photography, documentaries, per person, per week or part thereof (composite fees) (5)	125	250	1000
13. Filming: advertising, feature films, per person, per week or part thereof (composite fees) (5)	1000	2000	5000

II. FEES FOR MOTOR VEHICLES, AIRCRAFT AND BOATS (1)

Description	Botswana Registered	Foreign Registered
A. MOTOR VEHICLES		
1. Motor vehicles under 3500 kg, private, per day (6)	10	50
2. Motor vehicles under 3500 kg, commercial, per day (6)	30	200
3. Motor vehicles under 3500 kg, commercial, annual fee (6)	1500.00 (7)	N/A (8)
4. Motor vehicles between 3500 and 7000 kg, per day (6)	500	1000
5. Motor vehicles between 3500 and 7000 kg, supply/ utility, annual fee (6)	3000.00(7)	N/A (8)
6. Motor vehicles more than 7000 kg, per day (6)	800	1500
B. AIRCRAFT AND BOATS		
7. Aircraft, per day	50	250
8. Aircraft, annual fee	1500.00 (7)	3000.00 (8)
9. Boat, power, per day	10.00	N/A (8)
10. Boat, power, annual fee	1500	N/A (8)

Note: Items marked with an asterisk on page 209 indicate that persons between 8 and 15 years of age pay 50 per cent of the fees listed and persons under 8 years of age pay nothing. The rates shown above, for both the KTP and all the other parks, were published in April 2000. It is unlikely that they will change again for several years.

Explanatory notes for tables I and II:

1. These fees do not apply to the Kgalagadi Transfrontier Park (for which see page 211) or the educational reserves in Gaborone, Francistown and Maun. Separate fees are set for these parks and reserves.
2. The phrase 'Botswana Tour Operator' in terms of this schedule means a tour operator with a valid Tourism Enterprise Licence under the Tourism Act allowing off-site operations.

FEE STRUCTURE: KGALAGADI TRANSFRONTIER PARK

These entry fees apply to all visitors, whether they are overnight or day only, regardless of residential status.

Category	Pula Rate	Rand Rate
Adults (over 15 years old) – per person per day	20.00	25.00
Children (2 to 15 years old) – per person per day	10.00	12.00
Children under two years – per person per day	free	free
Vehicles – per car per day	4.00	5.00

OPENING TIMES: KGALAGADI TRANSFRONTIER PARK

January and February	06.00–19.30
March	06.30–19.00
April	07.00–18.30
May	07.00–18.00
June and July	07.30–18.00
August	07.00–18.30
September	06.30–18.30
October	06.00–19.00
November and December	05.30–19.30

3. This fee is applicable to citizen and resident professional guides and staff members of Botswana Tour Operators on official duty only. Permits will be provided upon application accompanied by appropriate proof of guide status, employment, tour operator status and payment of fees as may be applicable.
4. The fees include a 10 per cent sales tax.
5. The composite fees include park/reserve and camping fees. The fee applies to each individual named on the permit and any support staff.
6. The onus will be on the owner of the vehicle to prove that his/her vehicle falls within a particular category. If no proof is provided, the fees of the more expensive category will apply.
7. The annual fee payable for the use of vehicles and aircraft will authorise their use in all parks and game reserves.
8. Yearly fees are not applicable for this category.

Fishing permits

Permits were in the past required for fishing in national parks (that is, the Chobe), but not for fishing elsewhere. For the moment, though, all but subsistence fishing in national parks has been suspended while the situation is reviewed. It is expected that some decision on this matter will be made during 2001.

Public rest-camps: Kgalagadi Transfrontier Park (KTP)

There is excellent accommodation at the three public rest-camps on the South African side of the park, namely Nossob, Twee Rivieren and Mata Mata (note: there are no plug points or air-conditioning at the last two mentioned). If necessary, one can reserve a fully equipped safari tent at Twee Rivieren, but this must be booked in advance; tel (54) 5610021. Accommodation comprises:

Twee Rivieren A six-bed family cottage with two bedrooms, bathroom (shower), living room, air-conditioned and a fully equipped kitchen. Three-bed and four-bed cottages with one bedroom, bathroom (shower), living room, air-conditioning, and fully equipped kitchen. Bungalows with two single beds and a double sleeper-couch, bathroom (shower) air-conditioning, and fully equipped kitchen.

Mata Mata A six-bed family cottage with two bedrooms, bathroom (shower), living room and a fully equipped kitchen. Three-bed huts with communal ablution facilities and equipped communal kitchens. No air-conditioning; ceiling fans only.

Nossob A six-bed family cottage with two bedrooms, two bathrooms (shower), living room and a fully equipped kitchen. A six-bed family cottage with three bedrooms, bathroom (shower), living room and a fully equipped kitchen. Three-bed bungalows, bathroom (shower) and equipped kitchen. Three-bed huts, communal ablution facilities and equipped communal kitchens. No air-conditioning; ceiling fans only.

Camping Facilities available; see Campsites in national parks and reserves on page 213.

Other facilities

• Laundry tubs and ironing facilities (no irons) in all three camps.
• Twee Rivieren, the largest rest-camp and administrative base for the park, has a swimming pool, restaurant, information centre, shop and public telephones.
• All three rest-camps have a shop where basic commodities such as meat, vegetables, fruits, soft drinks, alcoholic drinks, ice, firewood, film, curios and dairy products can be purchased. Fresh bread is only available at

the 'lapa' at Twee Rivieren. The operating hours for the shops is from 7:30 am until 30 minutes after the gates close.

- There are five picnic spots within the park. Please note that there are no fences and that visitors alight from their vehicles at own risk. Braai (barbecue) facilities and gas are available for day visitors at all three rest-camps.
- Fuel: petrol, both leaded and unleaded, and diesel are available at all rest-camps.
- All roads within the park are gravel and in good condition. However, certain parts may be difficult to negotiate during the rainy season.
- Light aircraft may land on a tarred runway at Twee Rivieren. Length: 1900 m; co-ordinates 26.26.53.6S/ 20.36.24.8E. Altitude: 3000 mamsal. Prior permission to land must be obtained from the park manager at (054) 5610021.

Adventure and outdoor activities
- Game-viewing (daytime), in own vehicle.
- Night drives with experienced rangers aboard park vehicles. Also conducted drives in later afternoon/evening, with sundowner drinks. Booking essential, at park reception.
- Swimming pool at Twee Rivieren only.
- Information Centre, at Twee Rivieren: lectures, video and slide shows, photo gallery and holiday programmes.

Campsites in national parks and reserves

Note: Collect your own firewood, or carry it in from outside the area. Wood will either be non-existent, exceedingly scarce or expensive.

Chobe National Park

Savute The public camping ground at Savute is a temporary one, close to the original site. There are pit latrines enclosed by reed walls, a protected water standpipe but no showers. A completely new camping ground is planned. Water here is a problem: Savute Channel in the 1970s was a place of hippos and pools. Since the 1980s, however, it has been totally dry. Permanent water points have been established away from the campsite for the elephants. Savute is still a fine place to see game of all kinds, which is part of the reason for its popularity. Take care not to keep fruit, especially oranges, in your tent or vehicle as this can focus the elephants' unwanted attention on you.

Linyanti The area is a little off the beaten track and consequently appeals to those who prefer their wilderness to be more private. It has a small camping ground on the banks of the Linyanti River and looks into the Caprivi. Although it does have shower (with hot water!) and toilet facilities, the same provisos apply here as for all the other camps.

Nogatsha and Tjinga At present (November 2000) there are no ablution facilities at either Nogatsha or Tjinga. However, temporary camping grounds have been established and both sites are to be upgraded to standard permanent camping grounds. Water is usually available at both these sites.

Serondela Serondela exists no more as a campsite. It is now a picnic spot only (and what a beautiful place it is, too!).

Ihaha Much more remote than its predecessor Serondela, Ihaha (15 km further west than Serondela) was designed to reduce visitor impact on the western Chobe. It is purpose-built with modern facilities, including good showers, basins, flush toilets, water standpipes and an attractive reception office.

Moremi Game Reserve

South Gate (Maqwee) This has seven campsites, set among mopane trees. It is just outside the reserve and is generally only used by people who have arrived after the gate closes. Flush toilets, two water standpipes and showers are available.

Third Bridge This is probably the most popular campsite in Moremi. There are also seven campsites here, and a good ablution block with showers, water standpipes, basins and flush toilets. Water is available.

Xakanaxa Xakanaxa also has seven campsites. There are showers, basins, flush toilets, picnic tables, and water standpipes. A number of safari operators have camps here, from whom you may be able to hire a boat.

North Gate (Khwai) Here, again, there are seven campsites, which lie just within the reserve, across the river from Khwai village. The ground has showers, picnic tables, water standpipes, basins and flush-toilet facilities, as well as an ample supply of water – under normal conditions.

Nxai Pan and Makgadikgadi National Park

Nxai Pan

North Camp There are three campsites at North Camp, which is situated on the northern edge of the pan and has a standard ablution block with showers, hand basins and flush toilets. The water standpipe is centrally located. This camp is set among mopane trees, but there is not much shade and it can become very hot.

South Camp This camp is situated on the southern edge of the pan, not far from the entrance gate. It has four sites set among purple-pod Terminalia, which provide plenty of shade. There are ablution facilities, including showers and flush toilets, two water standpipes and picnic tables. Each campsite has a fire pit. This camp has one of the two viewing platforms within the park; each offers excellent views, especially the second one, high up on the top of the sand ridge.

Baines' Baobabs There are three informal, undeveloped campsites here. Each of them can accommodate a maximum of 12 persons and three vehicles. There is no water; bring your own.

Makgadikgadi

Xhumaga This camp is set on the Boteti River in a large sandy area beneath beautiful, mature *Acacia erioloba*. There are four sites with toilets, showers and water. An attraction is its position, overlooking the Boteti River. However, the river doesn't always have water in it, so check beforehand if you're set on a water camp.

Njuca Hills Views from this immense fossil dune are stunning. The camp has no water; there are two campsites, with pit latrines only.

Khutse Game Reserve

A total of 25 numbered campsites have been established at Khutse, located around various pans. Some of them have pit latrines, others have no facilities at all, so it is essential to carry all your own water. Camping is not allowed outside designated areas. A visitors' map is available at the gate, which shows the various campsites.

Central Kalahari Game Reserve

No campsites or facilities of any kind exist in the southern part of this reserve. In the northern half, however, there has been considerable investment and 13 separate campsites, accommodating 162 people, have been established. The campsites are merely designated places; be warned: they have no facilities whatsoever and you must be totally self-sufficient.

Kgalagadi Transfrontier Park: South African side

There is excellent accommodation at the three rest-camps of Nossob, Twee Rivieren and Mata Mata on the South African side; all of them offer comprehensive visitor facilities. See Public rest-camps: Kgalagadi

Transfrontier Park, on page 212. All three camps have barbecue (braai) facilities and communal ablution facilities with electricity points; caravan and campsites do not have power points. A maximum of six persons, one vehicle and one caravan/tent or one 'autovilla' (mobile home) are allowed per site.

Kgalagadi Transfrontier Park: Botswana side

Two Rivers This camping ground, situated in a fenced area near the entrance gate, offers ablution blocks and shade structures.

Rooiputs The Rooiputs camping ground is situated some 25 km up the Nossob River valley from the Two Rivers entrance gate. It offers six individual campsites, each of which has its own shade structure, fireplace, rustic pit latrine and shower.

Polentswa This camping ground lies in the northern section of the Nossob River valley and has three campsites with shade structures, pit latrines and shower shelters (you have to provide the water).

Note: Water for purposes other than drinking can be obtained at the game scout camp near the entrance gate at Two Rivers. Visitors are advised that petrol, diesel and food supplies are obtainable at Twee Rivieren on the South African side of the border. Payments may be made there in pula.

The Mabuasehube area

This area, formerly a separate game reserve, is now part of the Kgalagadi Transfrontier Park (see above).

Mabuasehube entrance There is a new campsite with ablutions just inside the entrance to the park and there are other campsites with a variety of facilities at the following pans in the interior of the park.

Monamodi Two shade structures, with pit latrines and showers with water.

Leshaloago Two shade structures, with pit latrines and showers with water.

Mpaathutlwa Two shade structures, with pit latrines and showers with water.

Mabuasehube Pan Four shade structures, with pit latrines and showers with water.

Khiding Pan Two shade structures, with pit latrines and shower shelters where the camper provides the water.

Bosobogolo Pan Two shade structures, with pit latrines and shower shelters where the camper provides the water.

For those people who prefer their wilderness without any facilities, there are some other campsites – at all the above pans – which have not been developed.

Smaller and private reserves

Mannyelanong Game Reserve

This reserve, created solely to protect a vulture nesting colony, has no facilities. It is located just a few kilometres outside the village of Otse, some 50 km south of Gaborone. Regrettably, protection came rather late and the number of birds now using the colony has plummeted from an estimated 300 pairs to something closer to 100. The game reserve includes much of the mountain on which the colony is situated as well as the fenced area that demarcates the actual nesting site.

Entrance is free but you are requested to stop at the game scout camp (tel 533-7181) and register when entering. The preference is to restrict access to the site during September and October and from the end of February to mid-April so as not to disturb the breeding birds, but, as a public road passes right under the site, this is proving a little impractical. Talk to the game scouts on duty and they will be very happy to arrange your visit.

No entry whatsoever is allowed into the fenced area. Even approaching it noisily or in haste can disturb the nesting birds, and this is detrimental to their proper conservation. A handy rule of thumb: if the birds take flight as you approach, you've upset them. Be more cautious.

Gaborone Game Reserve

This reserve opened in 1988 on the initiative of the Kalahari Conservation Society and the Department of Wildlife and National Parks. Created mainly for educational purposes, it consists of 5 km^2 of varied habitat on the edge of the Ngotwane River. Fees: P1 per person and P2 per car, plus 50 thebe per person picnic fee, all of which makes for an inexpensive outing (tel 318-4492).

Despite its tiny size, this remarkable reserve is one of the most visited protected areas in Botswana. Within it you'll find a wide range of mammals, including white rhino, kudu, eland, wildebeest, impala, gemsbok and zebra (among others). The rhino are kept in a separate area with strengthened fencing, although much of the other game is able to move freely between this area and the rest of the park.

There is a good network of roads, two picnic sites with toilets, water and braai sites, a visitor's information centre with a mini-museum, and a game-viewing hide overlooking a permanent artificial waterhole. There is also a bird hide in the marshy area of the park. Viewing is best in the early morning and is also quite good in the evenings. The reserve opens from 6.30 am to 6.30 pm each day.

Maun Game Reserve

This small (3 km²) reserve is situated on the banks of the Thamalakane River opposite Riley's Hotel. Like other sanctuaries of its type, the aim is to provide wildlife education facilities. At the moment (November 2000), entrance is free and visitors may walk around the park where it is possible to see a variety of antelope.

A visitor's centre has been completed; and there are plans to charge an entry fee. The reserve will be open seven days a week, probably from 6.30 am to 6.30 pm daily.

Francistown Game Reserve

Land has been allocated on the Shashe River to develop an educational game reserve, similar to those in other centres. At the time of writing (November 2000), fencing has been completed and a visitor's centre is at an advanced stage of construction. There will be a nominal entrance charge for vehicles, people and picnics. It is expected to open in 2001.

Khama Rhino Sanctuary

The sanctuary lies 29 km north of Serowe on the Orapa road in the central district of Botswana. The project, sustained by a community trust established in 1992, is dedicated to the safeguarding and breeding of some of Botswana's last rhinos (the rhino population was in danger of being poached out). At the moment, it conserves the largest herd (16 in November 2000) of white rhino in the country. It is situated on 4 300 hectares of Kalahari sandveld, and the Serwe pan, a large calcrete depression, lies in the centre of the reserve.

The reserve not only has the largest breeding herd of rhino in Botswana, but is also home to a diverse range of antelope and smaller mammals (such as bat-eared foxes). Leopard, although not common, have been seen. There is abundant bird life, with a large variety of raptors. A bird hide has been constructed (over 230 species identified) and one may join organised game drives and nature walks.

Entry fees are P10 per vehicle with an additional P10 per person per day; children under 12 are admitted free. On top of this there is a camping fee of P25, and a once-off booking fee of P50. The campsites all have ablution facilities.

The sanctuary offers delightful self-catering chalets as follows: two at P200 per night; three at P250 per night (each sleeps four people) and one at P350 per night (sleeps six people). The three 'squaredavels' (rectangular huts) suitable for backpackers at P120 each. All the campsites and other accommodation are situated in stands of mongongo trees (*Phytodendron rautanenii*), which provide privacy and shade.

The sanctuary is still being developed, and money has just (November 2000) been found for an education and conference centre. An ordinary car is suitable for getting to the chalets and campsites, but one either needs to join a conducted game drive or drive a bakkie (pick-up) or 4x4 to follow all the routes within the sanctuary.

Contact details: The Khama Rhino Sanctuary Trust, PO Box 10, Serowe; tel 463-0713/0420/0520; email krst@botsnet.bw.

Mokolodi Nature Reserve

Accommodation: Chalets, dormitory (booking essential), campsites.
Facilities: Restaurant, education centre, conference facilities, gift shop.
Activities: Game drives and walks, elephant walks, rhino walks, cheetah visit, night drives, giraffe tracking, bush barbecues, business bush lunch.
Tariff: Budget. **Contact details:** PO Box 170, Gaborone;. tel 316-1955, fax 316-5488. **Restaurant bookings:** Tel 316-1547, fax 316-5488 (closed on Mondays).

The reserve was established in 1994 by the Mokolodi Wildlife Foundation, whose aim it is to further environmental education and to conserve the flora and fauna of southeastern Botswana. It lies 15 km south of Gaborone on the Lobatse road. Animals you can see there include white rhino, giraffe, kudu, eland, impala, wildebeest, red hartebeest, warthogs and zebra. There are also four young African elephants that have been trained by mahouts from Sri Lanka. You may, at a price, organise to go on an elephant walk in the park with these elephants or with the rhino.

Accommodation is available in five thatched en-suite chalets set among rocky outcrops overlooking a waterhole. Each chalet is equipped with a small fridge, a gas stove and an outside braai area. Dormitory accommodation is also available for backpackers, at a very good rate (bed and breakfast).

There are eight campsites, all with flush toilets, hot water for under-the-stars showers, basins and a cooking area. Camping costs P40 per adult and P25 per child (5 to 12 years; under 5 years free). Bush braais (barbecues) cost P175 per person (minimum of six persons) but the price includes a game drive, braai at selected sites in the bush, meals and drinks.

Entry into the reserve costs P10 per person and P20 per vehicle. There is no entry fee for those patronising the restaurant. The gate opens at 7 am and closes at 6 pm. Only restaurant guests may enter after 6 pm. The restaurant closes at 6 pm on Sundays and is closed on Mondays.

Nata Sanctuary

See Places to Visit: the wilderness, page 103, and Route 8, page 173. The sanctuary has camping facilities that include hot water, basins, showers, flush toilets and a braai area. Firewood is sold at P10 a bundle. Entry fees per person: Citizens P5, residents P15, non-residents P25. Camping fees per person: citizens P15, residents P20, non-residents P25.

St Clair Lion Park

The park lies about 20 km south of Gaborone on the road to Lobatse in a large tract of private land. It provides facilities for camping and caravans with communal ablution blocks, braai stands and electricity points. Kennelling facilities are also available. A restaurant and bar are open 5 pm on weekdays, all day during the weekend (it is not usually necessary to book). There is a gate fee.

As the name suggests, the park contains lions, albeit in enclosures. The 4x4 Club, in association with the Lion Park, holds 4x4 challenges on specially laid out courses. Picnic spots have been established. The Lion Park Equestrian Club will also provide horses and lead game rides through the adjacent Mokolodi Nature Reserve (see page 219), or you could organise a game drive within the confines of the extensive park itself.

Private camping grounds

Francistown
The Marang Hotel and Casino (see page 223).
Tati River Lodge Caravan and Campsite (see page 96).
Gaborone
Citi Camp (budget tariff), PO Box 20222, Gaborone; tel and fax 391-1912.
St Clair Lion Park (budget tariff; see also above); PO Box 238, Gaborone; tel and fax 397-2711.
Gweta
Planet Baobab: A remarkable and innovative venture, the only permanent cultural/ecotourism one of its kind in the country; aimed at the independent traveller: camping, funkie bar, quad bikes on the pan (brilliant!); reasonable prices. Planet Baobab is located 4 km east of Gweta, towards Francistown. It is signposted, or call 241-2277/240-3575, email: unchar@info.bw.
Kasane
Chobe Safari Lodge (see page 225).
Kubu Lodge (see page 226).

Buffalo Ridge Campsites, PO Box 109, Kasane; tel and fax 625-0430. This new camping ground at Ngoma is set on the ridge overlooking the Chobe River 60 km from Kasane and 100 m from the Namibia border post. The camping ground is ideal for those who arrive too late at the Chobe National Park gate, or who are waiting to cross over into the Caprivi. There are ablution facilities, and each campsite has a tap. One can buy bags of very good firewood at the gate.

Maun
Audi Camp (see page 230).
Crocodile Camp Safaris (see page 231).
Island Safari Lodge (see page 232).
Sedia Hotel (see page 233).

Moremi and Central Delta
Gunn's Camp (see page 238).
Oddballs (see page 240).

Nata
Nata Lodge (see page 249).
Nata Sanctuary (see page 220, and Route 8, Option 1A, page 173).

Ngoma
Buffalo Ridge, PO Box 109, Kasane; tel and fax 625-0430.

Western Delta
Fish Eagle Lodge/Drotsky's Cabins (see page 246).
Guma Lagoon Camp (see page 246).
Shakawe Fishing Camp (see page 247).

Hotels in the major centres

Botswana has no grading system, but price is usually a reliable indicator of the quality. Many of the hotels are owned by the Botswana-based Cresta group, some are informally classed as Lodges (see page 222), and all are of a good standard. The following is a list of urban hotels, their addresses and telephone numbers.

Gaborone
President Hotel, PO Box 200, Gaborone, tel 395-3631, fax 395-1840.
Cresta Lodge, P/Bag 00126, Gaborone; tel 397-5375, fax 390-0635.
Gaborone Travel Inn, P/Bag 00127, Gaborone; tel 392-2777, fax 392-2727.
Gaborone Sun, P/Bag 0016, Gaborone; tel and fax 395-1111.
Oasis Motel, PO Box 30331, Gaborone; tel 392-8396, fax 392-8568.
Morning Star Motel, PO Box 177, Gaborone; tel 392-8301.
Grand Palm Hotel & Casino, P/Bag BR105, Gaborone; tel 391-2999, fax 391-2989.

Francistown
Thapama Hotel & Casino, P/Bag 31, Francistown; tel 241-3872, fax 241-3766.
The Marang Hotel and Casino (see page 223).
Tati River Lodge, P/Bag F333, Francistown; tel 240-6000, fax 240-6080.
Grand Lodge, PO Box 1713, Francistown; tel 241-2300, fax 241-2309.
Ghanzi
Kalahari Arms, PO Box 29, Ghanzi; tel 659-6298, fax 659-6311.
Lobatse
Cumberland Hotel, PO Box 135, Lobatse; tel 533-0281, fax 533-2106.
Mahalapye
Mahalapye Hotel, PO Box 526, Mahalapye; tel 471-0200.
Maun
Riley's Hotel (see Lodges and country hotels, below).
Palapye
Botsalo Travel Inn, PO Box 35, Palapye; tel 492-0245, fax 492-0587.
Selebi-Phikwe
Bosele Hotel, PO Box 177, Selebi-Phikwe; tel 261-0675, fax 261-1083.
Syringa Lodge, PO Box 254, Selebi-Phikwe; tel 261-0444/0019, fax 261-0450.
Serowe
Serowe Hotel, PO Box 150, Serowe; tel 463-0234.
Tshwargano Hotel, PO Box 430337, Serowe; tel 463-0377, fax 463-1700.
Cresta Central Reservations
Botswana: Tel 391-2431, fax 397-5376, email bwpresidenthotel@info.bw.
Zimbabwe: Tel Harare (263 4) 77-2886, fax 77-288.

Lodges and country hotels

It is impossible to give an exhaustive list of the lodges and country hotels (in some instances it's difficult to tell the difference between the two) as old ones are disappearing and new ones are emerging. Lodges that have been included in this guide however may all be relied on for their continuing hospitality and service.

Staying in a lodge is not the same as staying in a five-star establishment. A lodge will not offer the predictable sameness of hotel chains that you might find anywhere else in the world. Each lodge has its own character, and this is especially true of those that are owner-managed. You may well enjoy five-star service, but it will be very different from that which is laid down in the list of requirements for a grading system.

As you read through the descriptions of the lodges that follow, you should be able to develop a feel for what to expect. This section is intended to help you choose where to stay and how to construct the kind of

Botswana holiday experience that will suit both your interests and your pocket. The lodges are grouped by area; the latter are arranged in alphabetical order. At the beginning of each section there is a brief description of the area. Heading each lodge description is a brief summary; this is for quick reference to determine the type of accommodation offered, the tariff level, facilities and activities. Most if not all are licensed to serve alcoholic beverages.

Francistown area

Francistown is not a major port of call for tourists. It is one of the older towns in the country and the hub of economic activity in the region (see page 96). It has good road and rail links to major sources of supply so, from the visitor's point of view, it's a good place to pick up motor spares and basic necessities.

The Marang Hotel and Casino

Accommodation: Hotel rooms, chalets, campsites. **Facilities:** Restaurant, shop, satellite TV, swimming pool, conference facilties, tourist advice and maps, packed lunches. **Activities:** Walks, bird life. **Tariff**: Medium (hotel), budget (camping). **Contact details**: PO Box 807, Francistown; tel 241-3991/2/3, fax 241-2130.

You'll find the Marang – the 'place of sunbeams' – just outside Francistown, on the banks of the Tati River. Huge acacia trees, lush green lawns, thatched roofs and genuine comfort combine to make it an outstanding venue. Choose from wood and thatch chalets by the river bank, or air-conditioned rooms. Whichever you decide on, you will enjoy the hotel's beauty and tranquillity. The atmosphere is relaxed and friendly and, in these surroundings, you will leave intending to return.

The Marang also has a beautiful, shady campsite with hot water and clean ablution blocks. There is a terrace and an à la carte restaurant, a swimming pool, conference room and a most attractive bar constructed out of kiaat wood from Nata. The Marang has become the place to stop over on the long road to the Okavango and Chobe.

Gweta area

Gweta is a small, appealing village, just off the main tourist route – off the main road from Francistown to Maun, some 99 km west of Nata. The rest-camp is well signposted. The village is set among tall palm trees and serves as the gateway to the Makgadikgadi pans and game reserve.

Gweta Rest-camp

Accommodation: Rondavels, campsites. **Facilities:** Restaurant, swimming pool, bottle (liquor) store, curios on sale. **Activities:** Pan excursions. **Tariff**: Medium. **Contact details**: PO Box 124, Gweta; tel 621-2220, fax 686-0493.

The rest-camp's rondavels are thatched; the camping ground pleasant, although being in a village, somewhat noisy at night especially. There is an open-air restaurant and bar under thatch. Game drives into the Makgadikgadi pans and game reserve can be organised; also trips on 4-wheeler motor bikes (the so-called 'quad-bikes').

Kasane (Chobe) area

The Chobe National Park is the major drawcard of international visitors and the Kasane region is a fast-growing tourism centre. With an international airport and good access from four countries, as well as close proximity to Victoria Falls, it is set to become increasingly popular.

Chobe Chilwero

Accommodation: Chalets (booking essential). **Facilities:** Licensed, swimming pool, gift shop. **Attractions/activities**: game-viewing drives, game flights, river cruises, bird-watching, boating. **Tariff**: High. **Contact details**: Abercrombie & Kent, tel: 626-2688, email akbots@info.bw. **Reservations**: tel (27 11) 781-1497.

Chobe Chilwero, a small, luxurious safari lodge, is perched on top of the escarpment between Kasane and the main entrance to the Chobe National Park. Take the old road out of Kasane to the park. Just past Chobe Safari Lodge, look for a road to the left that crosses a small culvert bridge and heads up the hill. Follow this road for 5 km. Kasane is also accessible by air and guests can arrange to be collected from the airstrip.

The lodge offers some of the best views in Botswana. All meals, beverages, accommodation, game-viewing activities, park fees, laundry and transfers between Chilwero/Kasane airport are included in the tariff.

Chobe Game Lodge

Accommodation: Hotel rooms (booking essential). **Facilities**: Restaurant, swimming pool, conference centre, shop, first-aid facilities. **Attractions/ activities:** Game-viewing drives, boating, river cruises, birding. **Tariff**: High; the hotel has an accommodation discount system for all bona fide citizens and residents of Botswana, and for those using their own four-wheel-drive vehicles. **Contact details**: PO Box 32, Kasane; tel 625-0340, fax 625-0280, email cgl@info.bw. **Reservations**: tel (27 11) 706-0862, fax (27 11) 706-0863, email chobe@fast.co.za.

Chobe Game Lodge is 12 km west of Kasane; drive west towards Ngoma on the tarred road. Six kilometres from Kasane is the entrance to the national park. You will have to stop at the gate, fill in the appropriate forms and pay the park entrance fees. Visitors arriving at the gate and producing proof of their reservations will be charged the lower, 'operators', park fees. There is a sandy road that leads directly to the game lodge, or you can choose various scenic route options.

The lodge is a tranquil enclave of luxury in the midst of the African bush. Green lawns and lush gardens contrast with dry, dusty, wintry landscapes (the roads are, however, only passable by four-wheel-drive vehicles). The main building steps down to the river vista from the spacious entrance hall to a gallery of striking African art – a place of romance that has worked its magic on many people, perhaps the best-known of them actors Liz Taylor and Richard Burton, who celebrated their second marriage here in 1976.

Accommodation is in pleasingly appointed, air-conditioned rooms, each with bathroom en suite. For those who desire privacy, there are four luxury suites, each with its own private swimming pool. Other guests have access to the large lodge pool set in lawns on the river bank.

Amidst this luxury, it is all too easy to forget that you are a guest in the domain of the animals. Be prepared for such reminders as bushbuck and warthog, and even troops of baboons, elephants and hippos, who come to feed on the lawns and among the trees. The bird life is colourful. If the lure of big game has brought you to Chobe, you'll enjoy the game-viewing by boat or by open motor vehicle. Early mornings and late afternoons are the best times for this.

The hotel has a Cessna 207 at Kasane airstrip and can provide flights to Moremi, Savute, Okavango and Victoria Falls. For the rest, there is the appeal of relaxing beside the pool, or taking a sundowner cruise, which combines game-viewing, watching the sunset and enjoying light snacks and ice-cold refreshments after the heat of the day.

Chobe Safari Lodge

Accommodation: Hotel rooms, chalets, campsites; booking essential. **Facilities**: Restaurant, 'local' (pub), swimming pool, gift shop, conference room, bottle (liquor) store, fuel outlet. **Attractions/activities**: Game-viewing drives and flights, boating, birding, river cruises, fishing. **Tariff**: Medium. **Contact details**: PO Box 10, Kasane; tel 625-0336, fax 625-0437.

Chobe Safari Lodge is on the western outskirts of Kasane, overlooking the Chobe River. Once you have reached Kasane, take the main road towards the national park and you will see the hotel on the right-hand side of the road, just before you leave town. It is conveniently located close to a bank, garage and general store.

Apart from the hotel itself, there are 22 thatched rondavels and a grassed campsite. It is not unusual for elephants to stroll through the campsite at night, browsing on the trees. They are quite awesome close up but unlikely to harm campers if they are not disturbed. This is a popular spot for fishermen but you don't have to stick to the riverbanks: you can hire boats to take you further afield.

Game drives can be arranged, and, when you are neither game-viewing nor fishing, you can cool off in the residents' pool. The hotel arranges a daily sunset cruise (on a 25-seater double-decker boat). The vessel has bar facilities and is an excellent floating venue for bird-watching and game-viewing.

Remember, if you go into the neighbouring national park, the entrance ticket you pay for is valid for any number of visits on that day. It therefore makes sense to do a river visit on the evening of that day also – and you can do this very conveniently from the steps of the hotel.

Kubu Lodge

Accommodation: Hotel rooms, chalets, rondavels, campsites. **Facilities**: Restaurant, swimming pool, gift shop, store, fuel outlet. **Attractions/activities**: Game-viewing drives and walks, mobile safaris, boating, birding, river cruises, fishing, crocodile farm. **Tariff**: Medium. **Contact details**: PO Box 43, Kasane; tel 625-0312, fax 625-1092, email kubu@info.bw.

Take the tarred road from Kasane to Kazungula and, some 10 km along the road you'll see the signs to Kubu Lodge (they direct you down towards the river). The lodge is about 1 km from the main road.

Kubu Lodge used to be the site of the Employment Bureau of Africa (TEBA) recruitment office for the Kasane area, and it bears many signs of the old colonial era – for instance, exotic trees such as jacarandas and flamboyants have been planted around the settlement. The old houses have wide verandas closed in with mosquito gauze.

Among the large and ancient trees are 11 wooden chalets with thatched roofs overlooking the lower Chobe River and offering comfortable accommodation. Kubu Lodge boasts a restaurant of wood and thatch, with a small cocktail bar, a lounge and an extensive balcony with a superb and refreshing view. This is the perfect place for a sundowner! The kitchen produces excellent home-cooked meals.

The swimming pool is a delight in the heat of a Kasane summer, and a welcome facility even in the middle of winter. Scenic boat trips on a skimmer (flat-bottomed boat), down to the confluence of the Zambezi and the Chobe rivers, can be arranged and are particularly beautiful at sunset and sunrise. A trail has been laid out among the trees, allowing close-up views of the birds and the many bushbuck resident at Kubu Lodge. In addition, there are daily game drives to and through Chobe National Park with professional guides in open Land Rovers.

The campsites, which are laid out along the river, have brick and thatch ablution facilities of a high standard. This is 'quality' camping life; numbers are restricted, and it is advisable to book during the busy seasons of Easter, June and July.

Steve Griesel of African Odyssey organises safaris into the Chobe area from Kubu Lodge.

Cresta Mowana Safari Lodge

Accommodation: Hotel rooms. **Facilities**: Restaurant, cocktail lounge, swimming pool, poolside coffee shop and bar, shops, conference facilities. **Activities/attractions**: Game drives, game-viewing by helicopter, day-trips to the Victoria Falls. **Tariff**: High. **Contact details**: PO Box 266, Kasane; tel 625-0300, fax 625-0301, email Mowana@info.bw. **Central reservations**: South Africa: tel (27 12) 342-2810, fax (27 12) 342-2833, email crestasa@iafrica.com. Botswana: tel 391-2431, fax 397-5376.

Mowana Safari Lodge is located on the eastern outskirts of Kasane, overlooking the Chobe River: its entrance gate easily identified by the large baobab which grows next to it (mowana means 'baobab' in Setswana). The hotel is a stately double-storey building facing out on the banks of the Chobe River. The thatch and wood, which has been used so abundantly in the building, blends in with the environment.

Try to time your arrival for the sunset hour so that the baobab growing in the main amphitheatre of the hotel is backlit by the setting sun – a truly breathtaking sight.

Accommodation is in luxurious air-conditioned rooms, each with en suite bath and shower. Each room also has its own mini-bar, tea/coffee facilities, mosquito nets and electric mosquito protectors. The cocktail lounge is situated high above the Chobe and affords sweeping vistas of the river and, across it (in Namibia), of the floodplain.

On offer are game drives, in open safari vehicles, into the Chobe National Park; game-viewing boat trips and helicopter trips. For those who would rather lounge by the pool there are poolside bar facilities and a coffee shop.

Baobab Lodge

Accommodation: Chalets. **Facilities:** Restaurant, swimming pool, gift shop. **Activities/attractions:** Game-viewing drives and walks, birding, night drives, fishing, mokoro (traditional canoe) trips, crocodile farm. **Tariff:** Medium. **Contact details:** PO Box 109, Kasane, tel and fax 625-0430.

Baobab Lodge is a 12-bed camp, located 63 km from Kasane on the tarmac road to Savute and the Ngoma bridge (at the Botswana/Namibia border). It is built out of weathered basalt under thatch, and the six cabins, all raised above the ground, blend perfectly with the environment. There are magnificent views across the Chobe floodplain from the large restaurant-lounge.

The Chobe area's only klipspringer antelope are resident in the vicinity. A natural plunge pool has been built into the rock above the lodge's waterhole, which itself attracts all manner of game to provide excellent viewing opportunities.

Rates are fully inclusive, covering most activities, meals and refreshments, game drives and transfers to and from Kasane airport or the Namibia border. Not included are: the bar account, transfers to the Zimbabwe/Zambia border, mokoro (treaditional canoe) trips, crocodile farm and other optional activities.

Impalila Island Lodge (in Namibia)

Tariff: High. **Contact details:** PO Box 70378, Bryanston 2121, South Africa; tel. (27 11) 706-7207, fax (27 11) 463-8251, email: louise@ impalila. co.za.

Ichingo Chobe River Lodge (in Namibia)

Tariff: *To be ascertained.* **Contact details:** Tel (267) 65-0143, or cellphone (mobile) (267) 7130-2439, fax 625-0223 or (27 82) 903-2490, email ichingo@iafrica.com.

These Namibian lodges are included in a book about Botswana because they are convenient alternatives in the event that the Kasane and Kazungula lodges and hotels are fully booked (and this does happen!). I have not visited them, but I'm told they are both top-quality establishments. They are located on Impalila Island, just a few hundred metres beyond the Botswana–Namibia border (on the wedge of land that sits between Zambia and Botswana, and which divides the Chobe from the Zambezi right down to the junction).

Makgadikgadi area

This huge area which incorporates both the immense grasslands to the west of Ntwetwe Pan as well the vast emptiness of Sowa Pan is largely unexploited from a tourism point of view. As such, there are few places where the ordinary traveller can enjoy it. Most can be enjoyed only by independent travellers.

Jack's Camp & San Camp

Accommodation: Luxury tents (booking essential). **Activities/attractions**: Game-viewing, guided walks, Bushman walks, birding, 4x4 and quad-bike trips. **Tariff**: High. **Contact details**: PO Box 173, Francistown; tel 241-2277, fax 241-3458.

Uncharted Africa, the moving spirits behind this enterprise, operate the only two permanent camps in the Makgadikgadi, and into these sometimes harsh surrounds they have introduced luxury unparalleled.

In Jack's Camp the tents are fashioned in an enticing 1940s style – authentic, spacious and exceptionally comfortable. Bucket showers, Persian carpets and cool cotton sheets create a striking contrast with the area's rugged wilderness.

San Camp nestles among scattered clusters of palm trees on the edge of Ntwetwe Pan. For the first time ever in southern Africa, white canvas tents in the style of Jack's, twinned with a dramatic location, distinguish one of the most romantic camps in Africa.

Using four-wheel-drive quad-bikes, guests are able to explore the hitherto unknown and impenetrable area in an ecologically sensitive manner and, in the dry season, observe the relic of one of the earth's largest super-lakes. In the wet season the grass plains team with zebra, wildebeest and flamingo. A San (Bushman) tracker also takes guests on interesting and informative walks.

Guests may fly into Jack's Camp, or drive to Gweta, where they will be met and escorted to camp.

Leroo-La-Tau

Accommodation: Luxury tents (booking essential). **Activities/attractions**: Guided walks, game drives, night drives, cultural experiences; for longer-staying guests there are day-trips into Nxai and Makgadikgadi National Park, and the Central Kalahari Game Reserve. **Tariff**: Medium. **Contact details**: Private Bag 0047, Serowe; tel 463-4556, cellphone (mobile) 7130-6184, fax 463-4557, email attract@mopane.bw.

Located high on the banks of the Boteti River on its great bend to the south, and hidden among tall, shady trees, this new camp is ideally located for access to three of the country's national parks. Accommodation is in tented chalets, each with two double beds and bathroom en suite. The rate is inclusive of all activities, including drinks, meals, laundry and park fees. It is accessible by road (see Route 7A, Part 1, Mopipi–Maun, page 162; turn off and follow the signs at Xhumaga). Sean Watson is the owner and deserves to be congratulated on his choice of site: it combines, in unique fashion, grassland and riverine environment. The proximity of rural communities on the Boteti River adds another unusual element. Easy to get to, reasonably priced, this is a lodge for everyone.

The Ngamiland (Southern Okavango) region

The Okavango – soon, we hope, to become a World Heritage Site – is indeed unique. Some 6000 km² of permanently flooded land, set in a swirl of green that, at its greatest extent can spread to 15 000 km², it is a magnificent maze of rivers, streams, lagoons, islands and secret channels. It is home to all kinds of game and hosts a kaleidoscope of stunning birds. It is here that Botswana's tourist industry has its roots and from here that the visitor can take home memories and photographs of one of earth's great unspoilt wilderness areas.

Audi Camp

Accommodation: Tents, campsites (power-points installed, firewood available). **Facilities:** Restaurant, bar, swimming pool, laundry, boats. **Activities/attractions:** game-viewing and game flights, budget safaris. **Tariff:** Budget. **Contact details:** Private Bag 28, Maun; tel 686-0599, fax 686-0581.

Audi Camp is situated on the bank of the Thamalakane River. To get there, leave Maun on the Shorobe road and turn left at the circle (after crossing the bridge over the Thamalakane). The camp is situated 12 km from Maun.

For those who are too weary to put up their own tents, the camp offers erected two-person tents with fold-up mattresses. There is plenty of space, though, for your own tents, plus showers with lots of hot water.

Audi camp also hires equipment for mokoro (traditional canoe) excursions, including tents, mattresses, pots, pans, cool-boxes and so forth. A restaurant provides both a regular menu and light snacks; for the morning meal you can choose between a Continental breakfast and the full traditional English fare.

This is a good place to stop over on your way to the Moremi Game Reserve. Or let Audi Camp arrange a safari to Moremi, Chobe, the Central Kalahari or Nxai Pan for you.

Cresta Riley's Hotel

Accommodation: Hotel rooms (booking essential). **Facilities**: Restaurant, small shopping complex, hair salon, fuel outlet, bottle (liquor) store. **Activities/attractions**: See text below. **Tariff**: Medium plus. **Contact details**: PO Box 1, Maun; tel 686-0204, fax 686-0580, email rileys@info.bw.

Riley's Hotel is in the centre of Maun, on the banks of the Thamalakane River. The original hotel, with its unique frontier atmosphere, has been substantially renovated. Ever expanding to meet the energetic growth of the town, it now has 16 double air-conditioned rooms, three air-conditioned executive suites and 32 twin rooms, 12 of which have air-conditioning. All have en-suite facilities. The large and immaculate swimming pool is extremely popular, as are Harry's Bar and the Motswiri Pool Bar. Deep, shady verandas surround two sides of the hotel and overlook the river.

Riley's is within easy walking distance of banks, gift shops, garage, supermarket and liquor stores.

Crocodile Camp Safaris

Accommodation: 10 chalets (8 en suite), campsites (with showers); booking essential. **Facilities**: Restaurant, bar, swimming pool. **Activities/attractions**: Game drives, mobile safaris throughout Botswana, trips by mokoro (traditional canoe), fishing, boating, canoeing, birding. **Tariff**: Medium. **Contact details**: PO Box 46, Maun; tel 686-0265, fax 686-0793. *Safari reservations*: tel 686-0796, email sales@botswana.com.

'Croc Camp' is the oldest established campsite in Maun. Founded in 1968 by the legendary crocodile hunter Bobby Wilmot, it has become a favourite destination for overnighters and watering hole for tourists and Maun residents alike. The camp is situated on the banks of the Thamalakane River, the level of which varies according to the time of year and the strength of the annual flood.

The camp lies on the Shorobe road approximately 12 km from the traffic circle in Maun. Accommodation is in en-suite brick and thatch chalets that overlook the river. The bar, set next to a fragrant potato bush (*Phyllanthus reticulatus*), and a magnificent russet bushwillow (*Combretum hereroenses*), is the focal point for pre-dinner drinks, and a place for quenching your thirst with icy cold beverages after a hot, dusty drive. One can also order reasonably priced meals and snacks from the bar attendant. The restaurant is adjacent to the bar and serves breakfast and dinner.

The campsites are set back from the river among huge camelthorn acacia (*Acacia erioloba*) trees and have clean ablution facilities with hot and cold showers and flush toilets.

Crocodile Camp Safaris' primary business is the operation of mobile safaris, by boat and custom-designed safari vehicles. Safaris depart throughout the year from either Maun or Victoria Falls and are accompanied by a licensed professional guide. Itineraries for safaris are tailor-made to suit the needs of guests. For more details contact the safari reservations office by phone, fax or e-mail.

Island Safari Lodge

Accommodation: Chalets, campsites; booking advisable. **Facilities**: Restaurant, bar, swimming pool, shop. **Activities/attractions**: Safaris, mokoro (traditional canoe) trails, game flights by helicopter, light-aircraft scenic flights, walks, birding, boating. **Tariff**: Medium. **Contact details**: PO Box 116, Maun; tel 686-0300, fax 686-2932, email island@info.bw.

Starting from Maun, take the tar road northwest from the junction near the airport, and carry on along the tarred road for some 10 km. Just before the Matlapaneng bridge you will see, on your left, signposts directing you towards Island Safari Lodge.

The lodge is situated under a canopy of fine old trees, a place where one hears constant birdsong and the chatter of squirrels. The two-, three- and four-bedded brick cottages are thatched; all have hot and cold showers. There is a restaurant and bar.

The campsite is also set among the trees lining the river, and there are good ablution facilities. The bird life is a constant delight, even if you are not a keen bird-watcher.

Okavango River Lodge

Accommodation: Chalets, tents, caravan sites; booking essential. **Facilities**: Restaurant, swimming pool, small golf course. **Activities/attractions**: Trips into the Delta, walking safaris, fishing; safari excursions tailored to suit clients. **Tariff**: Budget. **Contact details**: Private Bag 28, Maun; tel and fax 686-3707.

Okavango River Lodge is situated on the Shorobe road, 15km from Maun, and overlooks the Thamalakane River. It currently (November 2000) offers four double, en-suite chalets and camping facilities, with good ablution facilities. Cut-off time for reservations is 6 pm on the evening of the stay unless a deposit has been paid. The lodge also hires out caravans and tents.

Sedia Hotel

Accommodation: Hotel rooms, chalets, campsites. **Facilities**: Restaurant, Internet café, swimming pool, volleyball court, conference facilities, mobile safaris on request. **Tariff**: Medium. **Contact details**: Private Bag 058, Maun; tel and fax 686-0177, email sedia@info.bw; website www.info.bw/~sedia.

The hotel is located 5 km out of Maun on the road to Matlapaneng, on the southwest side of the Thamalakane River. Take the road northwest from the airport junction. Sedia has 24 double rooms and a restaurant, and, for the self-catering guest, six cottages, each with a double bed and two single beds. There is a swimming pool and a volleyball court. Camping facilities, at the newly enlarged campsite, are also available; hot and cold showers are provided.

Maun Lodge

Accommodation: Hotel rooms. **Facilities**: Restaurant, bar, swimming pool, shop. **Tariff**: Medium. **Contact details**: PO Box 376, Maun; tel 686-3939, fax 686-3969, email lodge@info.bw.

The lodge is located on the banks of the Thamalakane River 2.5 km from the town centre and 4 km from the airport. A courtesy bus meets all Air Botswana scheduled flights.

New Moon

Tariff: Budget. **Contact details**: Private Bag 210, Maun; tel and fax 686-1665, email newmoon@info.bw.

Alongside the usual participation tours through the national parks (Moremi, Chobe, Central Kalahari, Makgadikgadi, and so on), New Moon offers adventure canoeing and walking/backpacking safaris through the Delta and through big-game country, hunter/gatherer excursions with San (Bushmen), elephant walking safaris through national parks (minimum four days), tailor-made safaris for families or groups to wherever in Botswana the clients wish to go, and for whatever duration, mokoro trips, and vehicle and guide hire (minimum two days).

New Moon's springboard to the western Delta is the new fishing camp, Sepupa Swamp. Here, at the northwestern edge of the Okavango (ideally situated on the panhandle en route to and from Namibia), it offers budget camping, luxury tented and chalet accommodation, mokoro (traditional canoe) trips, fishing boat and tackle hire, river safaris and full-moon night river safaris and safaris to Tsodilo Hills. Also offered are Bushman safaris to Aha Hills, which involve hunting and gathering activities and even lessons on traditional songs! Clients can build their own itineraries from the various options on offer.

The Booking Company

Contact details: Private Bag 198, Maun; tel 686-0022, fax 686-0037, email book@info.bw.

The Booking Company arranges excursions to, and activities and accommodation in, the Okavango Delta and surrounds. Situated close to the Maun airport, on the main road (opposite Nhabe Museum), the company specialises in one-, two- and three-day budget mokoro (traditional canoe) safaris, which include a scenic flight across the Delta. It will also arrange camping safaris into the Moremi and Chobe areas, day trips from Maun and Kasane, and walking trips with elephants, and will handle reservations for accommodation and light-aircraft flights.

Moremi area and central Delta

The heart of the Delta itself is found in the permanently flooded areas and in the Moremi Game Reserve. Most of the good lodges will be found in or near the former area and game-viewing is always good in the Moremi.

The Moremi reserve is something of a mecca for wildlife enthusiasts. There are no places to buy food or fuel in the area so, once you leave Kasane or Maun, you have to be fully self-contained. A four-wheel-drive vehicle is essential. The country is flat and well vegetated, with extensive areas under water after the annual flooding. There are four camping areas in the reserve – at North and South gates, Third Bridge and Xakanaxa.

Abu Camp

Renowned for its elephant-back safaris. **Accommodation**: Luxury tents; booking essential. **Facilities**: Air transfers. **Activities**: Game-viewing excursions on elephants, game drives, night drives, guided walks, trips by mokoro (traditional canoe). **Tariff**: High. **Contact details**: Private Bag 332, Maun; tel 686-1260, fax 686-100, email ebs@info.bw.

Abu Camp is located on the banks of the Nxabega River in the south-western part of the Okavango Delta and named after Randall Moore's legendary elephant celebrity, Abu. This splendid animal has starred in films such as *Circles in the Forest* and *The Power of One*, and here, in the Delta, he leads a herd of 13 adults and young.

Travelling with this elephant family, which blends naturally into their surrounds, allows visitors a unique opportunity to approach and interact with a wide variety of wildlife. Guests are transported on the backs of the four adult elephants in custom-made two-seater saddles. The younger elephants accompany the adults, play, swim and provide a constant source of interest and amusement.

Abu Camp nestles under African ebony trees overlooking a lagoon. Accommodation is in five luxurious en-suite safari tents. Sundowners and meals are eaten out in the shade of a giant fig tree. Access is by air only – a 20-minute flight – followed by a short drive. Tariffs include air transfers, accommodation, all activities, all meals and drinks and a daily laundry service.

Camp Moremi

Accommodation: Tented camp; booking essential. **Facilities**: Restaurant, swimming pool, gift shop, observation platform. **Activities/attractions**: Game-viewing drives and walks, boating, canoeing, river cruises, fishing. **Tariff**: High. **Contact details**: Private Bag 198, Maun; tel 686-1243, fax 686-0037; or Desert & Delta Safaris, PO Box 1200, Paulshof 2056, South Africa; tel (27 11) 807-3720, fax (27 11) 807-3480.

Camp Moremi is situated on the beautiful Xakanaxa Lagoon in the Moremi Game Reserve. Only 22 guests can be accommodated in walk-through safari tents (with open-air private hot showers and flush toilets; they can be covered in the rainy season!). Each tent is pleasantly appointed with Rhodesian teak furniture, colourful woven rugs, designer linen and matching interior blinds.

The main building, the magnificent Moremi Tree Lodge, which is shaded by giant ebony trees, is an elegant thatch and timber structure comprising a main lounge, wildlife reference library, dining room and cocktail bar cooled by overhead punkah fans. The large sundeck affords an excellent view of the lagoon.

Camp Moremi provides the complete lodge experience, including rewarding game drives through the Moremi reserve, opportunities for good fishing and visits by boat to the heronries on the Gadikwe and Xakanaxa lagoons.

Daily rates include all accommodation, meals, drinks, all scheduled game-viewing activities, park entrance fee and a laundry service. The place is popular among honeymooners.

Camp Okavango

Accommodation: Tented camp, deluxe suite; booking essential. **Facilities:** Restaurant, bar, swimming pool. **Activities/attractions**: Game-viewing drives and walks, boating, canoeing, river cruises, fishing, birding. **Tariff**: High. **Contact details**: Private Bag 198, Maun; tel 686-1243, fax 686-0037; or Desert & Delta Safaris, PO Box 1200, Paulshof 2056, South Africa; tel (27 11) 807-3720, fax (27 11) 807-3480.

Camp Okavango is situated on remote Nxaragha Island in the heart of the Okavango Delta. Unashamed luxury combines with the Africa of yesteryear in the elegant thatch and lethaka (reed) main building, which houses a cocktail bar, lounge and dining room, while the expansive open-air patio caters for al fresco meals and evenings around a blazing fire. The camp's silver-service dinner, served by candlelight, is renowned among seasoned travellers.

Shaded hammocks, reading benches and a delightful sundeck and plunge pool provide relief during the hot midday hours.

Camp Okavango accommodates just 22 guests in walk-through safari tents with open-air (but private) hot showers and flush toilets (which can be covered in the rainy season!). Each tent is pleasantly appointed with Rhodesian teak furniture, colourful woven rugs, designer linen and matching interior blinds.

Honeymooners are well catered for, and for those who demand the ultimate in exclusivity, Camp Okavango offers the 'Jessie Suite' (among other things, these guests enjoy private game-viewing excursions). Camp Okavango is the ideal base from which to discover the Delta's wetland ecosystem. All game-viewing activities are conducted by experienced resident naturalist guides and include canoe and boat trips. Guided nature walks on neighbouring islands can be arranged, and the fishing is superb.

Daily rates include all accommodation, meals, drinks, scheduled game-viewing activities, park entrance fee and a laundry service.

Camp Okuti

Accommodation: Chalets; booking essential. **Facilities**: Restaurant, gift shop. **Activities/attractions**: Game-viewing excursions, birding, boating, fishing. **Tariff**: Medium. **Contact details**: PO Box 39, Maun; tel 686-0220, 686-0339, fax 686-0589, email okavango@info.bw.

Situated in the northeastern corner of the Okavango Delta, this small, exclusive camp caters for a maximum of 20 guests in insect-proof thatched chalets, each with en-suite facilities. Each twin-bedded chalet (there is also a family unit which sleeps four) faces onto the river, providing the visitor with spectacular sunset viewing. The central dining and lounge area offers a welcome retreat from the hot midday sun, as does the bar, which is situated around a giant ebony tree.

The area is home to a wide range of flora and fauna; guided drives into forests and the open plains of Moremi reserve afford guests an excellent game-viewing experience; specially designed open vehicles allow the perfect photo opportunity. Elephant, lion, wild dog, giraffe, zebra, and a large variety of antelope can be seen. The bird life is explosive, with many migrant varieties seen during the rainy season. Excursions upstream by motorboat take you into the further reaches of the Delta, where you will have time to explore hidden waterways and conduct walks on one of the area's many islands. All meals, park fees, teas/coffees and game activities are included in the daily tariff.

Delta Camp

Accommodation: Chalets; booking essential. **Facilities**: Licensed to serve drinks. **Activities/attractions**: Game-viewing excursions, trips by mokoro (traditional canoe), fishing, birding. **Tariff**: High. **Contact details**: PO Box 39, Maun; tel 686-0220/0339, fax 686-0589, email okavango@info.bw.

There is no road access to this camp, so it's not the place for a casual visit; arrangements must be made to fly in on the daily Delta Air flights to the camp's private airstrip. Delta Camp is a luxury camp with traditionally reeded thatched chalets, each with en-suite facilities. The central feature is the thatched lounge and dining area, which also has a viewing deck that affords a most impressive view of the Delta. The whole camp faces west, which offers the most spectacular sunsets as distant islands and palm trees catch and diffuse the golden evening light.

Activities at and from the camp include guided mokoro (traditional canoe) trails that probe deeper into the Delta, along twisting narrow channels rich with diverse flora and fauna, game walks on adjacent islands, with your personal professional licensed guide, in search of the wealth of animals and bird life resident in this area. Motorboats are not used, as the emphasis is on preserving the pristine natural environment – which creates a relaxed, peaceful atmosphere for the safaris. Visitors can also take a longer trail and camp out with a guide on one of the many islands (camping on islands is by special arrangement only and must be booked in advance) and explore the Moremi Game Reserve. The Sitatunga Trail can be arranged exclusively for groups of four people (minimum) who wish to explore this wondrous area for six nights or more.

All meals, drinks, laundry, park fees and excursions are included in the daily tariff.

Eagle Island Camp (formerly Xaxaba)

Accommodation: Luxury tents; booking essential. **Facilities**: Swimming pool, gift shop. **Activities/attractions**: Game drives, river cruises, trips by mokoro, scenic flights, birding. **Tariff**: High. **Contact details**: Gametrackers, PO Box 100, Maun; tel 686-0302, fax 686-0153, email gtres@iafrica.com, website www.orient-expresshotels.com.

This camp lies deep in the Okavango Delta, and to get there you have to travel by air, usually from Maun. Booking is most important for Eagle Island (Xaxaba) as it is a very popular camp, especially during the busier months of the tourist season.

It offers a range of facilities, including mokoro trips, fishing and walks through the incredibly beautiful floodplains of the Delta. Aircraft flights can be arranged on request. The luxury tented camp, recently refurbished, is set in this 'place of tall trees' (which is the meaning of the old name) most of the trees in and around the camp have been discretely identified with their common, scientific and Setswana names.

The daily tariff is fully inclusive.

Gunn's Camp

Accommodation: Luxury tents, campsites; booking essential. **Facilities**: meals, bar. **Activities/attractions**: Game-viewing excursions, walks, sunset cruises (water level permitting), fishing, birding. **Tariff**: Medium. **Contact details**: Private Bag 033, Maun; tel 686-0023, fax 686-0040, email gunnscamp@info.bw.

Gunn's Camp is situated on the Boro River, adjacent to Chief's Island in the Moremi Game Reserve. The camp is set on two small neighbouring islands, each densely wooded and graced with tall palms. There is no access by water or air; the management tries to schedule flights as close as possible to your preferred time.

On one island is Gunn's Bush Camp, which caters for the budget conscious traveller. The camping area has toilets and showers, barbecue facilities, a bar and supply store. Camping and cooking equipment are available for hire, and you can buy basic non-perishable provisions. The second island, Gunn's Camp, offers seven large twin-bedded tents, each with its own en-suite facilities, plus a raised honeymoon suite. Accommodation is on a fully inclusive basis.

Mokoro (traditional canoe) safaris can be arranged while in camp. The trips are flexible: you can go out for anything from a few hours to a few days. It's also possible to take a powerboat excursion along the many channels and lagoons, and to walk on the islands.

Khwai River Lodge

Accommodation: Luxury tents; booking essential. **Facilities**: Swimming pool, gift shop. **Activities/attractions**: Game-viewing drives, walks, birding. **Tariff**: High. **Contact details**: Gametrackers, PO Box 100, Maun; tel 686-0302, fax 686-0153, email gtres@iafrica.com, website www.orient-expresshotels.com.

Khwai is not a casual, drop-in destination, so ensure you make firm arrangements if you intend to spend at least a night there. Intrepid self-drivers head in from the Moremi reserve's North Gate in an easterly direction for 8 km. However, most guests are flown in, to be met by their guide at the private airstrip.

Khwai, which overlooks the Khwai River, is one of the largest lodges in the Delta. It was completely refurbished in early 1999 and boasts a new thatched main complex of dining room, bar and lounge which, when open, makes the most of the stunning views of the river and the animals drinking and playing there. After your evening meal there's coffee, liqueurs and tales of the day around the fire.

Accommodation is in luxury tents scattered along the riverbank, under trees. Each has teak flooring and accessories, and en-suite facilities.

Game drives take clients into surrounding reserves to see the abundant wildlife. The rest of the time can be spent around the pool, or viewing the birds and game from the grounds of the lodge. Keep an eye out for elephants and resident hippo (it's sometimes hard to believe that hippos, which look so somnolent in the water, kill more humans than any other animal in Africa!). Rates are fully inclusive.

Machaba

Accommodation: Luxury tents; booking essential. **Facilities**: Restaurant. **Activities/attractions**: Game drives, night drives, birding. **Tariff**: Medium. **Contact details**: Ker & Downey, PO Box 27, Maun; tel 686-0375, fax 686-1282, email safari@kerdowney.bw.

Machaba lies on the banks of the Khwai River, right opposite Moremi Game Reserve – the heart of big-game country. Guests may drive to the camp, but most people fly in (there is a short transfer from the airstrip).

Accommodation is in luxury tents with every convenience, including really good showers and ablutions. You can look forward to long evenings of conversation and convivial company around a blazing campfire.

For the photographer, there is an enormous range of game animals to choose from, both in the reserve and outside it; among the wildlife to be seen are leopard, cheetah, wild dog, elephant, buffalo, lion and giraffe.

The rich bird life also offers excellent photographic opportunities. Night game-drives are fascinating, revealing another intriguing dimension of the wilderness experience.

Mombo Camp

Accommodation: Luxury tents; booking essential. **Facilities**: Dining room, bar, gift shop, plunge pool. **Activities/attractions**: Game drives, birding, walks. **Tariff**: High. **Contact details**: Private Bag 14, Maun; tel 686-0086, fax 686-0632. **Central reservations**: PO Box 5219, Rivonia 2128, South Africa; tel (27 11) 807-1800, fax (27 11) 807-2100.

Mombo Camp is situated on Mombo Island, which adjoins the northern tip of Chief's Island, within the Moremi Game Reserve. The camp overlooks a floodplain where the savannah meets the Delta, and is best known for its excellent game-viewing.

The camp accommodates 18 guests; Little Mombo a further six, in luxurious tents with en-suite facilities. The entire camp is on a raised deck; a separate lounge/dining/bar area overlooks the open plain in front of the camp. Morning and afternoon game drives produce good sightings of the abundant game, and of some of the more unusual bird species found in this area. A drive out to the waterhole is a pleasant excursion in the heat of the day, or one can cool off in the plunge pool.

Guests are flown in to the private airstrip, where they are met and escorted to camp.

Oddballs

Accommodation: Chalets (minimum two nights), campsites; booking essential. **Facilities**: Restaurant, bar, shop. **Activities/attractions**: Game-viewing excursions by mokoro (traditional canoe), conducted walks, fishing, birding. **Tariff**: Budget–Medium. **Contact details**: PO Box 39, Maun; tel 686-0220/0339, fax 686-0589, email okavango@info.bw.

To get to this camp you have to be flown in, usually from Maun – which is quite an experience: the aerial views of the Delta are fascinating and, particularly in winter, offer a complete contrast from the barren dryness of the area around the town.

Oddballs is situated on the edge of Chief's Island; guests camp and explore the Delta by mokoro. The décor is quaint and original. The bar is built around a tall tree and leaky mekoro (the plural of mokoro) are given a new lease of life, ingeniously serving as cupboards. At the campsite you will find hot showers and flush toilets. Self-catering chalets are available but you are requested to book a minimum stay of two nights.

On offer are camping trails, which last a minimum of two nights; all camping equipment is provided (tent, mattress, pillow, mokoro seat, cutlery, can-opener, crockery, pots, braai/barbecue grid and cooler-box) and food (on a self-prepare basis). Oddballs is very environment conscious, admirably so: every scrap of waste accumulated by staff and guests anywhere in the Delta is assiduously collected, bagged and removed.

Rates include all meals, guided walks and mokoro excursions.

Pom Pom Camp

Accommodation: Luxury tents; booking essential. **Facilities**: Restaurant, swimming pool. **Activities/attractions**: Game drives (day and night), game walks, trips by mokoro (traditional canoe), birding, fishing. **Tariff**: Medium. **Contact details**: Ker & Downey, PO Box 27, Maun; tel 686-0375, fax 686-1282, email safari@kerdowney.bw.

This is a fly-in island camp in the heart of the permanent Delta. Part of the Ker & Downey group, it meets all that enterprise's well-known standards of excellence and concern for clients' needs. Exploring the area and its wildlife is a delight – from the hippo which inhabit the lagoon fronting the camp to the game that you will encounter further afield, either on excursions by vehicle or on game walks, all of which allow a closeness to the Okavango and its inhabitants that you'll find hard to match. It's certainly a wonderful place for the enthusiastic photographer. Like the rest of the Okavango, the bird life is enormously varied and plentiful and one does not have to be a fanatic to enjoy this startling variety.

Shinde Island

Accommodation: Luxury tents; booking essential. **Facilities**: Restaurant, swimming pool. **Activities/attractions**: Game-viewing drives, conducted game walks, trips by water (mokoro, powerboat), birding, fishing. **Tariff**: Medium. **Contact details**: Ker & Downey, PO Box 27, Maun; tel 686-0375, fax 686-1282, email safari@kerdowney.bw.

Shinde, nestled on a lush palm island in the heart of the northern Okavango Delta, is surrounded by clear, permanent waterways teeming with bird life and game, and offers you every type of activity that is available in the Delta. The latter range from game drives in open four-wheel-drive safari vehicles, powerboat excursions, forays to witness the spectacular evening roosts, walks in the company of an armed ranger equipped with radio, fishing expeditions from the riverbank or from boats to the serene experience of gliding noiselessly through the papyrus-lined channels and lagoons in a mokoro poled by an expert guide.

Tsaro Elephant Lodge

Accommodation: Chalets; booking essential. **Facilities**: Swimming pool, covered hide, gift shop. **Activities/attractions**: Game drives, birding. **Tariff**: Medium. **Contact details**: Private Bag 48, Maun; tel 686-1805, fax 686-1087, email xugtsa@info.bw. Also Hartley's Safaris, PO Box 69859, Bryanston 2021, South Africa. **GPS co-ordinates:** 19 10' South 23 44' East 1026 m altitude.

Tsaro is situated on the banks of the Khwai River on the eastern side of Moremi Game Reserve. Access is by road or light aircraft. It's graciously luxurious and quite different from the majority of lodges in the Delta: here brick and mortar take the place of the more usual reeds and poles. The impression you get on arrival is of an elegant private home, and of your status as a guest of the family – an impression which lasts throughout your stay. Walk through the front door and your eye is drawn from a sparkling pool in a white-walled courtyard to a suspended mokoro, now no longer plying the waters of the Delta but used for the buffet. From the U-shaped courtyard you look through shady trees and across lush green lawns to the wild beyond. There is a shop that stocks a selection of clothes and curios, local artifacts, books and film.

Guests are taken out on early-morning game drives, which surprise and delight the receptive visitor. It's worth setting out just before sunrise to appreciate the rhythms of the bush to the full. Tsaro's game drives have many delightful surprises; bird-watching and boat excursions are a speciality, and start from a second camp at Xugana Lagoon.

Xakanaxa

Accommodation: Luxury tents; booking essential. **Facilities**: Dining room, lounge, swimming pool, gift shop. **Activities/attractions**: Game drives, river cruises, boating trips, scenic flights, fishing, birding. **Tariff**: Medium. **Contact details**: Private Bag 26, Maun, or Moremi Safaris and Tours, PO Box 2757, Cramerview 2060, South Africa; tel (27 11) 465-3842/3, fax (27 11) 465-3779, email Moremi@yebo.co.za, website http://www. Moremi.co.za. **Airstrip co-ordinates:** S19 11'53,8" E23'25'53,1".

One may fly in to Xakanaxa (by arrangement) from Maun, or drive there. The camp is 130 km from the town. If you're driving, turn west inside Moremi Game Reserve, just a short distance from North Gate and continue for about 50 km to Xakanaxa Lagoon. The route is signposted. Xakanaxa is situated on the edge of the lagoon, one of the most beautiful in the Delta. You'll find, set beneath a canopy of giant trees, luxurious accommodation in twin-bedded safari tents, each with en-suite facilities.

A relaxed, rustic and friendly atmosphere prevails in the camp. Indigenous building materials have been used wherever possible; the dining room and lounge are elevated and open-fronted with reed walls and thatched roof, and the open decks have a wonderful view of the river to the distant islands. The tents and the reception, office, shop and dining area have been carefully positioned to maintain privacy.

This is one of the few Botswana lodges that can offer all-year-round boating trips as well as extensive 4x4 drives into outstanding game country. Game-viewing trips can be organised to suit a client's preferences.

Xugana Lodge

Accommodation: Huts on stilts; booking essential. **Facilities**: Bar, swimming pool, gift shop. **Activities/attractions**: Walks, fishing, boating, birding. **Tariff**: Medium. **Contact details**: Private Bag 48, Maun; tel 686-1805, fax 686-1087, email xugtsa@info.bw. Also Hartley's Safaris, PO Box 69859, Bryanston 2021, South Africa. **GPS co-ordinates:** 19 5' South 23 6' East 1027 m altitude.

Access to Xugana is by air only (please note that the luggage weight restriction is 10 kg per person). The lodge is located on one of the Delta's largest lagoons; the record tiger-fish catch was made within hailing distance of the lodge's bar! Bream and catfish are also plentiful. Tackle is available. Many rare birds can be seen in the area; over 400 bird species have been identified. The sitatunga, a water-adapted antelope, is also resident here.

The lodge provides accommodation for no more than 16 guests at a time, in eight reed-and-thatch mesasa (huts) built on stilts and set among indigenous trees and overlooking the lagoon. Each mesasa is mosquito-proofed and has en-suite facilities. The Okavango Delta has attracted some of the world's celebrities. Xugana's most notable guest was Prince Charles, who spent several days at the lodge in 1984.

Savute area

A fuller description of Savute and its special attractions appears on page 133. Here the landscape differs from that of the Moremi and Chobe areas. After the flatness of the latter it's refreshing to find yourself in a landscape of hills. You'll see Bushman (San) paintings on some of the rocky outcrops. Savute can be very dry, and you should carry water.

Savute is a fine place to see game of all kinds, which is partly why it is so popular. Take care not to keep fruit, especially oranges, in your tent or vehicle as this can focus the unwanted attention of elephants on you.

Savute Elephant Camp

Accommodation: Luxury tents; booking essential. **Facilities**: Swimming pool, gift shop. **Activities/attractions**: Game-viewing drives, birding. **Tariff**: High. **Contact details**: Gametrackers, PO Box 100, Maun; tel 686-0302, fax 686-0153, email gtres@iafrica.com, website www.orient-expresshotels.com.

Savute typifies the eternal contrasts of Africa. Where the other two Gametrackers' camps (see Khwai River, page 239, and Eagle Island/Xaxaba, page 238) celebrate the Delta's water and lush vegetation, Savute is the epitome of aridity. It lies in the Chobe National Park in the far north of Botswana, in the Kalahari sandveld, and in this dry place rain is rare and water is precious. It's situated on the mysterious Savute Channel (an eccentric waterway with cycles that lurch between bone-dry terrain and floodwater).

Accommodation is under airy canvas: large, spacious, fully appointed luxury tents complete with air-conditioning, electric fan and heater, plenty of hot water on tap, private game-viewing deck, electric shaver plugs and facilities for charging your video camera batteries! Opportunities to view game and the astonishing bird life are superb throughout the year.

In Savute, one animal reigns supreme: the elephant. This is the place to see the earth's largest land creatures in their full, dusty magnificence (in fact the campsite suffers their close attention: they have a habit of digging up the plumbing, leaving it without water).

Kingspool

Accommodation: Luxury tents; booking essential. **Facilities**: Plunge pool, gift shop. **Activities/attractions**: Game-viewing drives, birding. **Tariff**: High. **Contact details**: Private Bag 14, Maun; tel 686-0086, fax 686-0632. **Central reservations**: PO Box 5219, Rivonia 2128, South Africa; tel (27 11) 807-1800, fax (27 11) 807-2100.

Kingspool is situated in the Linyanti Swamp, bordered by the Linyanti River and Chobe National Park, and was named after King Gustav of Sweden, who honeymooned here, in the 1970s, with Queen Sylvia.

It's a luxurious tented camp with en-suite facilities, and accommodates 20 guests. Each tent is situated on a deck that overlooks a lagoon (which is home to hippos). This area is renowned for its large herds of elephants and for the rare roan antelope. Hides are sited in and around the camp.

Guests are flown in on air charters.

Selinda Camp

Accommodation: Luxury tents; booking essential. **Facilities**: Gift shop. **Activities/attractions**: Game-viewing drives both by day and night, walks, limited fishing. **Tariff**: High. **Contact details**: Linyanti Explorations, PO Box 22, Kasane; tel 625-0505, fax 625-0352, email info@linyanti.com.

The camp is located on the banks of the eastern Selinda Spillway overlooking open floodplains, within a private wildlife area known as the Selinda Reserve. Less than a kilometre away is the exit point on the Linyanti (Chobe) River, from which the famed Savute Channel leaves (in those years when it mysteriously chooses to flow). Equally enigmatic in its unpredictable flow patterns is the Selinda Spillway, which also enters the Linyanti near here.

This camp can accommodate no more than 12 people at a time in its twin-bedded luxury safari tents. Each tent has its own en-suite facilities.

This is big-game country and there are few animals occurring in Botswana that you will not spot as you drive or walk in the care of your professional guide. The two-night three-day walking safaris are a must for those with an adventurous spirit and a desire for a different and rewarding African experience!

Selinda can be reached by air or by road, but this is definitely four-wheel-drive territory. The daily rate includes all meals, accommodation, game-viewing activities, and laundry. The camp is closed from December to the end of February.

Zibadianja Camp

Accommodation: Luxury tents; booking essential. **Facilities**: Bar area, gift shop. **Activities/attractions**: Game-viewing drives both by day and night, walks, limited fishing. **Tariff**: High. **Contact details**: Linyanti Explorations, PO Box 22, Kasane; tel 625-0505, fax 625-0352, email info@linyanti.com.

Zibadianja is a small, exclusive six-bed tented camp situated near the Zibadianja Lagoon in the private Selinda Reserve. Each tent is mounted on a raised wooden platform and has en-suite facilities. The tents also have a fly-sheet and shade-net cover. The bar area is outside, beside the campfire. Professional guides conduct all day and night game drives, and daily walks, through this private wildlife area.

Quality and service are the keynotes.

This camp can be reached by air, or by four-wheel-drive vehicle. It is closed from December to February.

The daily rate includes all meals, accommodation, game-viewing activities, laundry, sales tax, and refreshments (excluding imports).

Western Delta area

The western part of the Delta is the place for fishing enthusiasts, and the location of several fishing camps. This is also the home of Botswana's famous basket-makers, and a visit to villages such as Nokaneng, Gomare and Etsha, and meetings with the basket-makers, are fascinating experiences (the trips require time and patience, but the effort will be rewarded with some really special basketware). Two other attractions of the general area are the Tsodilo Hills (see Chapter 7, Places to Visit: the wilderness, page 141) and Drotsky's Cave (page 111). A quick way through the Caprivi is also described in Chapter 2 (page 24).

Fish Eagle Lodge/Drotsky's Cabins

Accommodation: A-frame chalets, campsites. **Facilities**: Boat hire, telephone and fax. **Activities/attractions**: Fishing, trips to Tsodilo Hills, birding, boating, boat hire. **Tariff**: Medium. **Contact details**: PO Box 115, Shakawe; tel 687-5035, fax 687-5043.

Drotsky's is probably the most distant of the Okavango lodges from Maun, but it can be reached by tarred road as well as by air. If you're into fishing on the big rivers of the Okavango, this is the place for you: the camp overlooks the main watercourse as it flows down the 100-km Panhandle. This is also a bird-watcher's paradise; the bird life is good all year round but particularly spectacular from September to December.

The rates are moderate for the choice of very comfortable accommodation. Five-metre powerboats are available for daily or hourly hire to provide an ideal opportunity – especially for independent travellers visiting the western Delta by road – to take a day or two off, camp and explore the waterways.

Guma Lagoon Camp

Accommodation: Luxury full-accommodation tents, self-catering tents, campsites; booking essential. **Facilities**: Restaurant, airstrip, powerboat hire, telephone and fax. **Activities/attractions**: Birding drives and walks, trips by mokoro (traditional canoe), fishing. **Tariff**: Budget (camping), medium (tents). **Contact details**: PO Box 66, Maun; tel 686-0351 and 686-0978, fax 686-0571.

This camp, surrounded by palm trees, papyrus and reed beds, is situated on the banks of Guma Lagoon, one of the area's biggest, in the northwest Delta. Guma has a warm family atmosphere (most of the clients are returnees). There is a choice of facilities: camping, self-catering accommodation in furnished and serviced wilderness tents, and full accommodation in nine luxury en-suite tents. The main activity of this camp is fishing, which is excellent all year round.

Those camping or staying in self-catering accommodation may book meals. Special rates are available for large groups or families staying for six days or more during the fishing season.

You can get to Guma by air or by road. The road is tarred to Etsha-13, but the last 11 km must be done by four-wheel-drive. The camp provides parking for saloon cars that cannot make the last stretch – under shade-cloth with a watchman – and arranges a four-wheel-drive transfer to camp.

Geoff Randall manufacturers 'real' fibreglass mokoro (traditional canoes) here in an attempt to minimize use of powerboats and so preserve the environment.

Nxamaseri Lodge

Accommodation: Thatched en-suite chalets; booking essential. **Facilities**: Restaurant, gift shop, airfield, game drives (in Mahango Game Reserve, over the border in Namibia), aquatic game-viewing, fishing (including fly-fishing), conducted walks, boating, horseback safaris, mokoro (traditional canoe) trails, trips to Tsodilo Hills. **Tariff**: Medium. **Contact details**: Private Bag 23, Maun; tel 686-1671, fax 686-1671, email ohsnx@info.bw. **Direct bookings:** tel 687-8016, fax 687-8015. **Airstrip co-ordinates**: 18 36-02S and 022-0444E.

This island lodge, set among giant riverine trees on the northwest Okavango Panhandle, is accessible by air or vehicle, followed by a short boat ride to camp.

Nxamaseri Lodge is a small, intimate camp accommodating 12 guests in luxury en-suite chalets, each with its own private wooden deck. It is a mecca for both the fisherman and the bird-watcher. Day trips to Mahango Game Reserve and Tsodilo Hills can be arranged. The lodge is renowned for its excellent cuisine, and for the remarkable horse safaris, further down the Delta, organised by Barney Bestelink (they are either five- or ten-day trips, with a three-day extension at the lodge, and they're memorable).

Shakawe Lodge

Accommodation: Chalets; booking essential; campsites. **Facilities**: Mains power, swimming pool, shop and bar at camping ground. **Activities/attractions**: Swimming, boating and boat trips, fishing, conducted walks, trips to Tsodilo Hills. **Tariff**: Medium. **Contact details**: PO Box 12, Shakawe; tel 686-0822/3, fax 686-0493, email t.wild@info.bw.

Shakawe Lodge, one of the first tourist camps to be established in the region, has been in operation since 1969. It lies 375 km from Maun, 15 km south of Shakawe village and 30 km from Mohembo on the Botswana/Namibia border. The routes are tarred, so access by road is no problem. There is also a good airstrip at Shakawe, and a Customs and Immigration post has been established. The lodge will organise transfers to and from the airstrip. It is perched on a high bank overlooking a bend in the Okavango River. It has ten spacious double rooms of brick under thatch, each with electric lights and fan. All bathrooms (shower and bath) are en-suite.

Bird-watching in the area is outstanding – here there is a wide range of habitats (riverine bush, savannah and semidesert). Other activities include boat trips and fishing and, at management's discretion, trips to the Tsodilo Hills. The best time for fishing generally is from April to November; bream are good in June, and the fighting tigerfish from August to October.

Shakawe camping ground is adjacent to, but operates as a separate entity from, the lodge. It is in a lovely lawned setting, right on the banks of the Okavango River, and shaded by large riverine trees. Hot water, showers and flush toilets are standard. An office, bar and shop complex have been constructed. Current prices (November 2000) are P35 per person; children under 12 free.

Jao

Accommodation: Luxury tents; booking essential. **Facilities**: Dining room and bar, plunge pool, gift shop. **Activities/attractions**: Game-viewing drives, walks, boating, mokoro (traditional canoe) trips. **Tariff**: High. **Contact details**: Private Bag 14, Maun; tel 686-0086, fax 686-0632. **Central reservations**: tel (27 11) 807-1800, fax (27 11) 807-2100.

Jao is situated on the western side of the Delta, among a thicket of sycamore fig and mangostene trees, and can accommodate 16 people in luxurious units built on decks overlooking a small river. These and the lounge/dining/bar area are situated among the trees on a split level with a superb view. Game drives enable you to see incredible herds of red lechwe, a water-adapted antelope, on almost every open floodplain.

Nata area

Nata village has really expanded and now boasts three filling stations. The Shell garage is attached to Sua Pan Lodge, which also has a take-away shop and bottle store. The lodge, owned by Thompson Masuku, is a good overnight venue on your journey further afield. Among the area's principal attractions are Nata Lodge and Nata Sanctuary (see pages 220 and 249).

Nata Lodge

Accommodation: Two-bed chalets, luxury safari tents, campsites. **Facilities**: Restaurant, family room, cocktail bar, swimming pool, gift shop, fuel outlet. **Activities/attractions**: Excursions (4x4) to the Makgadikgadi Pans, birding. **Tariff**: Budget. **Contact details**: Private Bag 10, Francistown; tel 621-1260, fax 621-1265.

The lodge lies some 10 km south of Nata on the main, tarred road from Francistown, and is strategically situated as a stopover point for visitors to Maun, the Okavango Delta, Chobe National Park, Victoria Falls and Zambia. It's clearly signposted, so keep your eyes open for the distinctive logo (a helmeted guineafowl).

The attractive A-frame cottages, each with a private shower and toilet, and the luxury en-suite safari tents, stand among tall palm, marula and monkey-thorn trees. The site is near the northeastern edge of the great Makgadikgadi Pans, an area of unique beauty.

In periods of good rains, this portion of the pans floods and might retain an initial metre or more of water for several years. At such times flamingo, pelican and other waterbirds appear in tens of thousands. The lodge will organise sunrise and sunset pan trips into Nata Sanctuary.

Nata Lodge has a thatched cocktail bar next to the large attractive swimming pool. There is also an excellent à la carte restaurant that serves breakfast, a snack menu and dinner. On Saturday nights a traditional braai (barbecue) is organised.

The area is generally considered to be excellent for bird-watching as the countryside around supports a diversity of habitats. Campers are particularly welcome at Nata Lodge; the attractive campsite offers brick-and-thatch ablution blocks in cool and shady surrounds.

Tuli area

Tuli is an area of Botswana that deserves far more attention than it gets at present. It lies to the east of the Kalahari sands, and the rocky landscape is full of interesting hills and valleys. It also has great historical and archaeological interest, and is rich in game. The landscape is very favourable for game-viewing.

All game reserves are on private land. Historically, they were part of the original Tuli Block – land set aside for Rhodes' great railway to the north. In the event, the large number of bridges required and the discovery of gold in Francistown caused a re-alignment and the Tuli Block, no longer needed for the railway line, was carved up into large cattle ranches. It is those former ranches that now form the private game reserves.

Mashatu Game Reserve

Accommodation: Luxury chalets and tents; booking essential. **Facilities**: Fully catered, private bar, plunge pool, conference centre. **Activities/ attractions**: Game-viewing drives (day and night), walks, birding, mountain biking (among the animals!). **Tariff**: High. **Contact details**: Private Bag X284, Hillcrest, KwaZulu-Natal 3650; tel (27 31) 765-2900, fax (27 31) 675-3365. (**Note**: All bookings must be made through the address given here or through travel agents in Botswana.)

Located in the northeast Tuli Block, the Mashatu Game Reserve's closest border crossing into South Africa is at Pont Drift. Fly-in facilities are available; Customs and Immigration clearance at the local airfield can be arranged when booking. Charter flights and accommodation may be booked through your travel agent in Botswana or South Africa. The drive time from Johannesburg via Pietersburg and Alldays is roughly 4 to 5 hours; the drive from Gaborone is approximately the same. Self-drive guests are met at the border by the game reserve staff and then transported to the camps.

Mashatu is the largest privately owned conservation area in southern Africa, and is remarkable for its diversity of landscape, and wildlife; its elephants are particularly well known. Other large animals to be found there include lion, leopard, cheetah, giraffe and many of the antelopes. There are two commercial camps at Mashatu.

Main Camp accommodates a maximum of 34 guests in luxuriously appointed air-conditioned standard rooms and superior rooms, and is an ideal venue for corporate clientele and senior management seminars. It also caters well for the needs of foreign and local travellers who enjoy a certain amount of luxury during their bushveld holiday.

A feature of the camp is a thatched observation bar, the 'Gin Trap', overlooking a floodlit waterhole. There is also a filtered plunge pool. Day and night game drives are conducted in open four-wheel-drive vehicles. Also on offer are walking tours led by experienced rangers.

Tent Camp is a luxury tented camp accommodating a maximum of 14 guests. Its character is entirely rustic, although every convenience is available to guests – the tents are insect-proof and each has an en-suite shower and toilet. Other notable features of the camp are its very personalised atmosphere, and the sense of wilderness it imparts. It has a swimming pool. Game-viewing outings are conducted in the same manner as at Main Camp.

The tariff includes all meals, teas, coffees, snacks, accommodation, game drives, transfers to and from the Tuli airstrip and from the Pont Drift border post.

Tuli Safari Lodge

Accommodation*:* Chalets, guest-house (self-catering). **Facilities***:* Luxury facilities, conference centre, swimming pool, viewing hides. **Activities/ attractions***:* Game-viewing drives (day and night), bush walks, birding. **Tariff***:* Medium. **Reservations***:* tel and fax 264-5303, email tuli@ tulilodge.co.za. Website: www.tulilodge.co.za.

Tuli Lodge is accessible both from air and by road; guests may fly in from anywhere; Customs and Immigration facilities are organised by the lodge, and guests picked up from the airstrip (S:22.11; E: 29.07). If driving from South Africa, one goes through the Pont Drift border post (vehicles can safely be left there). Guests are transferred to the lodge by Tuli vehicles; if you want to drive through, though, simply follow the well-placed signs to Tuli Lodge (it's about 7 km from the border). Should the mighty Limpopo be in flood – which does happen in the rainy season (November to March) – guests will negotiate the waters by cableway.

Tuli remains a symphony in contrasting colours: in winter, the best time to visit this wildlife area, the bush is dry, dusty and brown, and Tuli is like an oasis of contrasting colours, a green haven surrounded by a protective layer of boulder-strewn koppies (rocky hills).

The rooms have been sensitively laid out to reflect the tranquillity of the bush. The bar and rest area are situated under the arms of a huge 500-year-old nyalaberry tree. The dining area seems to be part of the large garden that embraces the lodge, although guests are often surprised to find themselves transported to a venue under the African skies.

Tuli Lodge can accommodate 26 people, and conference facilities.

Mawana Nature Reserve

Accommodation*:* Chalets (self-catering), tented camp. **Activities/attractions***:* Game-viewing, bush walks, game drives (day and night), holiday adventures for children, koppie (rocky hill) climbing, swimming, birding, horseback riding**.** **Tariff***:* Budget (self-catering). **Reservations***:* Tel and fax 316-1390, cellphone (mobile) 7131-1229, email mawana@info.bw.

Set in country very similar to the Matobos in Zimbabwe, this private nature reserve offers two enchanting types of accommodation: a beautiful self-catering luxury lodge, Malope, which is right on the edge of the Limpopo River, and a luxury tented camp called Mokowe, in an equally charming setting under large scotia trees. Like Malope, Mokowe is self-catering. In both cases visitors will be requested to leave their vehicle at the main reception under shade-cloth parking. They will be transferred in a game-drive vehicle to the camp.

The route to the reserve is via Bobonong, and is about 5.5 hours from both Johannesburg and Gaborone. It's tar all the way except for the last few kilometres.

Despite being on private land, there is a big variety of game, including elephant (plentiful), lion, leopard, hippo, crocodile and a variety of antelope, among them kudu, eland and impala, and zebra, wildebeest and waterbuck. Bird life is fantastic, with the Pels fishing owl a major attraction to serious birders. Horse trails are another of the reserve's specialities, but only for the more experienced rider. They are either multi-day safaris, or morning or afternoon rides that cost in the region of P440 per 3.5-hour ride. Mawana also hosts a special educational camp called Tswee, which is aimed specifically at schoolchildren.

As at November 2000, the rate for Malope was P240 per night per person; children under 12 pay 50 per cent. The Mokowe rate is P175 per night per person, and, again, children under 12 pay 50 per cent. Included in the rates are game drives and game walks, both morning and evening.

Kwa Nokeng

Accommodation: River cottages, chalets, luxury safari tents, campsites. **Facilities**: Restaurant, bar, swimming pool, air-conditioning, nature trails, bottle (liquor) store, satellite television, fuel outlet, superette, bureau de change. **Activities/attractions**: Game drives, birding, mountain biking, adventure trails (motor cycle, quad-bike, 4x4), horseback riding. **Tariff**: Medium to budget (self-catering or restaurant). **Contact details**: PO Box 23, Sherwood, Botswana (Clinton and Michelle van Vuuren). **Reservations**: Tel and fax 494-0221 or 494-0234, cellphone (mobile) (27 82) 871 1230.

This lodge, both a holiday destination and an overnight stop for travellers, is located on the banks of the famous Limpopo River (aptly, the Setswana name means 'at the river'). The accommodation units enjoy fine river views. The campsite has power points, wash-up basins and hot water.

Tumelo Lodge

Accommodation: Chalets (bathroom en suite), safari tents; booking essential. **Facilities**: Restaurant, bar, children's room, gift shop, swimming pool, conference centre, airstrip. **Activities/attractions**: Game drives, (day and night), river walks, mountain-bike trails, boating. **Tariff**: Medium. **Contact details**: Tel (27) (21) 6898962, or tel and fax (27) (15) 2914889, cellphone (mobile) (27) 83 2728424 (Lanice and Mark Thorp), email tumelo@imaginet.co.za.

This is an exclusive, private lodge nestling on the banks of the Limpopo close to the confluence with the Shashi, at the most eastern extremity of Botswana (two hours' drive from Selebi-Phikwe, six from Johannesburg). The place is owner-managed and deliberately kept small (12 beds maximum, not counting children) so that your hosts can provide genuine personal service at an individual level.

Lanice and Mark pride themselves on the cuisine. I am told the 'hunter's pot' that awaits guests on their return from a game drive is something to remember and (not so) 'Tiny', the cook, can work magic with her potjies.

Set in the cool shade, beneath the towering canopies of ancient riverine forest, Tumelo offers a wide range of habitats from the river itself and the on-bank forest to the sparse thornveld beyond. This diversity is reflected in the wide variety of wildlife and birds. Pel's fishing owl nest near the lodge, elephant are constant visitors, and plenty of game can be found all year round.

The conference centre is open-sided and under thatch, but many find their inspiration in the shade beneath the trees. It is, I am told, the biggest, coolest and most beautiful conference centre in this part of Africa!

The Shashi-Limpopo confluence has profound significance in the pages of African history: it is here that the first of the early Bantu-speaking 'states' emerged. It became the hub of an Africa trade network that spanned the hinterland and maintained centuries-long links with the Middle East, India and China (see page 19). It's an area full of fascinating archaeological interest.

USEFUL CONTACTS

Government addresses

The following is a useful list of postal addresses and telephone numbers of a number of government ministries and departments:

Ministry	Gaborone address	Telephone/s
Office of the President	P/Bag 001	395-0800
Agriculture	P/Bag 003	395-0500
Commerce & Industry	P/Bag 004	360-1200
Finance & Development	P/Bag 008	395-0100
Health	P/Bag 0038	395-2000
Labour & Home Affairs	P/Bag 002	361-1100
Local Govt, Lands & Housing	P/Bag 006	395-4100 & 395-2091
Director of Vet. Services	P/Bag 0032	395-0500
Dept Wildlife & National Parks	PO Box 131	397-1405
Registrar of Companies	PO Box 102	318-0754
Central Statistics Office	P/Bag 0024	395-2200
National Archives	PO Box 239	391-1820
National Museum and Art Gallery	P/Bag 0014	397-4616
Dept of Immigration	PO Box 942	361-1300
Dept of Surveys & Mapping	P/Bag 0037	395-3251
Police Headquarters	P/Bag 0012	395-1161
Dept of Civil Aviation	PO Box 250	397-1397
Dept Customs & Excise	P/Bag 0041	392-2855
Central Arms Registry	P/Bag 0012	395-1161x2466
Tourism Department	P/Bag 0047	395-3024

Diplomatic representatives

Embassy of the Republic of Angola, Private Bag BR 111, Gaborone; tel 390-0204, fax 397-5089.

British High Commission, Private Bag 0023, Gaborone; tel: 395-2841, fax 395-6105, email british@bc.bw.

Embassy of The People's Republic of China, PO Box 1031, Gaborone; tel 395-2209, fax 390-0156, email chnemb@info.bw.

Embassy of the Federal Republic of Germany, PO Box 315, Gaborone; tel 395-3143/3806, fax 395-3038.

Embassy of France, PO Box 1424, Gaborone; tel 395-3683/397-3863, fax 395-6114, email ambbots@info.bw.

High Commission of India, Private Bag 249, Gaborone; tel 397-2676, fax 397-4636, email hicomind@global.bw.

The People's Bureau of the Socialist Peoples Libyan Arab Jamahiriya, PO Box 180, Gaborone, tel 395-2481, fax 395-6928.

High Commission of the Federal Republic of Nigeria, PO Box 274, Gaborone, tel 391-3561 fax 391-3738.

NORAD: Norwegian Agency for Development Corporation, Private Bag 0017, Gaborone, tel 395-3912, fax 395-3942.

Embassy of the Russian Federation, PO Box 81, Gaborone, tel 395-3389/3739, fax 395-2930, email embrus@info.bw.

South African High Commission, Private Bag 00402, Gaborone, tel 390-4800/1/2/3, fax 390-5502.

Embassy of Sweden, Private Bag 0017, Gaborone; tel 395-3912, fax 395-3942, email ambassaden.gaborone@foreign.ministry.se.

Embassy of the United States of America, PO Box 90, Gaborone; tel 395-3982, fax 395-6947, email usembgab@mega.bw.

High Commission of the Republic of Zambia, PO Box 362, Gaborone; tel 395-1951, fax 395-3952.

High Commission of Zimbabwe, PO Box 1232, Gaborone; tel 391-4495, fax 390-5863.

Consular offices and trade missions

Royal Danish Consulate, PO Box 1973, Gaborone; tel 395-3505.

Consulate Office of the Republic of Cuba, PO Box 40261, Gaborone; tel and fax 395-1750.

Consulate of the Republic of Kenya, PO Box 287, Gaborone; tel 395-1408.

Honorary consuls

Belgium Honorary Consul, PO Box 821, Gaborone; tel 395-7438, fax 395-7476, email gabdelta@info.bw.

Honorary Consul of Italy & Spain (combined), PO Box 495, Gaborone; tel 391-2641, fax 397-3441, email icc@iccrdc.info.bw.

Honorary Consul of Ireland, Private Bag 00347, Gaborone; tel 390-3333, fax 390-3400.
Honorary Consul of Netherlands, PO Box 457, Gaborone; tel 390-2194, fax 395-1200, email nederland:info.bw.

International organisations based in Botswana

United Nations Development Programme, tel 395-2121, fax 395-6093 and 390-1459.
European Commission, tel 391-4455, fax 391-3626.
United Nations High Commissioner for Refugees, tel 395-6917, fax 397-5131.
World Health Organisation, tel 397-1505/6, fax 395-9483.
Southern African Development Community, tel 395-1863, fax 397-2848.
United Nations Children's Fund, tel 395-2752/1909, fax 395-1233.

Clubs, societies and service organisations

Alliance Française, Plot 2939, Pudulogo Crescent, PO Box 1817, Gaborone; tel 395-1650, fax 318-4433.
American Women's International Association, Meets every second Wednesday of the month in Gaborone; call US Embassy, CLO tel 395-3982.
Botswana Bird Club, Private Bag 00300, Gaborone; tel and fax 397-1584.
National Museum, Independence Ave, PO Box 71, Gaborone; tel 397-4616, fax 390-2797.
Botswana Orientation Centre, Plot 2930, Pudulogo Crescent, PO Box 1482, Gaborone; tel and fax 397-2964.
Botswana Red Cross Society, Red Cross Building, Plot 135, Independence Ave; PO Box 485, Gaborone; tel 395-2465, fax 391-2352.
The Botswana Society, PO Box 71, Gaborone; tel 391-9673, fax 391-9745, email botsoc@botsnet.bw.
Kalahari Conservation Society, Independence Ave, PO Box 859, Gaborone; tel 397-4557, fax 391-4259.
Lions Region 5, Clubs in all major towns; the Gaborone club meets every fourth Tuesday of the month at 7 pm at the Gaborone Sun; guest Lions welcome.
Rotary, Clubs in all major towns; Gaborone club meets every Friday except public holidays, 12.30 pm, Gaborone Sun Hotel.
Round Table, Gaborone No 26 meets at 7 pm every fourth Thursday of the month.
Photographic Society, tel 391-4460.

List of lodges in Botswana (by area)

Francistown   The Marang

Makgadikgadi
Jack's Camp
San Camp
Leroo-La-Tau

Maun
Audi Camp
Cresta Riley's Hotel
Crocodile Camp Safaris
Island Safari Lodge
Okavango River Lodge
Sedia Hotel
Maun Lodge

Savute
Savute Elephant Camp
Kings Pool
Selinda Camp
Zibadianja Camp

Nata   Nata Lodge

Tuli
Mashatu Game Reserve
Tuli Lodge

**Moremi and
Central Delta**
Abu Camp
Camp Moremi
Camp Okavango
Camp Okuti
Delta Camp
Eagle Island Camp (the old Xaxaba)
Gunn's Camp
Khwai River Lodge
Machaba
Mombo Camp
Oddballs
Pom Pom Camp
Shinde Island
Tsaro Elephant Lodge
Xakanaxa
Xugana Lodge

Gweta	Gweta Rest-camp
Kasane	Chobe Chilwero
	Chobe Game Lodge
	Chobe Safari Lodge
	Cresta Mowana Safari Lodge
	Kubu Lodge
	Baobab Safari Lodge
	(In Namibia) Impalila Island Lodge
	Ichingo Chobe River Lodge

Travel agents in Botswana

You may well want to seek some professional advice on the logistics of travel within Botswana, and to make use of local booking services. A list of travel agencies, together with their contact details, appears below.

Maun
Bathusi Travel & Safaris, Private Bag 44, Maun; tel 686-0647, fax 686-0664, email bathusi@info.bw.
Merlin Travel, Private Bag 13 Maun; tel 686-0351/635, fax 686-0036, email mack.air@info.bw.
Okavango Wilderness Safaris, Private Bag 14, Maun; tel 686-0086, fax 686-0632, email ldikgole@ows.bw.
Travel Wild, PO Box 236, Maun; tel 686-0822/823, fax 686-0493, email t.wild@info.bw.

Francistown
VIP Travel, Private Bag 225, Francistown; tel 241-6600, fax 241-4526.

Gaborone
Manica Travel, PO Box 1188, Gaborone; tel 395-2021, fax 390-5552, email: travelco@info.bw.
Kudu Travel, Private Bag 00130, Gaborone; tel 397-2224, fax 397-4224, email: kudutravel@info.bw.
Travel Centre, PO Box 1950, Gaborone; tel 390-4360, fax 390-5840, email: travel.ctr@info.bw.
Travel Promotions, Private Bag 00130, Gaborone; tel 390-5283, fax 397-4224.
Travel Wise, PO Box 2482, Gaborone; tel 390-3244, fax 390-3245, email: travelwise@galileosa.co.za.
Adventure Safaris, Private Bag 00352, Gaborone; tel 395-2705/6, email: advensaf@global.bw.

Kasane
Kasane Enterprises, PO Box 55, Kasane; tel 625-0234, fax 625-0223, email chobe@botsnet.bw.

Selebi-Phikwe
Travel Bags, PO Box 556, Selebi-Phikwe; tel 261-4106, fax 261-4107.

Air charter companies in Botswana

Gaborone
Executive Charter, Private Bag SK6, Gaborone; tel 397-5257, fax 397-5258, email nacexecutive@info.bw.
Kalahari Air Services & Charter, PO Box 41278, Gaborone; tel 395-1804/3593, fax 3912015, email kasac@info.bw.

Maun
Aer-Kavango, PO Box 169, Maun; tel 686-0393, fax 686-0623.
Air Xaxaba Gametrackers, Private Bag 100 Maun; tel 686-0302, fax 686-0153, email gtb.mngr@info.bw.
Bushfree Air, Tel 686-3599, fax 686-3599, email bushfree@global.bw.
Delta Air, PO Box 39, Maun; tel 686-0044, fax 686-1703, email synergy@info.bw.
Elgon Air, Private Bag 198, Maun; tel 686-0654, fax 686-0037, email book@info.bw.
Mack Air, Tel 686-0675, fax 686-0675, email mack.air@info.bw.
Moremi Air Charter, Tel 686-2078, fax 686-2078, email moremi.air@info.bw.
Ngami Air, PO Box 119, Maun; tel & fax 686-0530.
Northern Air, PO Box 27, Maun; tel 686-0385, fax 686-1559, email nair@kerdowney.bw.
Sefofane Air Charter, Private Bag 159, Maun; tel 686-0778, fax 686-1649, email garyk@sefofane.bw.
Swamp Air, tel 686-0569, fax 686-0040, email: gunnscamp@info.bw.
Wildlife Helicopters, Private Bag 161, Maun; tel & fax 686-0664, email:wildheli@info.bw.
Xugana Air, tel 686-0921.

ROUTE MAPS

This edition of the *African Adventurer's Guide to Botswana* is innovative in several ways. Among these is the inclusion of GPS reference points and route maps (see page 72). Users should be quite clear on the role of these maps. I am assuming that everybody who uses this guide will either be well acquainted with the main road network in Botswana or will have with them a standard national road map of some sort.

For this reason, few of the main roads are included on the maps in this section. Those maps that do appear are mostly of remote, off-road sections about which ordinary maps say nothing or provide insufficient detail. The maps are mostly schematic; they are not to scale. North is always shown, but it may not point to the top of the page, as convention demands, due to the need to fit the route into a prescribed paper size (you can, of course, always rotate the book!). They have been tested out on a number of users, who have found them satisfactory, and I believe you will have no difficulty with them.

Key to the route maps

Xaxa	Place with water (often)		Pan
	River	**A**	GPS Waypoint
	Cut-line		Gate
	Roads & tracks		Bridge
	Vet Fence		Lodge
	Reserve boundary		
	International boundary		Village
6.2	Distances in kilometres		Border post
u/k	This symbol on a GPS table implies that the Datum of the recording GPS is unknown	?	A road or track the ultimate destination of which is unknown
	Mountains		Plain

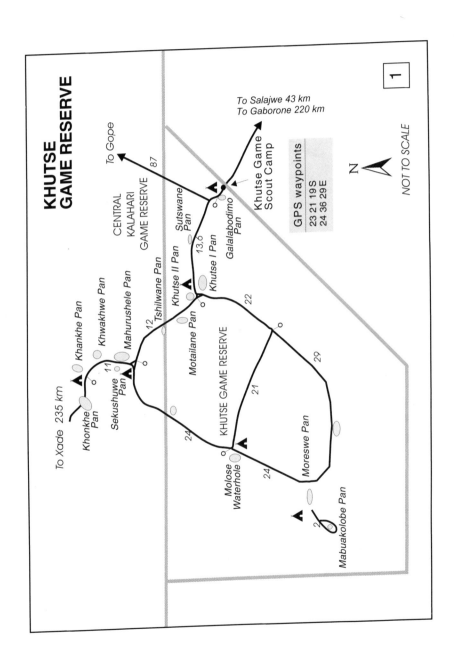

KHUTSE
GAME RESERVE

To Salajwe 43 km
To Gaborone 220 km

To Gope

87

CENTRAL
KALAHARI
GAME RESERVE

Khutse Game
Scout Camp

Sutswane
Pan

13,6

GPS waypoints

23 21 19S
24 36 29E

N

NOT TO SCALE

Khutse II Pan

Tshilwane Pan

Khutse I Pan

Galalabodimo
Pan

Khankhe Pan

Khwakhwe Pan

Mahurushele Pan

12

Motailane Pan

22

To Xade 235 km

Khonkhe
Pan

Sekushuwe
Pan

11

KHUTSE GAME RESERVE

21

29

24

Molose
Waterhole

Moreswe Pan

24

Mabuakolobe Pan

1

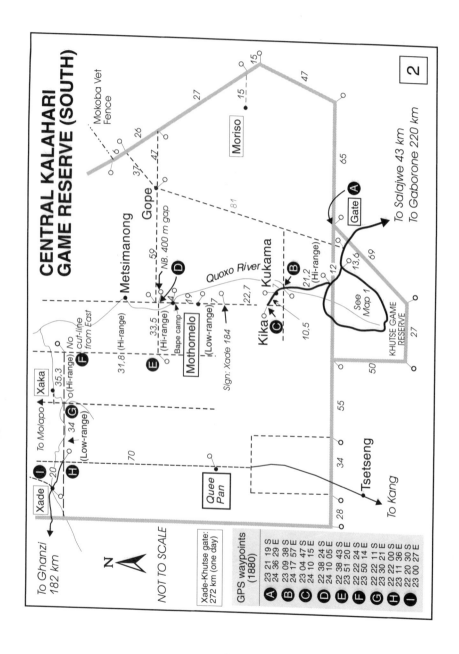

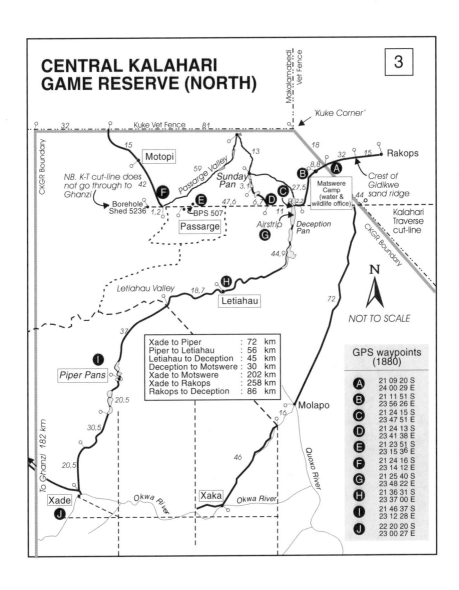

CENTRAL KALAHARI GAME RESERVE (NORTH)

3

'Kuke Corner'

Makalamabedi Vet Fence

Kuke Vet Fence

32   81

15   Motopi

CKGR Boundary

NB. K-T cut-line does not go through to Ghanzi   42

59   Passarge Valley

Sunday Pan   3,1

13

18

32   15   Rakops

8,8   B   A

27,5   Crest of Gidikwe sand ridge

Borehole Shed 5236   1,2   E   BPS 507   47,6   6,2   D   C

Passarge

Airstrip   G   11   Deception Pan

Matswere Camp (water & wildlife office)   44   Kalahari Traverse cut-line

44,9

CKGR Boundary

N

NOT TO SCALE

Letiahau Valley   18,7   H

Letiahau

72

37

I

Piper Pans

20,5

30,5

20,5

To Ghanzi 182 km

Molapo

16

46   Quoxo River

Okwa River   Xaka   Okwa River

Xade

J

Xade to Piper	: 72	km
Piper to Letiahau	: 56	km
Letiahau to Deception	: 45	km
Deception to Motswere	: 30	km
Xade to Motswere	: 202	km
Xade to Rakops	: 258	km
Rakops to Deception	: 86	km

GPS waypoints (1880)

A	21 09 20 S 24 00 29 E
B	21 11 51 S 23 56 26 E
C	21 24 15 S 23 47 51 E
D	21 24 13 S 23 41 38 E
E	21 23 51 S 23 15 36 E
F	21 24 16 S 23 14 12 E
G	21 25 40 S 23 48 22 E
H	21 36 31 S 23 37 00 E
I	21 46 37 S 23 12 28 E
J	22 20 20 S 23 00 27 E

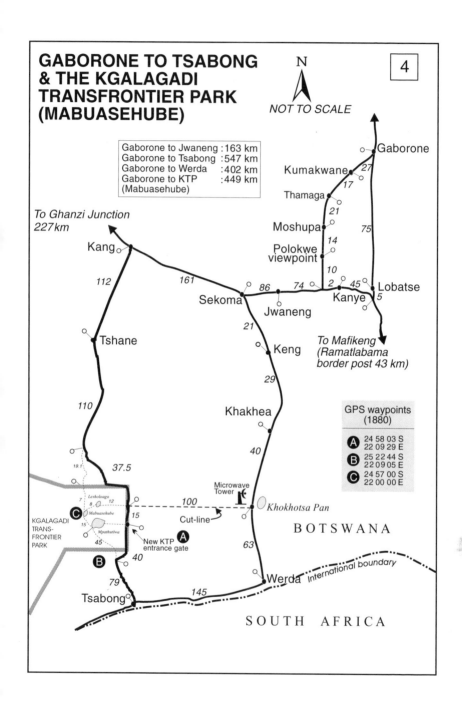

GABORONE TO TSABONG & THE KGALAGADI TRANSFRONTIER PARK (MABUASEHUBE)

N

NOT TO SCALE

4

Gaborone to Jwaneng	:163 km
Gaborone to Tsabong	:547 km
Gaborone to Werda	:402 km
Gaborone to KTP (Mabuasehube)	:449 km

Gaborone

Kumakwane 27

Thamaga 17

21

Moshupa

Polokwe viewpoint 14

To Ghanzi Junction 227km

Kang 75

112 161

Sekoma 86 74 2 45 Lobatse

Jwaneng Kanye 5

21

Tshane Keng

To Mafikeng (Ramatlabama border post 43 km)

29

110

Khakhea

40

GPS waypoints (1880)

A 24 58 03 S
22 09 29 E
B 25 22 44 S
22 09 05 E
C 24 57 00 S
22 00 00 E

19.1 37.5

Lesholoago
7 8 12
C Mabuasehube 15

KGALAGADI TRANS-FRONTIER PARK

Microwave Tower

100

Cut-line Khokhotsa Pan

B O T S W A N A

Mpathutlwa 15

45 New KTP entrance gate **A** 63

B 40

79 145

Tsabong Werda International boundary

S O U T H   A F R I C A

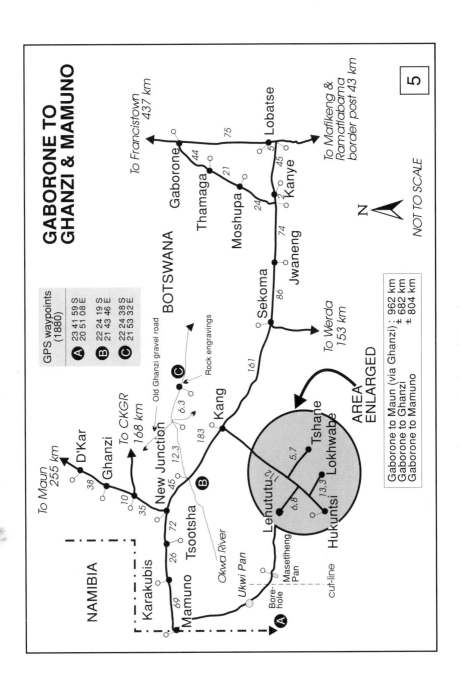

GABORONE TO GHANZI & MAMUNO

5

NOT TO SCALE

BOTSWANA

NAMIBIA

GPS waypoints
(1880)
A 23 41 59 S
    20 51 08 E
B 22 24 19 S
    21 43 46 E
C 22 24 38 S
    21 53 32 E

To Francistown
437 km

To Mafikeng &
Ramatlabama
border post 43 km

To Maun
255 km

To CKGR
168 km

To Werda
153 km

Gaborone to Maun (via Ghanzi) : 962 km
Gaborone to Ghanzi ± 682 km
Gaborone to Mamuno ± 804 km

AREA
ENLARGED

Old Ghanzi gravel road

Rock engravings

Gaborone

Thamaga

Moshupa

Lobatse

Kanye

Jwaneng

Sekoma

Kang

New Junction

Ghanzi

D'Kar

Tsootsha

Mamuno

Karakubis

Okwa River

Ukwi Pan

Masetlheng
Pan

Bore-
hole

cut-line

Lehututu

Tshane

Lokhwabe

Hukuntsi

44

21

75

5

45

24

74

86

161

183

45

12.3

6.3

35

10

38

72

26

69

5.7

6.8

13.3

A

B

C

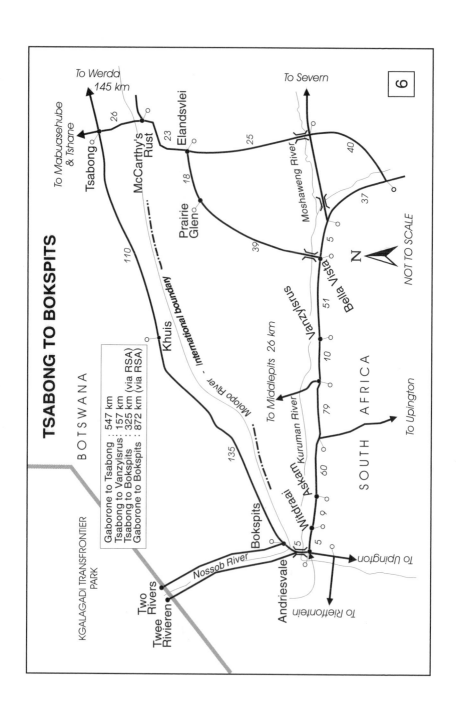

TSABONG TO BOKSPITS

Gaborone to Tsabong : 547 km
Tsabong to Vanzylsrus : 157 km
Tsabong to Bokspits : 325 km (via RSA)
Gaborone to Bokspits : 872 km (via RSA)

BOTSWANA

KGALAGADI TRANSFRONTIER PARK

To Werda 145 km

To Mabuasehube & Tshane

To Tsabong

McCarthy's Rust

To Severn

Elandsvlei

Prairie Glen

Moshaweng River

Bella Vista

Khuis

International boundary

Molopo River

Vanzylsrus

To Middlepits 26 km

Kuruman River

Askam

To Upington

Witdraai

SOUTH AFRICA

Bokspits

Nossob River

Andriesvale

Two Rivers
Twee Rivieren

To Upington

To Rietfontein

N

NOT TO SCALE

6

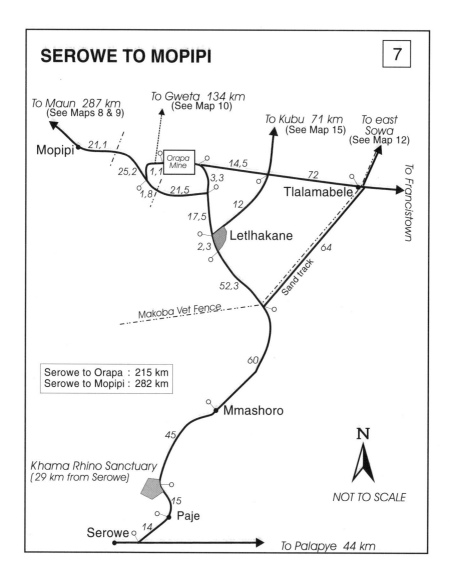

SEROWE TO MOPIPI

7

To Maun 287 km
(See Maps 8 & 9)

To Gweta 134 km
(See Map 10)

To Kubu 71 km
(See Map 15)

To east
Sowa
(See Map 12)

Mopipi

21,1

25,2

1,1

1,8

21,5

Orapa
Mine

3,3

14,5

72

To Francistown

Tlalamabele

17,5

12

Letlhakane

2,3

52,3

64

Sand track

Makoba Vet Fence

60

Serowe to Orapa : 215 km
Serowe to Mopipi : 282 km

Mmashoro

45

Khama Rhino Sanctuary
(29 km from Serowe)

15

Paje

Serowe

14

To Palapye 44 km

N

NOT TO SCALE

MOPIPI TO MOTOPI

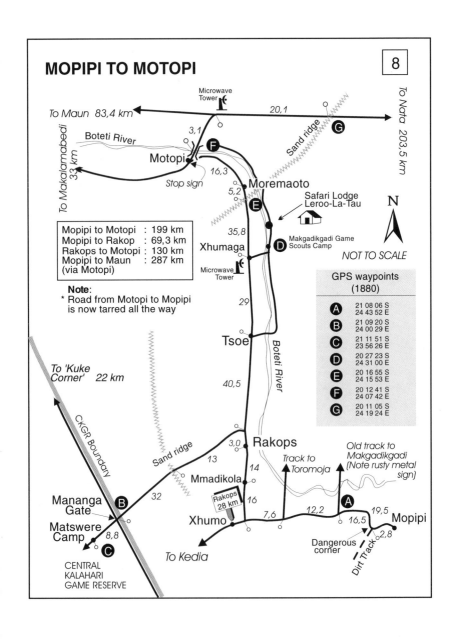

8

To Maun 83,4 km

Microwave Tower

20,1

To Nata 203,5 km

Boteti River

3,1

Sand ridge

G

Motopi

To Makalamabedi 33 km

16,3

F

Stop sign

Moremaoto

5,2

Safari Lodge
Leroo-La-Tau

E

N

NOT TO SCALE

Mopipi to Motopi	: 199 km
Mopipi to Rakop	: 69,3 km
Rakops to Motopi	: 130 km
Mopipi to Maun	: 287 km
(via Motopi)	

35,8

Xhumaga

D

Makgadikgadi Game
Scouts Camp

Microwave Tower

Note:
* Road from Motopi to Mopipi
is now tarred all the way

29

GPS waypoints
(1880)

A	21 08 06 S 24 43 52 E
B	21 09 20 S 24 00 29 E
C	21 11 51 S 23 56 26 E
D	20 27 23 S 24 31 00 E
E	20 16 55 S 24 15 53 E
F	20 12 41 S 24 07 42 E
G	20 11 05 S 24 19 24 E

Tsoe

Boteti River

To 'Kuke Corner' 22 km

40,5

CKGR BOUNDARY

3,0

Rakops

Old track to
Makgadikgadi
(Note rusty metal
sign)

Track to
Toromoja

Sand ridge

13

14

Mmadikola

Mananga Gate

B

32

16

Rakops
28 km

Matswere Camp

C

8,8

Xhumo

7,6

12,2

A

19,5

16,5

Mopipi

2,8

To Kedia

Dangerous corner

Dirt Track

CENTRAL
KALAHARI
GAME RESERVE

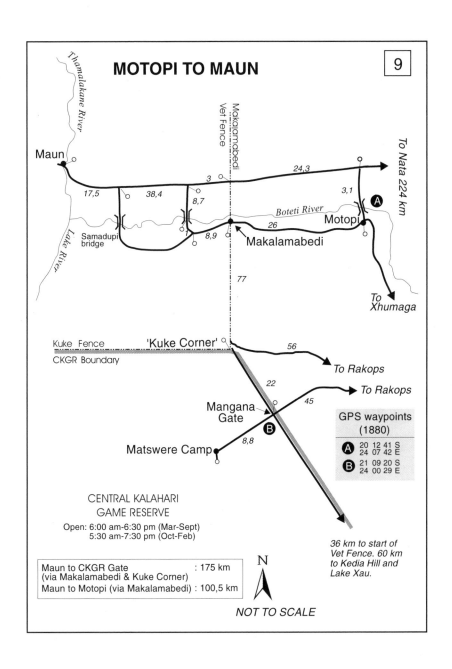

MOTOPI TO MAUN

9

Thamalakane River

Maun

Makalamabedi Vet Fence

Makalamabedi

To Nata 224 km

24,3

3

17,5   38,4   8,7   3,1   Ⓐ

Boteti River

26   Motopi

Samadupi bridge   8,9   Makalamabedi

77

To Xhumaga

Kuke Fence   'Kuke Corner'   56
CKGR Boundary   To Rakops

22   To Rakops

45

Mangana Gate   Ⓑ

Matswere Camp   8,8

GPS waypoints
(1880)
Ⓐ 20 12 41 S
   24 07 42 E
Ⓑ 21 09 20 S
   24 00 29 E

CENTRAL KALAHARI
GAME RESERVE
Open: 6:00 am-6:30 pm (Mar-Sept)
      5:30 am-7:30 pm (Oct-Feb)

36 km to start of
Vet Fence. 60 km
to Kedia Hill and
Lake Xau.

Maun to CKGR Gate   : 175 km
(via Makalamabedi & Kuke Corner)
Maun to Motopi (via Makalamabedi) : 100,5 km

N

NOT TO SCALE

Lake River

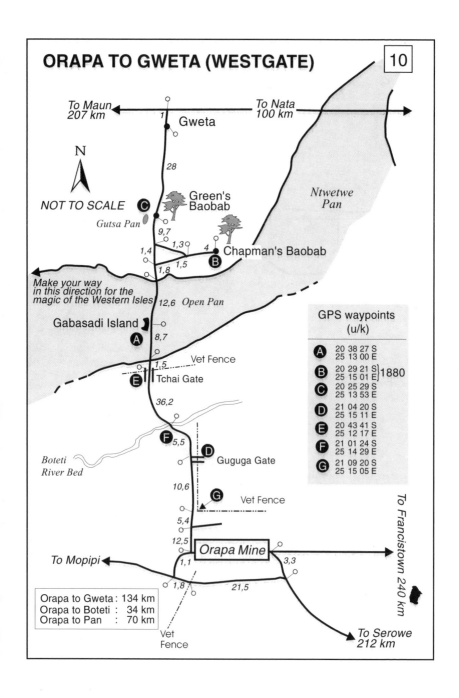

ORAPA TO GWETA (WESTGATE)

10

To Maun
207 km

To Nata
100 km

1 Gweta

N

28

NOT TO SCALE **C**

Gutsa Pan

Green's
Baobab

Ntwetwe
Pan

9,7

1,4   1,3

4   Chapman's Baobab

1,5

1,8 **B**

Make your way
in this direction for the
magic of the Western Isles

12,6   Open Pan

Gabasadi Island

A   8,7

1,5   Vet Fence

E   Tchai Gate

36,2

Boteti
River Bed

F 5,5

D   Guguga Gate

10,6

G   Vet Fence

5,4

12,5

To Mopipi

1,1   **Orapa Mine**

1,8   21,5

3,3

To Francistown 240 km

Vet
Fence

To Serowe
212 km

GPS waypoints (u/k)		
A	20 38 27 S	25 13 00 E
B	20 29 21 S	25 15 01 E } 1880
C	20 25 29 S	25 13 53 E
D	21 04 20 S	25 15 11 E
E	20 43 41 S	25 12 17 E
F	21 01 24 S	25 14 29 E
G	21 09 20 S	25 15 05 E

Orapa to Gweta : 134 km
Orapa to Boteti : 34 km
Orapa to Pan : 70 km

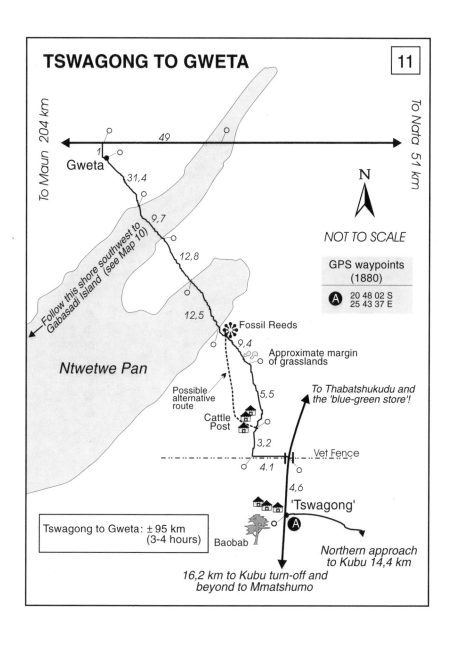

TSWAGONG TO GWETA

11

To Maun 204 km

To Nata 51 km

49

1

Gweta

31,4

9,7

12,8

12,5

N

NOT TO SCALE

GPS waypoints
(1880)

Ⓐ 20 48 02 S
25 43 37 E

Follow this shore southwest to Gabasadi Island (see Map 10)

Fossil Reeds

9,4

Approximate margin
of grasslands

Ntwetwe Pan

Possible
alternative
route

Cattle
Post

5,5

*To Thabatshukudu and
the 'blue-green store'!*

3,2

Vet Fence

4.1

4,6

'Tswagong'

Ⓐ

Tswagong to Gweta: ± 95 km
(3-4 hours)

Baobab

*Northern approach
to Kubu 14,4 km*

*16,2 km to Kubu turn-off and
beyond to Mmatshumo*

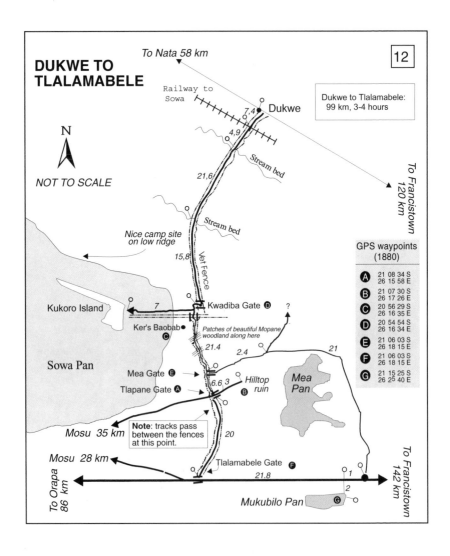

DUKWE TO TLALAMABELE

To Nata 58 km

12

Railway to Sowa

7,4
Dukwe

Dukwe to Tlalamabele:
99 km, 3-4 hours

N

NOT TO SCALE

4,9

Stream bed

21,6

To Francistown
120 km

Stream bed

Nice camp site
on low ridge

15,8

Vet Fence

GPS waypoints
(1880)

Kukoro Island

7

Kwadiba Gate **D**

?

Ⓐ 21 08 34 S
   26 15 58 E
Ⓑ 21 07 30 S
   26 17 26 E
Ⓒ 20 56 29 S
   26 16 35 E
Ⓓ 20 54 54 S
   26 16 34 E
Ⓔ 21 06 03 S
   26 18 15 E
Ⓕ 21 06 03 S
   26 18 15 E
Ⓖ 21 15 25 S
   26 25 40 E

Ker's Baobab ● **C**

Patches of beautiful Mopane
woodland along here

21.4   2.4

21

Sowa Pan

Mea Gate **E**

Tlapane Gate **A**

6.6, 3

Hilltop
ruin **B**

Mea
Pan

Mosu 35 km

Note: tracks pass
between the fences
at this point.

20

Mosu 28 km

Tlalamabele Gate **F**

1

To Orapa
86 km

21.8

2

To Francistown
142 km

Mukubilo Pan **G**

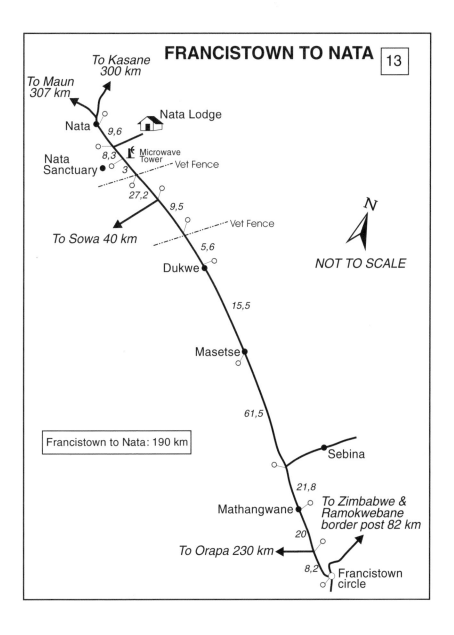

FRANCISTOWN TO NATA 13

To Kasane 300 km

To Maun 307 km

Nata Lodge

Nata 9,6

8,3

Nata Sanctuary 3

Microwave Tower

Vet Fence

27,2

9,5

Vet Fence

To Sowa 40 km

5,6

Dukwe

N

NOT TO SCALE

15,5

Masetse

61,5

Francistown to Nata: 190 km

Sebina

21,8

To Zimbabwe & Ramokwebane border post 82 km

Mathangwane

20

To Orapa 230 km

8,2

Francistown circle

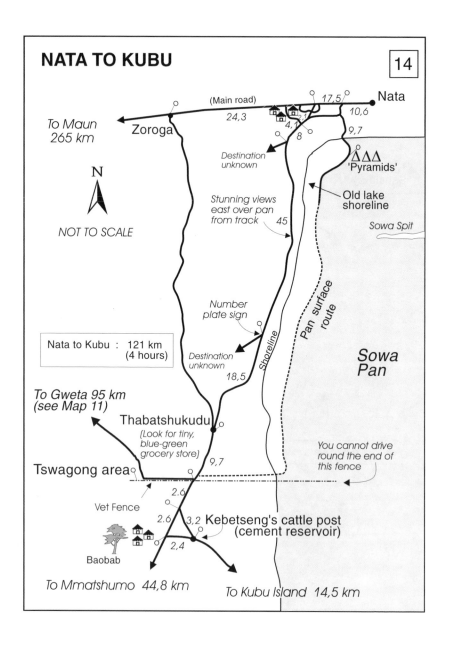

NATA TO KUBU

14

(Main road)
24,3
17,5
Nata
10,6

**To Maun
265 km**
Zoroga
4,1
9,7
8

*Destination
unknown*

△ △△
'Pyramids'

N

Old lake
shoreline

NOT TO SCALE

*Stunning views
east over pan
from track*   45

Sowa Spit

*Number
plate sign*

Shoreline

Pan surface route

**Sowa
Pan**

Nata to Kubu : 121 km
(4 hours)

*Destination
unknown*

18,5

To Gweta 95 km
(see Map 11)

Thabatshukudu
*(Look for tiny,
blue-green
grocery store)*

*You cannot drive
round the end of
this fence*

Tswagong area

9,7

Vet Fence

2,6

2,6   3,2 **Kebetseng's cattle post**
(cement reservoir)

2,4

Baobab

To Mmatshumo 44,8 km

To Kubu Island 14,5 km

LETLHAKANE TO KUBU

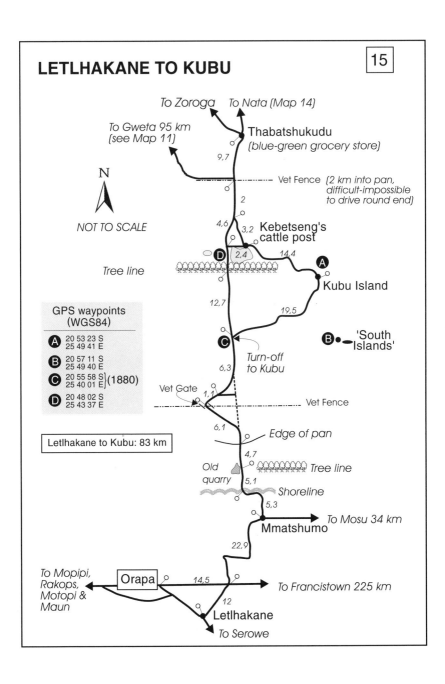

15

To Zoroga   To Nata (Map 14)

To Gweta 95 km
(see Map 11)

Thabatshukudu
(blue-green grocery store)

9,7

N

NOT TO SCALE

Vet Fence *(2 km into pan,
difficult-impossible
to drive round end)*

2

4,6   3,2

Kebetseng's
cattle post

D   2,4   14,4   **A**

Tree line

Kubu Island

12,7

19,5

GPS waypoints
(WGS84)

A 20 53 23 S
25 49 41 E

B 20 57 11 S
25 49 40 E

C 20 55 58 S
25 40 01 E }(1880)

D 20 48 02 S
25 43 37 E

C

Turn-off
to Kubu

B 'South
Islands'

6,3

Vet Gate   1,1

Vet Fence

Letlhakane to Kubu: 83 km

6,1

Edge of pan

4,7

Old
quarry   5,1

Tree line

Shoreline

5,3

To Mosu 34 km

Mmatshumo

22,9

To Mopipi,
Rakops,
Motopi &
Maun

Orapa   14,5

To Francistown 225 km

12

Letlhakane

To Serowe

NATA TO MAUN

16

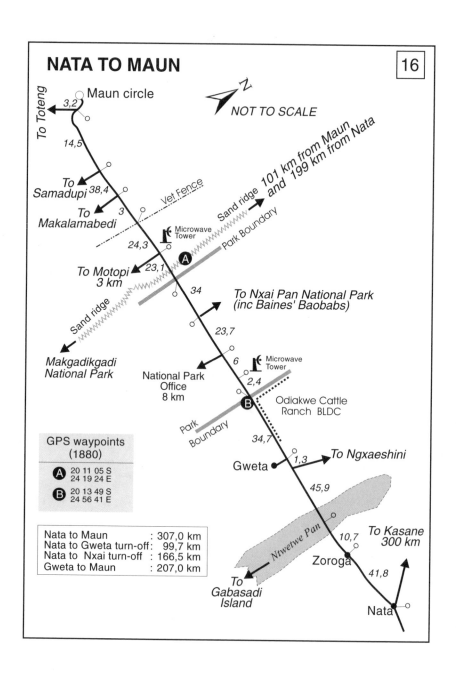

NOT TO SCALE

To Toteng

Maun circle

3,2

14,5

To Samadupi 38,4

To Makalamabedi 3

Vet Fence

Sand ridge 101 km from Maun and 199 km from Nata

Park Boundary

24,3

Microwave Tower

Ⓐ

To Motopi 3 km

23,1

Sand ridge

34

To Nxai Pan National Park (inc Baines' Baobabs)

Makgadikgadi National Park

23,7

6

Microwave Tower

National Park Office 8 km

2,4

Park Boundary

Ⓑ

Odiakwe Cattle Ranch BLDC

GPS waypoints (1880)

Ⓐ 20 11 05 S 24 19 24 E

Ⓑ 20 13 49 S 24 56 41 E

34,7

Gweta

1,3

To Ngxaeshini

45,9

Ntwetwe Pan

10,7

To Kasane 300 km

Zoroga

41,8

To Gabasadi Island

Nata

Nata to Maun	: 307,0 km
Nata to Gweta turn-off	: 99,7 km
Nata to Nxai turn-off	: 166,5 km
Gweta to Maun	: 207,0 km

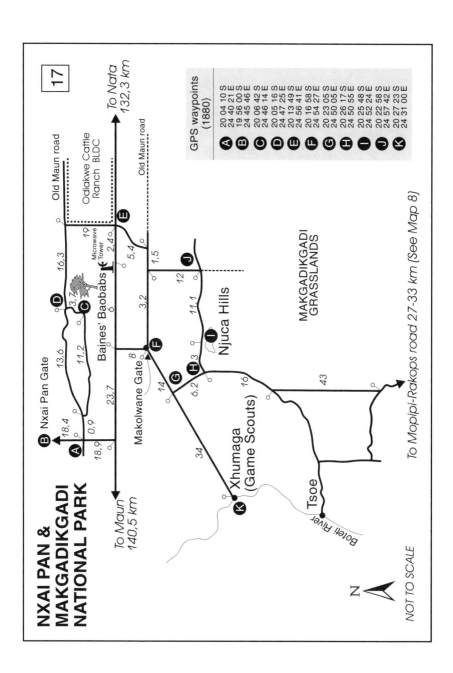

NXAI PAN & MAKGADIKGADI NATIONAL PARK

17

To Nata 132,3 km

Old Maun road

Odiakwe Cattle Ranch BLDC

Old Maun road

B Nxai Pan Gate

D

C

Baines' Baobabs

Microwave Tower

E

16,3

3,7

19

2,4

5,4

1,5

13,6

11,2

3,2

J

12

11,1

Njuca Hills

23,7

18,4

A

0,9

18,9

To Maun 140,5 km

Makolwane Gate

8

F

14

G

6,2

H 3

I

MAKGADIKGADI GRASSLANDS

43

To Mopipi-Rakops road 27-33 km (See Map 8)

16

Xhumaga (Game Scouts)

34

K

Tsoe

Boteti River

N

NOT TO SCALE

GPS waypoints (1880)

A	20 04 10 S 24 40 21 E
B	19 56 00 S 24 45 46 E
C	20 06 42 S 24 46 14 E
D	20 05 16 S 24 47 25 E
E	20 13 49 S 24 56 41 E
F	20 16 58 S 24 54 27 E
G	20 23 05 S 24 50 05 E
H	20 26 17 S 24 50 55 E
I	20 25 48 S 24 52 24 E
J	20 22 58 S 24 57 42 E
K	20 27 23 S 24 31 00 E

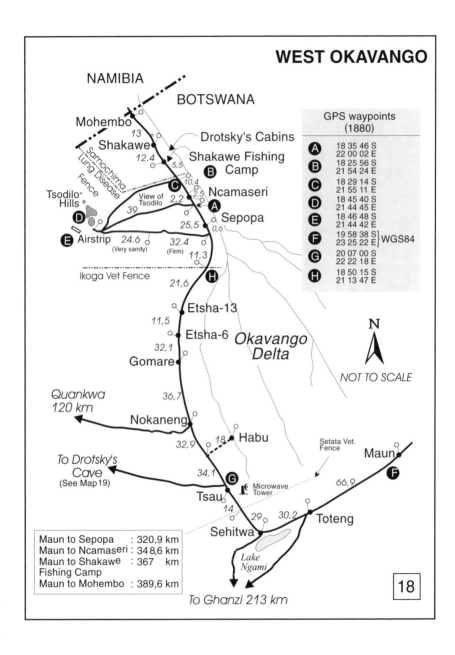

WEST OKAVANGO

NAMIBIA

BOTSWANA

Mohembo

Drotsky's Cabins

13

Shakawe

12.4

Shakawe Fishing Camp

B

5.5

C

10.4

Ncamaseri

2.5

Samochima Lung Disease Fence

Tsodilo Hills

2.2

A

View of Tsodilo

Sepopa

D

39

0.6

25.5

E Airstrip

24.6
(Very sandy)

32.4
(Firm)

11.3

H

Ikoga Vet Fence

21,6

Etsha-13

11,5

Etsha-6

Okavango Delta

32,1

Gomare

N

NOT TO SCALE

Quankwa
120 km

36,7

Nokaneng

32,9   *18*   Habu

Setata Vet. Fence

Maun

To Drotsky's Cave
(See Map 19)

34,1

G

Microwave Tower

66,9

F

Tsau

14

29   *30,2*

Toteng

Sehitwa

Lake Ngami

18

Maun to Sepopa	: 320,9 km
Maun to Ncamaseri	: 348,6 km
Maun to Shakawe Fishing Camp	: 367 km
Maun to Mohembo	: 389,6 km

To Ghanzi 213 km

GPS waypoints
(1880)

A	18 35 46 S 22 00 02 E
B	18 25 56 S 21 54 24 E
C	18 29 14 S 21 55 11 E
D	18 45 40 S 21 44 45 E
E	18 46 48 S 21 44 42 E
F	19 58 38 S } WGS84 23 25 22 E
G	20 07 00 S 22 22 18 E
H	18 50 15 S 21 13 47 E

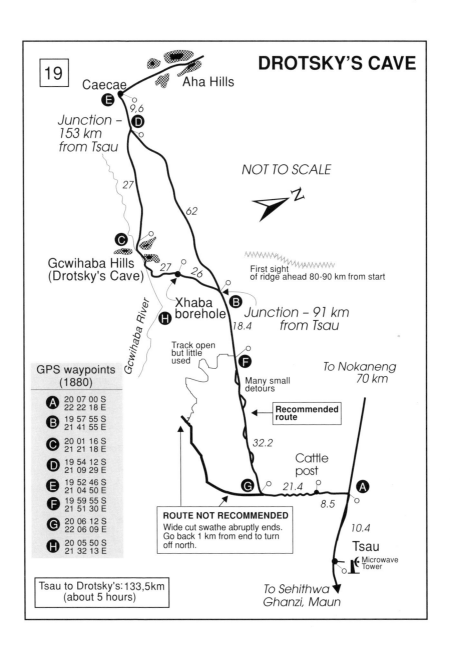

19

DROTSKY'S CAVE

Caecae

E

9,6

D

Aha Hills

Junction – 153 km from Tsau

NOT TO SCALE

N

27

62

C

Gcwihaba Hills
(Drotsky's Cave)

27

26

Gcwihaba River

First sight
of ridge ahead 80-90 km from start

B

Xhaba
borehole

H

18.4

Junction – 91 km from Tsau

*To Nokaneng
70 km*

Track open
but little
used

F

Many small
detours

**GPS waypoints
(1880)**

A	20 07 00 S
22 22 18 E
B	19 57 55 S
21 41 55 E
C	20 01 16 S
21 21 18 E
D	19 54 12 S
21 09 29 E
E	19 52 46 S
21 04 50 E
F	19 59 55 S
21 51 30 E
G	20 06 12 S
22 06 09 E
H	20 05 50 S
21 32 13 E

Tsau to Drotsky's: 133,5km
(about 5 hours)

**Recommended
route**

32.2

Cattle
post

G

21.4

A

8.5

ROUTE NOT RECOMMENDED
Wide cut swathe abruptly ends.
Go back 1 km from end to turn
off north.

10.4

Tsau

Microwave
Tower

*To Sehithwa
Ghanzi, Maun*

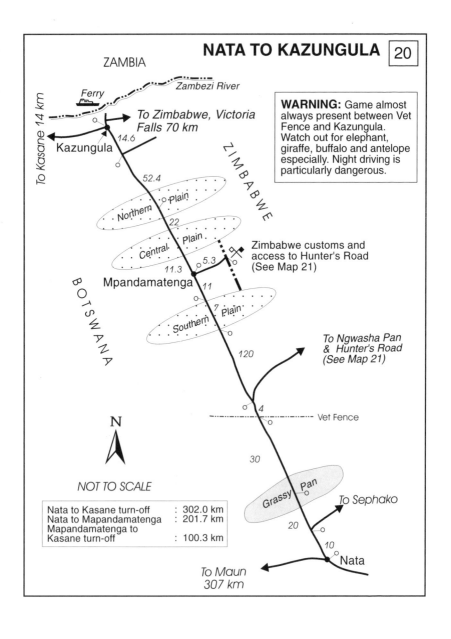

NATA TO KAZUNGULA 20

ZAMBIA

Zambezi River

Ferry

To Kasane 14 km

To Zimbabwe, Victoria Falls 70 km

14.6

Kazungula

WARNING: Game almost always present between Vet Fence and Kazungula. Watch out for elephant, giraffe, buffalo and antelope especially. Night driving is particularly dangerous.

52.4

Northern Plain

ZIMBABWE

22

Central Plain

Zimbabwe customs and access to Hunter's Road (See Map 21)

11.3   5.3

Mpandamatenga   11

7 Plain

Southern Plain

BOTSWANA

120

To Ngwasha Pan & Hunter's Road (See Map 21)

4

Vet Fence

N

30

NOT TO SCALE

Grassy Pan

To Sephako

20

Nata to Kasane turn-off	: 302.0 km
Nata to Mapandamatenga	: 201.7 km
Mapandamatenga to Kasane turn-off	: 100.3 km

10

Nata

To Maun 307 km

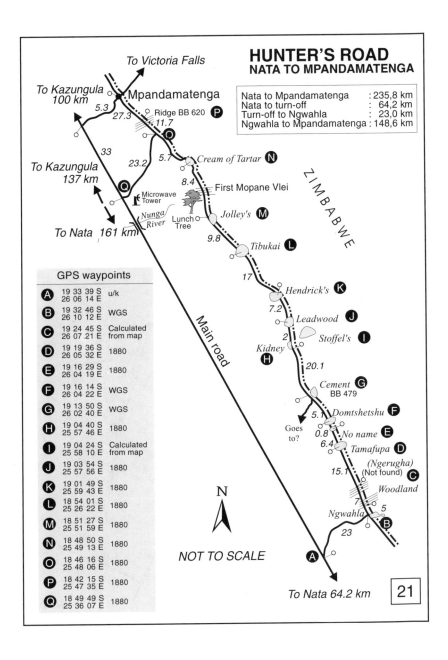

HUNTER'S ROAD
NATA TO MPANDAMATENGA

To Victoria Falls

To Kazungula
100 km
Mpandamatenga

Nata to Mpandamatenga	: 235,8 km
Nata to turn-off	: 64,2 km
Turn-off to Ngwahla	: 23,0 km
Ngwahla to Mpandamatenga	: 148,6 km

5.3
27.3
Ridge BB 620 **P**
11.7

33
23.2
5.7
Cream of Tartar **N**

To Kazungula
137 km
Q

Microwave
Tower
8.4
First Mopane Vlei

Nunga
River
Lunch
Tree
Jolley's **M**

To Nata 161 km
9.8
Tibukai **L**

GPS waypoints

17

Hendrick's **K**
7.2
Leadwood **J**
2
Stoffel's **I**
Kidney
H
20.1

A 19 33 39 S
26 06 14 E u/k

B 19 32 46 S
26 10 12 E WGS

C 19 24 45 S
26 07.21 E Calculated
from map

D 19 19 36 S
26 05 32 E 1880

E 19 16 29 S
26 04 19 E 1880

F 19 16 14 S
26 04 22 E WGS

G 19 13 50 S
26 02 40 E WGS

H 19 04 40 S
25 57 46 E 1880

I 19 04 24 S
25 58 10 E Calculated
from map

J 19 03 54 S
25 57 56 E 1880

K 19 01 49 S
25 59 43 E 1880

L 18 54 01 S
25 26 22 E 1880

M 18 51 27 S
25 51 59 E 1880

N 18 48 50 S
25 49 13 E 1880

O 18 46 16 S
25 48 06 E 1880

P 18 42 15 S
25 47 35 E 1880

Q 18 49 49 S
25 36 07 E 1880

Cement **G**
BB 479
5.1
Domtshetshu **F**
Goes
to?
0.8
No name **E**
6.4
Tamafupa **D**
15.1
(Ngerugha)
(Not found) **C**
Woodland
7
Ngwahla 5
B
23

A

ZIMBABWE

Main road

N

NOT TO SCALE

To Nata 64.2 km

21

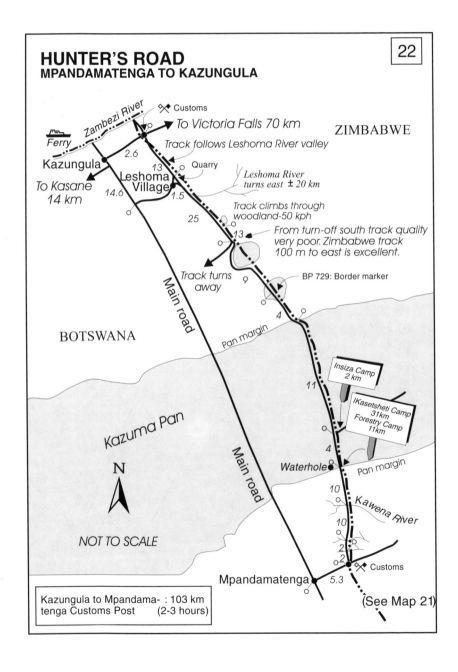

HUNTER'S ROAD
MPANDAMATENGA TO KAZUNGULA

22

Zambezi River

Customs

To Victoria Falls 70 km

ZIMBABWE

Ferry

Track follows Leshoma River valley

Kazungula

2.6

13

Quarry

Leshoma River turns east ± 20 km

To Kasane 14 km

Leshoma Village

14.6

1.5

Track climbs through woodland-50 kph

25

13

From turn-off south track quality very poor. Zimbabwe track 100 m to east is excellent.

Track turns away

9

BP 729: Border marker

BOTSWANA

4

Pan margin

Insiza Camp 2 km

11

IKasetsheti Camp 31km Forestry Camp 11km

Kazuma Pan

Main road

N

4

Waterhole

Pan margin

10

Kawena River

10

NOT TO SCALE

2

2

Customs

Mpandamatenga

5.3

(See Map 21)

Kazungula to Mpandama- : 103 km
tenga Customs Post   (2-3 hours)

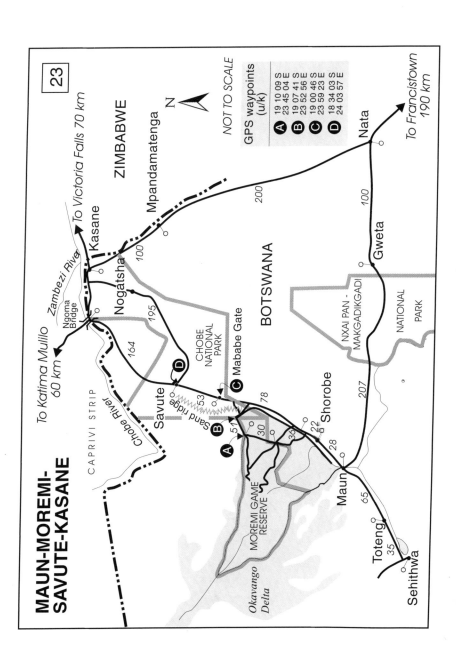

MAUN-MOREMI-
SAVUTE-KASANE

23

GPS waypoints
(u/k)
Ⓐ 19 10 09 S
   23 45 04 E
Ⓑ 19 07 41 S
   23 52 56 E
Ⓒ 19 00 46 S
   23 59 23 E
Ⓓ 18 34 03 S
   24 03 57 E

NOT TO SCALE

N

ZIMBABWE

To Victoria Falls 70 km

Mpandamatenga

Kasane

Zambezi River

To Katima Mulilo
60 km

Ngoma
Bridge

Nogatsha

CAPRIVI STRIP

Chobe River

Savute

Sand ridge

CHOBE
NATIONAL
PARK

Mababe Gate

BOTSWANA

Nata

To Francistown
190 km

Gweta

NXAI PAN -
MAKGADIKGADI

NATIONAL
PARK

Shorobe

Maun

MOREMI GAME
RESERVE

Okavango
Delta

Toteng

Sehithwa

200

100

100

195

164

53

78

51

30

36

22

28

207

65

35

Ⓐ

Ⓑ

Ⓒ

Ⓓ

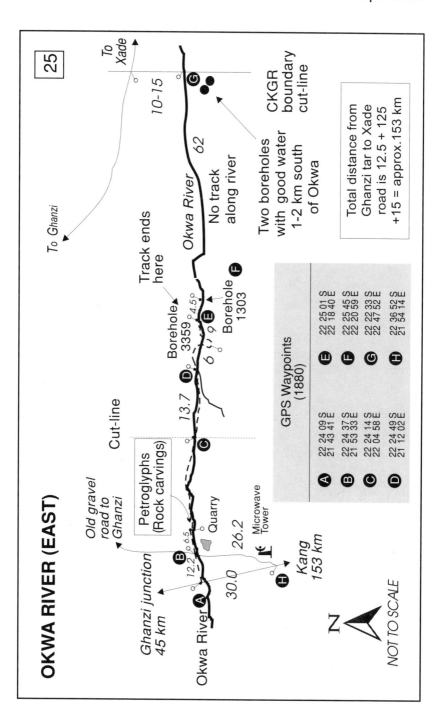

OKWA RIVER (EAST)

25

To Xade

To Ghanzi

10-15

CKGR boundary cut-line

Okwa River

62

No track along river

Two boreholes with good water 1-2 km south of Okwa

Total distance from Ghanzi tar to Xade road is 12.5 + 125 +15 = approx.153 km

Track ends here

Borehole 3359

4.5

Borehole 1303

6

Cut-line

13.7

D

C

9

E

F

G

GPS Waypoints (1880)

A	22 24 09 S	21 43 41 E	**E**	22 25 01 S	22 18 40 E
B	22 24 37 S	21 53 33 E	**F**	22 25 45 S	22 20 59 E
C	22 24 14 S	22 04 58 E	**G**	22 22 33 S	22 47 52 E
D	22 24 49 S	21 12 02 E	**H**	21 36 52 S	21 54 14 E

Old gravel road to Ghanzi

Petroglyphs (Rock carvings)

Quarry

Microwave Tower

Ghanzi junction 45 km

Okwa River

A

B

12.2

6.5

26.2

30.0

H

Kang 153 km

N

NOT TO SCALE

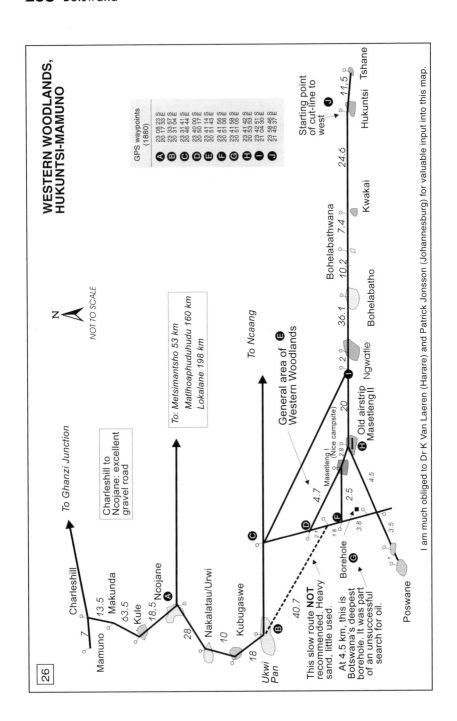

WESTERN WOODLANDS,
HUKUNTSI-MAMUNO

NOT TO SCALE

GPS waypoints
(1880)

A 23 08 23 S / 20 17 33 E
B 23 33 57 S / 20 31 04 E
C 23 31 41 S / 20 46 44 E
D 23 40 09 S / 20 51 43 E
E 23 41 14 S / 20 51 43 E
F 23 41 56 S / 20 51 06 E
G 23 41 58 S / 20 51 05 E
H 23 41 42 S / 20 53 51 E
I 23 41 25 S / 21 04 30 E
J 23 58 46 S / 21 45 37 E

I am much obliged to Dr K Van Laeren (Harare) and Patrick Jonsson (Johannesburg) for valuable input into this map.

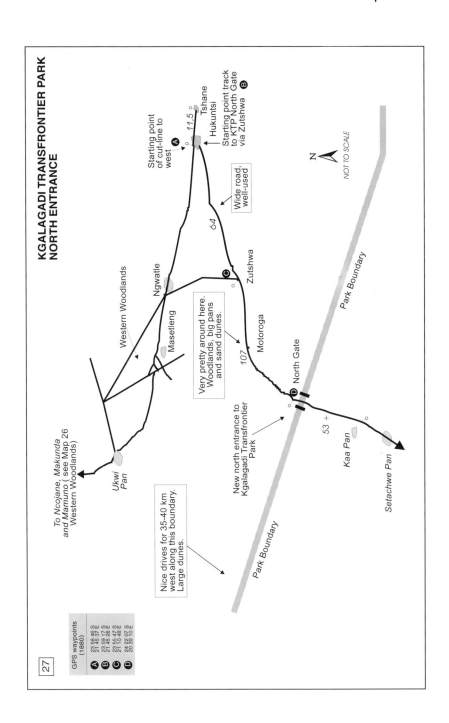

27

KGALAGADI TRANSFRONTIER PARK
NORTH ENTRANCE

Starting point of cut-line to west Ⓐ

Tshane
Hukuntsi

Starting point track to KTP North Gate via Zutshwa Ⓑ

11.5

Wide road, well-used

64

N
NOT TO SCALE

Western Woodlands

Ngwatle

Masetleng

Zutshwa Ⓒ

Very pretty around here. Woodlands, big pans and sand dunes.

Motoroga

107

Park Boundary

North Gate Ⓓ

New north entrance to Kgalagadi Transfrontier Park

53 +

Kaa Pan

To Ncojane, Makunda and Mamuno (see Map 26 Western Woodlands)

Ukwi Pan

Nice drives for 35-40 km west along this boundary. Large dunes.

Park Boundary

Setachwe Pan

GPS waypoints
(1880)

Ⓐ 23 56 46 SE
    21 45 37 E
Ⓑ 23 59 17 SE
    21 45 26 E
Ⓒ 23 55 47 SE
    21 10 48 E
Ⓓ 24 22 07 SE
    20 39 10 E

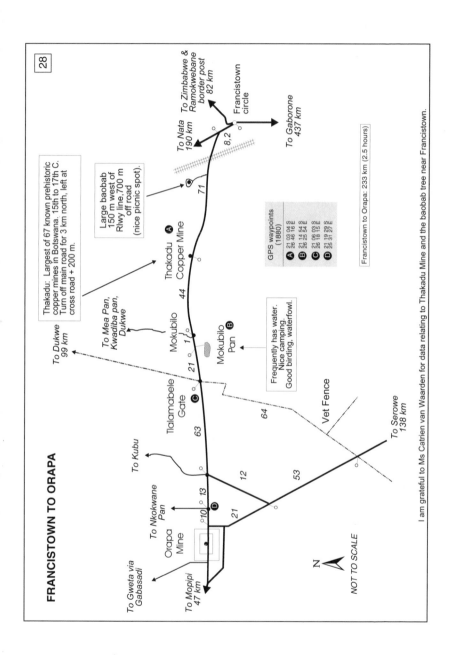

FRANCISTOWN TO ORAPA

Thakadu: Largest of 67 known prehistoric copper mines in Botswana. 15th to 17th C. Turn off main road for 3 km north, left at cross road + 200 m.

Large baobab 150 m west of Rlwy line, 700 m off road (nice picnic spot).

To Dukwe 99 km

To Mea Pan, Kwadiba pan, Dukwe

To Kubu

To Nkokwane Pan

Orapa Mine

To Gweta via Gabasadi

To Mopipi 47 km

Tlalamabele Gate

Mokubilo

Mokubilo Pan

Thakadu Copper Mine

Frequently has water. Nice camping. Good birding, waterfowl.

Vet Fence

To Serowe 138 km

To Zimbabwe & Ramokwebane border post 82 km

Francistown circle

To Nata 190 km

To Gaborone 437 km

GPS waypoints (1880)

Ⓐ 21 03 04 S   26 46 16 E
Ⓑ 21 14 54 S   26 25 54 E
Ⓒ 21 06 03 S   26 18 05 E
Ⓓ 21 19 29 S   25 31 29 E

Francistown to Orapa: 233 km (2.5 hours)

N

NOT TO SCALE

I am grateful to Ms Catrien van Waarden for data relating to Thakadu Mine and the baobab tree near Francistown.

28

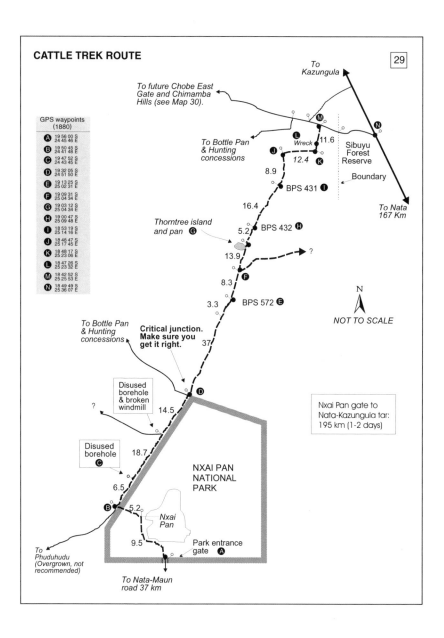

CATTLE TREK ROUTE

29

To Kazungula

To future Chobe East Gate and Chimamba Hills (see Map 30).

To Bottle Pan & Hunting concessions

Wreck

11.6

Sibuyu Forest Reserve

12.4

8.9

BPS 431 **I**

Boundary

16.4

To Nata 167 Km

Thorntree island and pan **G**

5.2 BPS 432 **H**

13.9

?

8.3 **F**

3.3 BPS 572 **E**

N

NOT TO SCALE

To Bottle Pan & Hunting concessions

Critical junction. Make sure you get it right.

37

Nxai Pan gate to Nata-Kazungula tar: 195 km (1-2 days)

Disused borehole & broken windmill

?

14.5

D

Disused borehole **C**

18.7

NXAI PAN NATIONAL PARK

6.5

B 5.2

Nxai Pan

To Phuduhudu (Overgrown, not recommended)

9.5

Park entrance gate **A**

To Nata-Maun road 37 km

GPS waypoints (1880)

A 19 56 00 S / 24 45 46 E
B 19 50 45 S / 24 41 48 E
C 19 47 52 S / 24 43 45 E
D 19 32 05 S / 24 51 50 E
E 19 13 25 S / 25 02 31 E
F 19 09 31 S / 25 04 34 E
G 19 03 12 S / 25 04 34 E
H 19 00 47 S / 25 09 48 E
I 18 53 19 S / 25 14 16 E
J 18 46 47 S / 25 17 45 E
K 18 48 17 S / 25 23 06 E
L 18 47 26 S / 25 23 32 E
M 18 42 53 S / 25 25 53 E
N 18 49 49 S / 25 36 07 E

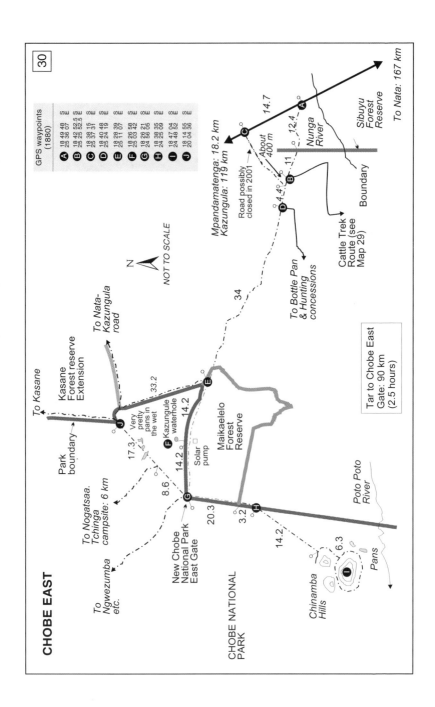

CHOBE EAST

30

GPS waypoints (1880)

A	18 49 48	S
	25 36 07	E
B	18 42 52.5	S
	25 25 52.5	E
C	18 38 15	S
	25 37 31	E
D	18 40 48	S
	25 24 09	E
E	18 28 39	S
	25 11 07	E
F	18 26 58	S
	25 03 42	E
G	18 24 56 05	S
	24 56 05	E
H	18 38 35	S
	24 25 09	E
I	18 47 04	S
	24 48 52	E
J	18 14 55	S
	20 04 36	E

To Nata: 167 km

Sibuyu Forest Reserve

Nunga River

14.7

12.4

About 400 m

Road possibly closed in 2001

Mpandamatenga: 18.2 km
Kazungula: 119 km

11

4.4

Boundary

Cattle Trek Route (see Map 29)

To Bottle Pan & Hunting concessions

34

N

NOT TO SCALE

To Nata-Kazungula road

Kasane Forest reserve Extension

To Kasane

Park boundary

33.2

17.3

Very pretty pans in the wet

Kazungule waterhole

14.2

14.2

14.2

Solar pump

Maikaelelo Forest Reserve

Tar to Chobe East Gate: 90 km (2.5 hours)

To Nogatsaa.
Tchinga campsite: 6 km

8.6

New Chobe National Park East Gate

20.3

3.2

Poto Poto River

CHOBE NATIONAL PARK

To Ngwezumba etc.

14.2

Chinamba Hills

6.3

Pans

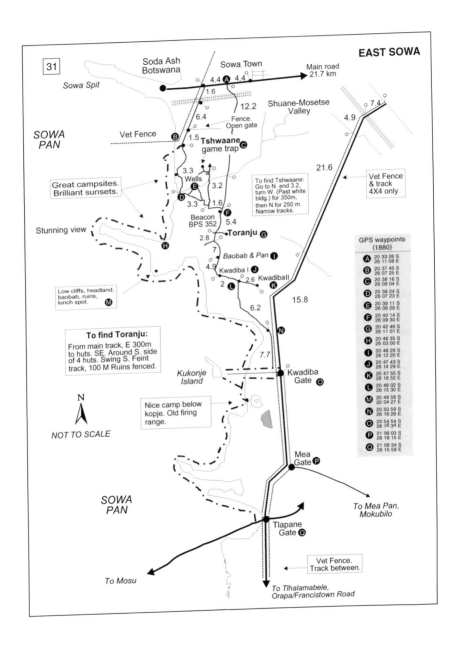

EAST SOWA

31

Soda Ash Botswana

Sowa Town

Main road 21.7 km

Sowa Spit

4.4 **A** 4.4

1.6

12.2

6.4

Fence. Open gate

Shuane-Mosetse Valley

7.4

4.9

SOWA PAN

Vet Fence

1.5 **Tshwaane** game trap **C**

21.6

Vet Fence & track 4X4 only

B

Great campsites. Brilliant sunsets.

3.3 Wells

E

3.2

To find Tshwaane: Go to N. end 3.2, turn W. (Past white bldg.) for 350m, then N for 250 m. Narrow tracks.

D

3.3

1.6

Stunning view

Beacon BPS 352

F

5.4

2.8 **Toranju** **G**

H

7

Baobab & Pan **I**

4.9 Kwadiba I **J**

2.6 Kwadiba II

Low cliffs, headland, baobab, ruins, lunch spot. **M**

2 **L**

K

6.2

15.8

N

7.7

GPS waypoints (1880)

A	20 33 26 S 26 11 08 E
B	20 37 45 S 26 07 25 E
C	20 38 16 S 26 09 04 E
D	20 39 24 S 26 08 28 E
E	20 39 11 S 26 08 28 E
F	20 40 14 S 26 09 30 E
G	20 41 51 S 26 11 01 E
H	20 46 35 S 26 03 00 E
I	20 46 29 S 26 12 20 E
J	20 47 43 S 26 14 29 E
K	20 47 55 S 26 16 52 E
L	20 48 02 S 26 15 30 E
M	20 49 56 S 20 04 27 E
N	20 50 59 S 26 16 28 E
O	20 54 54 S 26 16 34 E
P	21 06 03 S 26 18 15 E
Q	21 08 34 S 26 15 58 E

To find Toranju:
From main track, E 300m to huts. SE. Around S. side of 4 huts. Swing S. Feint track, 100 M Ruins fenced.

N

NOT TO SCALE

Kukonje Island

Nice camp below kopje. Old firing range.

Kwadiba Gate **O**

SOWA PAN

Mea Gate **P**

To Mea Pan, Mokubilo

Tlapane Gate **Q**

Vet Fence. Track between.

To Mosu

To Tlhalamabele, Orapa/Francistown Road

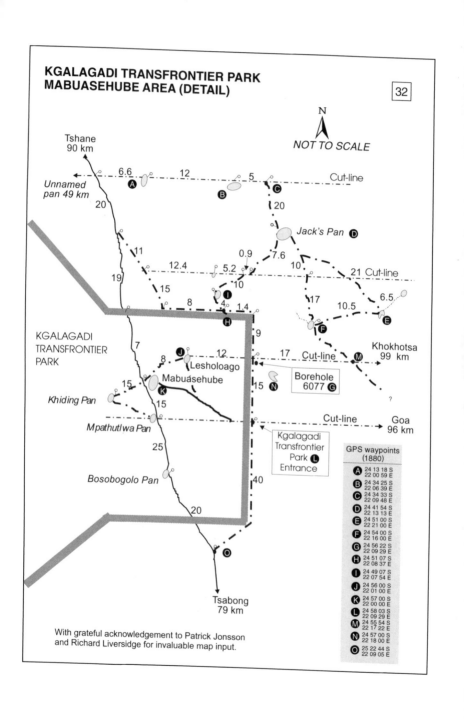

KGALAGADI TRANSFRONTIER PARK
MABUASEHUBE AREA (DETAIL)

32

N

NOT TO SCALE

Tshane
90 km

6.6   12   5   Cut-line

*Unnamed
pan 49 km*   20

A   B   C

20

Jack's Pan   D

11

0.9   7.6

12.4   5.2   10   21 Cut-line

19   15   10

8   I

4   1.4   17   10.5   6.5

H   F   E

9

KGALAGADI
TRANSFRONTIER
PARK   7   Khokhotsa
99 km

J   12   17 Cut-line   M

8   Lesholoago

15   Mabuasehube   15   Borehole
6077   G

Khiding Pan   K   N

15   Cut-line   Goa
96 km

Mpathutlwa Pan

Kgalagadi
Transfrontier
25   Park   L
Entrance

Bosobogolo Pan   40

20

O

Tsabong
79 km

With grateful acknowledgement to Patrick Jonsson
and Richard Liversidge for invaluable map input.

**GPS waypoints
(1880)**

A	24 13 18 S / 22 00 59 E
B	24 34 25 S / 22 06 39 E
C	24 34 33 S / 22 09 48 E
D	24 41 54 S / 22 13 13 E
E	24 51 00 S / 22 21 00 E
F	24 54 00 S / 22 16 00 E
G	24 56 22 S / 22 09 29 E
H	24 51 07 S / 22 08 37 E
I	24 49 07 S / 22 07 54 E
J	24 56 00 S / 22 01 00 E
K	24 57 00 S / 22 00 00 E
L	24 58 03 S / 22 09 29 E
M	24 55 54 S / 22 17 22 E
N	24 57 00 S / 22 18 00 E
O	25 22 44 S / 22 09 05 E

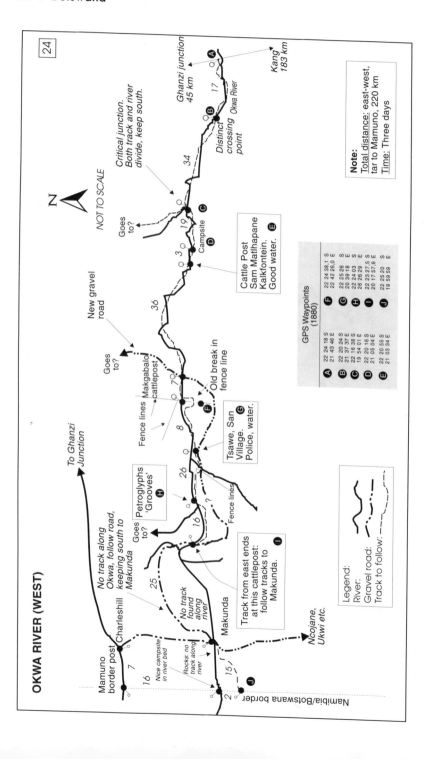

OKWA RIVER (WEST)

Mamuno border post

Charleshill

To Ghanzi Junction

No track along Okwa, follow road, keeping south to Makunda

7

16

Nice campsite in river bed

Rocks: no track along river

25

No track found along river

Makunda

15

J

2

Ncojane, Ukwi etc.

Namibia/Botswana border

Goes to?

Petroglyphs 'Grooves' **H**

Goes to?

26

16

8

Fence lines

Fence lines

Makgabalol cattlepost

7

Old break in fence line

F

Tsawe, San Village. Police, water. **G**

Track from east ends at this cattlepost: follow tracks to Makunda. **I**

New gravel road

36

Goes to?

3

19

Campsite **D**

C

Cattle Post Sam Matlhapane Kalkfontein. Good water. **E**

34

Critical junction. Both track and river divide, keep south.

Goes to?

N

NOT TO SCALE

17

Ghanzi junction 45 km

B

Distinct crossing point Okwa River

A

Kang 183 km

Note:
Total distance: east-west, tar to Mamuno, 220 km
Time: Three days

GPS Waypoints (1880)

A	22 24 18 S	**F**	22 24 38,1 S
	21 43 46 E		22 42 26,0 E
B	22 20 24 S	**G**	22 25 26 S
	21 37 37 E		20 39 18 E
C	22 16 38 S	**H**	22 24 03 S
	19 54 01 E		26 26 29 E
D	22 20 16 S	**I**	22 23 27,5 S
	21 05 04 E		20 17 57,6 E
E	22 20 55 S	**J**	22 25 20 S
	21 03 34 E		19 59 59 E

Legend:
River:
Gravel road:
Track to follow:

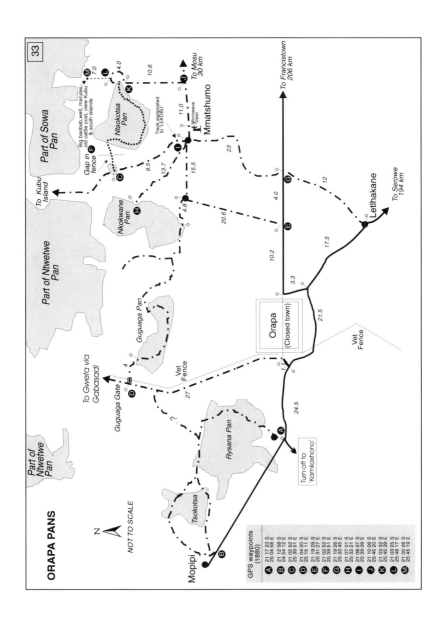

ORAPA PANS

33

NOT TO SCALE

N

Part of Sowa Pan

Part of Ntwetwe Pan

Part of Ntwetwe Pan

To Kubu Island

To Gweta via Gabasadi

To Mosu 30 km

To Francistown 206 km

To Serowe 194 km

Letlhakane

Mmatshumo

Ntsokotsa Pan

Nkokwane Pan

Guguaga Pan

Rysana Pan

Tsokotsa Pan

Mopipi

Orapa (Closed town)

Guguaga Gate

Vet Fence

Vet Fence

Turn-off to 'Kamkaxhana'

Big baobab, well, marulas, old cattle post, view Kubu & south islands

Gap in fence

Track signposted to 'LEKUBU'

Microwave tower

7.0
4.0
10.6
11.0
9.5
13.7
15.5
23
4.8
20.6
4.0
12
17.5
10.2
3.3
21.5
24.5
1.7
27
4
?

GPS waypoints (1880)

Ⓐ	21 17 23 S	25 04 58 E
Ⓑ	21 12 58 S	24 54 12 E
Ⓒ	20 52 52 S	25 39 51 E
Ⓓ	21 04 20 S	25 15 11 E
Ⓔ	21 19 29 S	25 31 27 E
Ⓕ	21 02 52 S	25 39 51 E
Ⓖ	21 19 26 S	25 33 45 E
Ⓗ	21 07 01 S	25 32 21 E
Ⓘ	21 08 37 S	25 39 09 E
Ⓙ	21 10 06 S	25 45 20 E
Ⓚ	21 03 32 S	25 45 39 E
Ⓛ	21 03 25 S	25 46 17 E
Ⓜ	21 00 26 S	25 45 19 E

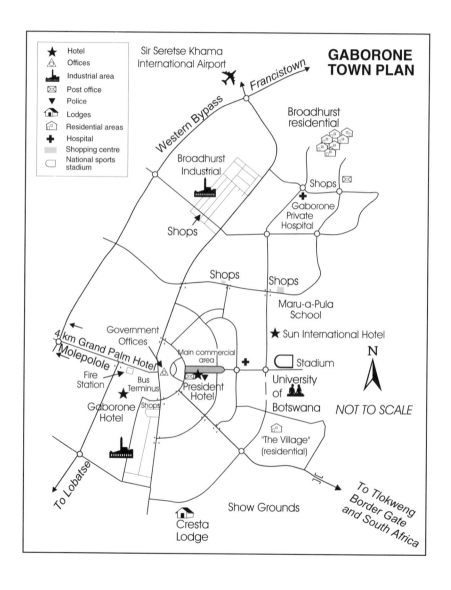

GABORONE TOWN PLAN

Legend:
- ★ Hotel
- △ Offices
- 🏭 Industrial area
- ⊠ Post office
- ▼ Police
- 🏠 Lodges
- 🏠 Residential areas
- ✛ Hospital
- ▦ Shopping centre
- ◯ National sports stadium

Sir Seretse Khama International Airport

Francistown

Western Bypass

Broadhurst residential

Broadhurst Industrial

Shops

Shops

Gaborone Private Hospital

Shops

Shops

Maru-a-Pula School

Government Offices

4 km Grand Palm Hotel / Molepolole

Fire Station

Bus Terminus

Gaborone Hotel

Shops

Main commercial area

President Hotel

★ Sun International Hotel

✛ Stadium

University of Botswana

N

NOT TO SCALE

"The Village" (residential)

To Lobatse

Show Grounds

Cresta Lodge

To Tlokweng Border Gate and South Africa

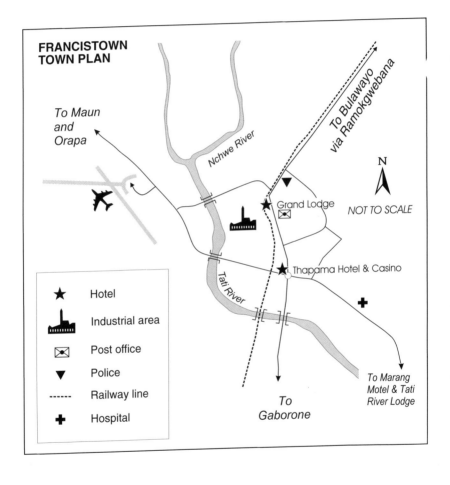

FRANCISTOWN TOWN PLAN

To Maun and Orapa

Nchwe River

To Bulawayo via Ramokgwebana

N

NOT TO SCALE

Grand Lodge

Tati River

Thapama Hotel & Casino

To Marang Motel & Tati River Lodge

To Gaborone

★ Hotel
Industrial area
⊠ Post office
▼ Police
------ Railway line
✚ Hospital

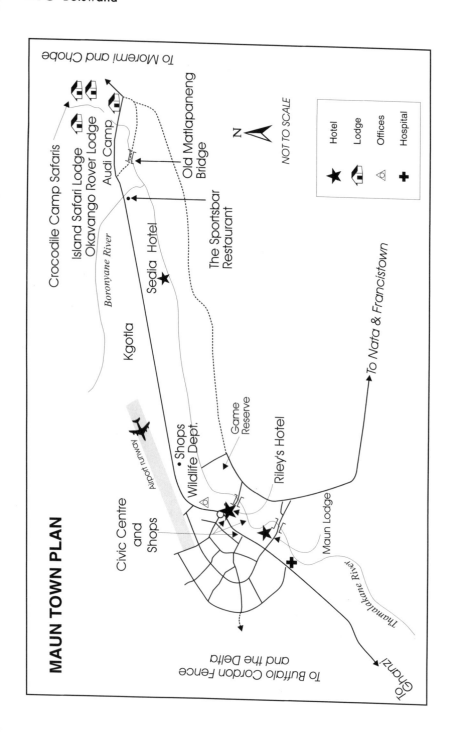

MAUN TOWN PLAN

To Moremi and Chobe

Crocodile Camp Safaris

Island Safari Lodge
Okavango Rover Lodge
Audi Camp

Old Matlapaneng Bridge

The Sportsbar Restaurant

Boronyane River

Sedia Hotel

Kgotla

N

NOT TO SCALE

Hotel
Lodge
Offices
Hospital

To Nata & Francistown

Game Reserve

Shops
Wildlife Dept.

Airport runway

Riley's Hotel

Civic Centre and Shops

Maun Lodge

Thamalakane River

To Ghanzi

To Buffalo Cordon Fence and the Delta

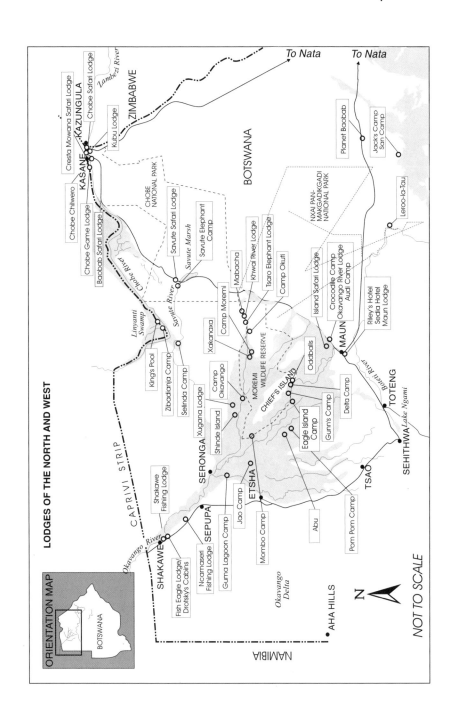

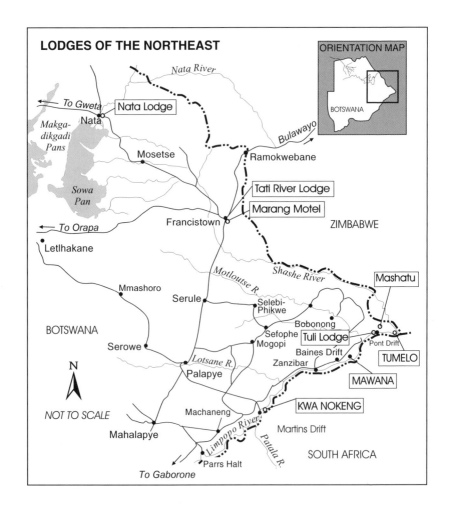

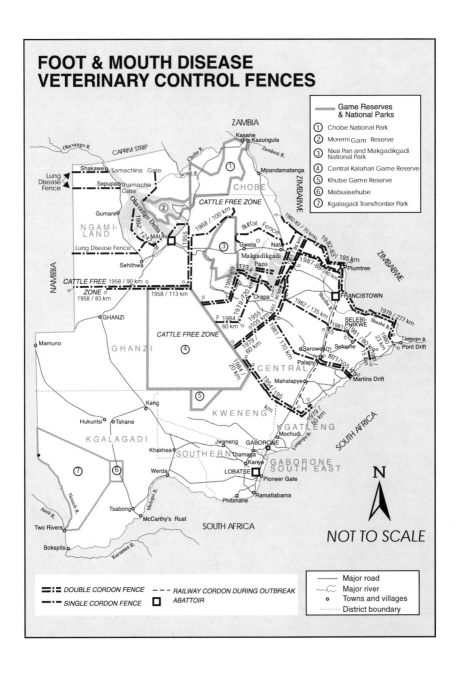

FOOT & MOUTH DISEASE
VETERINARY CONTROL FENCES

Game Reserves & National Parks

1. Chobe National Park
2. Moremi Gam Reserve
3. Nxai Pan and Makgadikgadi National Park
4. Central Kalahari Game Reserve
5. Khutse Game Reserve
6. Mabuasehube
7. Kgalagadi Transfrontier Park

NOT TO SCALE

DOUBLE CORDON FENCE — — — RAILWAY CORDON DURING OUTBREAK
SINGLE CORDON FENCE ☐ ABATTOIR

——— Major road
~~~ Major river
∘ Towns and villages
········ District boundary

INDEX